BEYOND THE
SOCIOLOGY
OF CONFLICT

BEYOND THE SOCIOLOGY OF CONFLICT

David Binns

ST. MARTIN'S PRESS   NEW YORK

Printed in Great Britain

Contents

Preface

This book, a critical examination of sociological theories of social conflict, grew out of a number of themes explored in my M. Litt. The initial work was undertaken at the University of Glasgow during 1973–5. In anticipation of two possible lines of criticism, it is intended neither to exhaust the range of sociological conflict doctrines, an impossible task in a single volume, nor to offer a full elaboration of the alternative approach which stands behind my discussion of the theories in question. More positively, what I have attempted to do is to explore the content, assumptions and implications of some Weberian-influenced approaches to class conflict, and to demonstrate their historical and theoretical relationship to Marxism, from which they often claim a direct or indirect descent.

I would particularly like to thank Paul Walton and Professor J. E. T. Eldridge of the University of Glasgow, whose discussions and comments have helped, I hope, to curb some of the initial excesses, stylistic and spatial, of my earlier efforts. Also, a word of thanks to Nelio Oliveira, now at the University of Oporto, Portugal; Derek Bryant of Bradford University; and Ian Roxborough at the London School of Economics. Should any other colleagues and friends, past or present, detect an unacknowledged debt, I offer both gratitude and apologies. The book, finally, is dedicated to my parents.

I

Max Weber and the Sociology of the Market

Weber, like Marx, saw class conflict to be an endemic feature of a capitalist society. This view is apparent from his early writings on East Prussia. In these, Weber examined the decline of patriarchal agricultural relations consequent upon the rise of capitalism on the land and in manufacture. The end of a common interest of workers and landowners in the success of the harvest meant the beginning of unavoidable conflict between classes whose only relations were those of the market. The Eastern landowners allied themselves with the nascent capitalist manufacturers and 'joined with them in common struggle against the demands of labour'.[1] In his lectures of 1919–20 on economic history, Weber similarly remarked that under the capitalist conditions of the free sale of labour, workers 'actually under the compulsion of the whip of hunger, offer themselves'.[2]

Weber's recurrent concern with class conflict as a central feature of economic and political life has led to much confusion on the part of later commentators. Giddens, for example, suggests that for both Weber and Marx 'ownership versus non-ownership of property is the most important basis of class division in a competitive market'.[3] Again, Beetham's important recent study of Weber's political writings concludes that, 'Both Marx and Weber . . . recognised the same power relationships, the same structure of power, in modern society; where they differed was the point at which they sought to apply the lever of political action to this structure'.[4] Our view, by contrast, is that for

Weber, unlike Marx, class is first and foremost defined at the level of market interaction, is primarily a distributive concept, and that this perspective may be shown to derive from his methodology of Verstehen sociology.

Weber initially defines class situation as the typical probability of procuring goods, gaining a position in life, and finding inner satisfaction. This class situation is seen to derive from 'relative control over goods and skills and . . . their income producing uses'.[5] Class itself is defined as the totality of people in the same class situation, and Weber's three-fold typology of classes (property, commercial and social classes) is derived accordingly. That Weber holds a market-oriented conception of class is apparent in his discussion of commercial classes: he includes workers who hold 'monopolistic qualifications and skills' in the positively-privileged category.[6] The concept of entrepreneurial activity is used by Weber in an idiosyncratic way which directs analysis to the monopolisation of attributes which effectively command privileged treatment at the level of market encounter. For Marx, the working class is an exploited and subordinated class because its members are objectively and structurally compelled to sell their labour power to capital, whereas Weber's criteria for negatively-privileged commercial classes are quite different. The classes he locates in this category are skilled, semi-skilled and unskilled labourers and, viewed merely empirically, are close to Marx's class of productive workers. But Weber's analytical equation of a given sector of workers with merchants, shipowners, industrial entrepreneurs and bankers indicates how he locates class in the sphere of the market, a single 'moment' which he abstracts from the total process of social production and reproduction. His criteria for property and social classes pose similar problems.[7]

SOCIAL SCIENCE AND SOCIAL ACTION

Weber's market-interactive orientation flows directly from his methodological starting point. He interpreted social action as conscious behaviour oriented directly or indirectly towards that of others; he viewed social action 'only as the behaviour of one or more individual human beings'.[8] As such, it constitutes 'the subjective meaning-complex of action'. Verstehen, or subjective understanding, is inseparable from Weber's wider conception of the nature of scientific activity and the philosophical problems associated with the social sciences. Around the time of Weber's earliest writings, evolutionistic social theories, such as those of Herbert Spencer, were gaining an increasing influence in academic circles. Weber's own *Roman Agrarian History* attempted to apply Meitzen's evolutionary categories in the analysis of a given historical problem.[9] This work, however, was an early and essentially experimental project on Weber's part, and his later studies are based on a quite different conception of history, eschewing the use of potentially value-laden constructs.

Weber observes that Eduard Meyer's distrust of the notion 'development' arose at least in part from his discussions with Wellhausen as to whether the growth of Judaism occurred like evolution 'from the inside outwards', or epigenetically, being conditioned by concrete historical forces which 'enter', so to speak, from the 'outside'. In the latter instance an adequate account would consider extrinsic (to the characteristics of the Jews) factors such as the influence of Persian politics, in particular the imposition of laws on the Jews by the Persian kings.[10] Weber criticises Meyer's position on the grounds that it sees the 'general', an abstract concept, to constitute the limiting condition within which 'the infinite possibilities of development' lie. In this way, an abstraction is 'hypostatized into an effective force operating behind the historical scene', which ignores the 'elementary fact', stressed by Meyer in other places, that 'reality is constituted only by the concrete and particular'.[11]

Weber thus opposed the evolutionary view of social and economic development as conceived by the Historical School from Roscher's seminal work in the 1840s. Important members of this school included Schmoller and Hildebrand, who depicted a series of stages of economic development centred on methods of exchange, with societies progressing from barter, through money, to credit. Karl Bücher alternatively emphasised the importance of the social and economic unit, envisaging the supersession of the family unit by the town economy, with the national economy emerging later.[12] Weber's conception of history, by contrast, affirmed the elucidation of specific cultural phenomena, their causes and consequences. Of particular importance is his distinction between progress of technical rationality and progress conceived as an 'increase in value'. For Weber, 'progress' as understood by the social sciences can only refer to technical problems, or the means of attaining an unambiguously given end. Progresss can never be legitimately used in relation to the development or realisation of absolute values: 'It can never elevate itself into the sphere of "ultimate evaluations".'[13]

The background intellectual context of Weber's view of history was the debate on methodology which took place, mainly in Germany, in the early years of the twentieth century. The neo-Kantian position, held by Windelband and Rickert among others, saw a sharp distinction between the methodologies of the natural and social sciences: natural science is first and foremost concerned with law-like phenomena and employs a generalising method, while the cultural sciences study unique meaning complexes by an individualising procedure.[14] As against this methodology-centred distinction, Dilthey opposed the natural to the social sciences in terms of their subject matter as such. While in the natural sciences, theory has become increasingly esoteric, the social sciences retain a close connection with life, so that 'thought arising from life remains the foundation of scientific activity'.[15] The experiential basis of social thought derives from the fact that the human world is permeated with meaning, and that knowledge of it in consequence takes a unique, interpretative form. Dilthey's conception of the social world is summed up by his dictum, 'Things we explain, the soul we understand'.[16]

Now while Weber challenged both of these positions, his conception of the methodology appropriate to the social sciences developed against the background of this Geisteswissenschaften debate. In particular, he adopted the distinction between the logic of statements of generalisation and the explanation of the unique, but denied the exclusive relevance of these two methods of analysis to distinct aspects of the world, as implied by Rickert's formulation. Weber proposed that valid knowledge in the social sciences takes the form of the analytical ordering of empirical reality. All such analysis, however, at least tacitly assumes that only a finite portion of the infinite range of potentially cognisable reality is 'important' in the sense of being 'worthy of being known'. Selection of a particular segment of the total reality is conditioned by the orientation of the analyst's interests, as it arises from the specific cultural significance he attributes to it. The point of departure of social scientific interest is thus the concrete, individually-structured configuration of cultural life, its relations and development.[17] Knowledge of laws is an indispensable heuristic stage in the analysis of significant configurations of cultural phenomena, which become cultural to us precisely because we are directed to them by, and relate them to, value ideas. Scientific knowledge is thus not, for Weber, morally neutral in its epistemological implications: that portion of concrete reality which is coloured by the social scientist's value-conditioned interest is significant because it expresses relations which are 'important' in that they connect with his values.[18]

The social sciences are distinguished by a qualitative aspect of their subject matter which has no direct counterpart in the exact or natural sciences, namely the empathic understanding of psychological and intellectual events. Weber avoids a rigid methodological dualism on two principal counts. Firstly, the natural sciences, with the exception of mechanics, also use qualitative as well as quantitative concepts in their account of the world: astronomical knowledge, for example, first and foremost constitutes not a system of laws, but rather the individual consequences of laws in unique configurations, since these are of direct cultural significance to the astronomer.[19] Furthermore, within the social sciences themselves, the phenomena characteristic of, for example, a money-economy are subject to formulation as laws. Exchange in the money-economy is significant in so far as it exists on a mass scale as a fundamental component of modern culture. To render its cultural significance *understandable*, however, it is necessary to explain causally the specificity of the money-economy as a historically unique phenomenon.[20]

As W. G. Runciman has stressed, Weber endorses the positivists' view that the social sciences can be value-free and causal, but at the same time holds that this position is consistent with a difference of kind between social and natural scientific procedure.[21] Knowledge of cultural phenomena centres on the significance to observers of their individuality – as 'historically unique configurations'.[22] These aspects of reality alone are the objects of causal analysis, which concerns unique, concrete relations rather than abstract laws. The scope of the social sciences is thus defined by 'the *conceptual* interconnections of problems' rather than 'the *actual* explanation of *things*',[23] and the ideal-typical form of concept construction is indispensable to their development. The ideal type is a generic concept which aims not to exhaustively reflect reality, but to bring together certain relations and events in an internally consistent conceptual complex which makes their characteristic features clear and understandable.[24] The heuristic status of the ideal type is underlined by its function in accentuating the essential aspects of the phenomena in question. Weber explicitly refers to it as a utopia which exists nowhere in reality. Neither is it a normative yardstick; as against the Historical School's 'classical scholastic epistemology', Weber's ideal types are analytical instruments for the intellectual mastery of empirical data, the conceptual and empirical orders not being automatically correspondent. Their one-sided, accentuated character is inseparable from Weber's neo-Kantian conception of reality as essentially a 'meaningless infinity' outside the will and capacity of human beings to take a deliberate attitude towards the world and lend it significance. He approvingly cites Goethe's observation that 'theory' is involved in the 'fact', and notes that the given empirical 'reality' is transformed into a mental construct in its constitution as 'historical material'.[25]

Weber thus rejects Locke's classical, empiricist, reflective epistemology and grounds cognition in the processes of culturally-structured meaning imputation. The general role of science in human affairs lies in the ordering and causal imputation of empirical data, and the elaboration of means appropriate to the attainment of an already given end or value, the content of which cannot be derived from empirical scientific analysis. Science may be of service to partisan political interests by clarifying both 'ultimate' positions conceivable with reference to particular practical problems and the facts that must be taken into account in rationally choosing between these positions. Nevertheless, the practical range of science ends at the point where the status of absolute values is at issue. Thus:

. . . every single important activity and ultimately life as a whole, if it is to be consciously guided, is a series of ultimate decisions through which the soul — as in Plato — chooses its own fate, i.e. the meaning of its activity and existence . . . There is no (rational or empirical) scientific procedure of any kind whatsoever which can provide us with a decision here.[26]

Conflict among rival absolute values is perennial and unavoidable. Compromise is, of course, pervasive in everyday life, but underlying the routine of daily existence is a Nietzschean complex of struggling and irreconcilable ultimate values, which Weber likens to 'the choice between "God" and the "Devil"'. Weber avoids a position of total ethical relativism, however, by grounding the value of scientific endeavour in the web of culture which gives it significance as a distinctive form of cognition. All knowledge is gained from a particular point of view, arising from evaluative ideas which are differentially graded by the criteria of significance between individuals at different points in time. Still, for Weber, this does not mean that cultural science is subjective in the sense of being valid for its researcher alone. History is concerned exclusively with those aspects of events which are of 'general significance', 'and *hence* of historical *interest* from general standpoints'.[27] It is in their 'general' cultural significance that Weber locates the criteria for intersubjectively valid knowledge of cultural phenomena. The choice of an object for investigation and the scope of a particular enquiry are 'determined by the evaluative ideas which dominate the investigator and his age'.[28] The disenchanted and intellectualised modern world is distinguished by providing conditions under which the influence of non-rational beliefs and forms of thought need no longer dominate social life: 'it means that principally there are no mysterious incalculable forces that come into play, but rather that one can, in principle, master all things by calculation. This means that the world is disenchanted.'[29]

Weber clearly saw the belief in the value of science to be itself the product of certain cultures rather than an invariant feature of human life.[30] In particular, he expressed concern at what he perceived to be a trend towards a negative evaluation of science by German youth in the early years of the twentieth century.[31] Despite this, he believed that the contemporary premium on the technical control of life, itself bound up with the development of scientific modes of thought, meant that science, while competing as only one ultimate standpoint towards life among many, represented an activity which in terms of intellectual integrity and courage corresponded to 'The fate of our times'.[32] For the cultural world this means the analytical ordering of empirical reality in terms of the specific historical configurations which are significant for cultural values. In this process of ordering, the empathic interpretation of social action is seen as an indispensable tool for sociological analysis. This tool was unique to the cultural sciences and the cornerstone of Weber's Verstehen methodology. Weber defines sociology as 'a science concerning itself with the interpretative understanding of social action and thereby with a causal explanation of its course and consequences'.[33] His dictum that sociological interpretation should be adequate at the levels of both meaning and causality is underpinned by an assumption that causal relations, expressed conceptually as generalisations of probability, are themselves grounded in and causally sustained by interpretable orientations in the sphere of social action. Weber, writing on the theme of socialist economy, suggests that:

> The real empirical sociological investigation begins with the question: What motives determine and lead the individual members in this socialistic community to behave in such a way that the community came into being in the first place and that it continues to exist?[34]

While commending the functionalist frame of reference as convenient for purposes of practical illustration and for provisional orientation, Weber warns against the illegitimate reification of collective concepts. His Verstehen sociology, that is to say, is rooted in the motives of social actors. His conception of class is, as we have seen, accordingly articulated at the 'interpretable' level of direct patterns of market interaction and distribution, as is his notion of social and economic action.[35]

WEBER AND CAPITALISM

Weber's conception of class as a market-centred phenomenon permeates and, in an important sense, structures his concern with rationalisation as the central developmental feature of contemporary society. This rationalisation, he believed, dominated the age:

> The fate of our times is characterised by rationalisation, intellectualisation, and above all by the "disenchantment" of the world.[36]

By this Weber meant a stage of social development where there are no mysterious forces at work and in which it is possible, at least in theory, to master all things by rational calculation. A key feature of this process is the conscious pursuit of individual interests, or

> . . . the substitution for the unthinking acceptance of ancient custom, of deliberate adaption to situations in terms of self-interest.[37]

Weber sought to elucidate the historical foundations of rationalisation and to show how it may historically assume different forms. He held, for example, that the very direction of the action deemed rational may vary: it may proceed positively as 'a conscious rationalization of ultimate values', negatively at the expense 'not only of custom, but of emotional values', or finally in favour of 'a morally sceptical kind of rationality'.[38] The very direction of rationalisation is just as significant in Weber's work as its degree or tempo.

Yet while Weber's formal view is that 'Rationalism is an historical concept that covers a whole world of different things',[39] his analysis in fact refers principally to the particular rationality of capitalist society; capitalist economic relations are, he argues, technically a vital precondition of a rational economy. He refers to the 'sheer superiority and actual indispensability of a type of management oriented to the particular market situations'.[40] Rational calculating activity is the ideal type of subjective meaning attributed by Weber to social action in his causal account of the capitalist class structure. In *The Protestant Ethic*, he defines capitalism as

> . . . identical with the pursuit of profit, and forever renewed profit, by means of continuous, rational, capitalistic enterprise.[41]

Conceptually set against the acquisition of profit by force, capitalist economic action rests on '(formally) peaceful chances of profit'. Thus, as Professor John Eldridge observes, it is not 'acquisitive activity as such' that is seen by Weber to define the nature of capitalism.[42] Rather, Weber identifies its essential characteristic to be a historically specific form of calculating activity. Noting its major requisite as the 'rational capitalistic organization of (formally) free labour', Weber indicates that in terms of cultural history the problem of the origins of capitalism is that of the origin of 'the Western bourgeois class and of its peculiarities'.[43] This problematic is explored in considerable detail in Weber's *General Economic History*, where he specifies the major objective preconditions for the development of rational capitalism to be the geographical factor of trade connections, the special demand generated by military requirements, luxury demand, and the 'rational permanent enterprise'. Above all, however, he stresses the absolute indispensability of 'the rational spirit, the rationalization of the conduct of life in general, and a rationalistic economic ethic'. Rational capitalism, Weber proposes, could not develop 'in an economic group . . . bound hand and foot by magical beliefs'[44] He notes in particular the 'decisive break' of the Lutheran Reformation, the ethical values of which served to generate a form of 'Asceticism within the world'. The notion of rational capitalistic activity as the fulfilment of a God-given task gave to the modern entrepreneur, Weber suggests, a 'fabulously clear conscience'.

Weber's thesis has been challenged from a variety of theoretical positions by such diverse writers as H. M. Robertson, Pitirim Sorokin and Talcott Parsons.[45] Tawney's influential account of the interrelations between religion and the rise of capitalism objects to Weber's underestimation of the economic bases of capitalist development and the role of non-religious economic movements in fostering individualist attitudes towards economic relations, as well as of the complexity and heterogeneity of Calvinist thought itself, much of which was in fact concerned, in its early stages at least, to propagate a conservative and collectivist doctrine of social organisation.[46] It should be noted that Weber discerns an affinity or congruence between the ethic of Puritanism and capitalist activity, rather than a unidirectional causal link. Thus, he proposes that the ascetic belief in a fixed calling provided an 'ethical justification' of the modern division of labour and the activities of the entrepreneur.[47] He suggests that wealth has a secularising influence and that the intense search for the Kingdom of God soon became transformed into 'sober economic virtue'; the ideology of rational capitalism, in other words, rapidly achieved autonomy from its religious origins.

The substantive historical validity of Weber's discussion of the Protestant Ethic is not our immediate concern, but what is of particular importance is his equation of capitalist activity with a particular type of rational calculation, and a corresponding ethos of social life in general. Capitalism is described as involving the 'method of enterprise', which consists primarily of capital accounting, or calculation by means of modern bookkeeping, and the 'striking of a balance' in undertakings concerned with the provision of satisfaction for everyday wants.[48] Weber identifies as aspects of this mode of accounting the institution of private property, freedom of market exchange, mechanised technology, 'calculable' law, and the commercialisation of economic life.

An unwarranted and unjustified theoretical transposition of this rationality from its original sense as a historically specific form of social action to the level of the system as a whole takes place in Weber's analysis. For instance, counterposing rational capitalistic enterprise to non-rational forms such as tax farming and trade speculation, he contends that the former is

> organized with a view to market opportunities, and hence to economic objectives in the real sense of the word, and the more rational it is the more closely it relates to mass demand and the provision for mass needs.[49]

Rational capitalism is thus seen to be at the heart of modern economic activity, rather than in any way accidental to or parasitic upon it. Moreover, the quality of calculability that Weber ascribes to particular capitalistic enterprise is perceived to engender a rationality in the system as a whole in the form of a correspondence between production and (mass) needs.

Weber saw the distinction between the 'formal' and the 'substantive' types of rationality to be of crucial importance for concrete historical analysis. In particular, an economic system is defined as formally rational 'according to the degree to which the provision of needs, which is essential to every rational economy, is capable of being expressed in numerical calculable terms and is so expressed'.[50] But even if one accepts the presence of this condition of formal rationality, one must also take into account that a given activity is oriented towards ultimate ends, whether they be ethical, political, hedonistic or whatever. It follows that even for Weber substantive rationality cannot be measured in terms of the presence of formal calculation alone but, in addition, involves a relation to absolute values or the content of a particular end. Action in the interest of a hierarchy of class distinctions or in furtherance of the power of a particular unit are, among many other possible standards of value, 'of potential "substantive" significance' in Weber's schema.[51]

As with his discussion of class, Weber's model of formally rational capitalism is dominated and structured by the subjectivist methodology of Verstehen; but here the consequence is that the empirically existent dominance of calculability in *particular* capitalist activity is theoretically reproduced at the level of the socio-productive system, at the level of *capital as a whole*. In both cases, Weber's conception of social action acts as an epistemological barrier to the understanding of economic relations in capitalist society. It confines the concept of class to the sphere of direct, immediate, market interaction. In the case of the wider system, it results in a mystified portrayal of the workings of the capitalist economy, essentially reformulating the empirically false equilibrium model as expressed, at its simplest, in Say's Law.

Structural aggregates such as class, state and capitalism are, in Weber's work, attributed with the rational essence that he discerns in the conscious strategies of their individual members. Social power, its distribution, source and social significance is, of course, the central theme of this dimension of Weber's work: he defines power, in its most general sense, as 'the possibility of imposing one's will upon the behaviour of other persons'.[52] His rather more limited notion of domination has two aspects, namely domination by virtue of interests and domination by virtue of authority. Weber is concerned primarily with situations involving an 'authoritarian power of command' or, viewed from the opposite perspective, of 'obedience'. Every highly privileged group, he adds, develops its own myth of natural superiority; for long periods, this myth is accepted almost unquestioningly but, when the nature of the class structure becomes unambiguously apparent, it is typically the target of 'powerful attacks'.

Within this framework, Weber identifies the three 'pure' or 'ideal' types of charismatic, traditional and legal rational authority. While the latter is of especial relevance for Weber's analysis of the modern state, the other two forms will be sketched briefly in order to indicate the scope of his typology. Bearers of charismatic authority are seen to be endowed with specific gifts of body and mind that are considered to be 'supernatural' and to satisfy all 'extraordinary' needs, that is those which transcend the sphere of everyday economic routines.[53]

Traditional domination, on the other hand, is derived from norms which are sanctified by tradition and custom. Weber cites the Talmudic maxim 'Men should never change a custom' in order to illustrate this power of tradition.[54] Interestingly for the women's movement, within this traditional category Weber devotes most space to patriarchal domination which, he claims, is ultimately based on 'nothing but purely subjective rights and privileges'.[55] It thus lacks the more objective 'matter-of-factness' of bureaucratic domination, Weber's third type.

Weber lists the basic characteristics of bureaucracy as the division of the field in question into official 'jurisdictional' areas which are generally ordered by formal rules, the establishment of 'office hierarchy' and of corresponding channels of appeal in order to stipulate a clear system of super- and sub-ordination, and the preservation and use of written documents ('the files'). There is a staff of subaltern officials and scribes whose work is formally segregated from their private lives. In addition, Weber's ideal typical model of bureaucracy incorporates thorough training in a field of specialisation, the demand for the full working capacity of the official during office hours, and the presence of more or less stable and exhaustive 'general rules'.[56] As a consequence of these factors, the office constitutes a 'vocation', and the position of the official is of the nature of a 'duty' in return for the grant of a secure existence. Officials are appointed rather than elected, their salaries are fixed according to rank, and there is an established line of career promotion in terms of, for example, seniority or examinations.

In order to understand fully Weber's theory of bureacracy it is necessary to view it in the context of his conception of domination. Marcuse stresses this when he points out that the 'formal analysis of capitalism' becomes, in Weber's work, 'the analysis of forms of domination'.[57] Weber himself asserts that:

> Without exception every sphere of social action is profoundly influenced by structures of dominancy.[58]

He adds that, from a historical viewpoint, domination has played 'the decisive role', particularly within the most important economic structures of the manor and the large-scale capitalist enterprise. Weber's work is permeated by an assumption that domination, in one form or another, will naturally accompany any enduring pattern of regular social interaction. C. J. Friedrich has justly questioned the 'authoritarian norms' which are embodied in Weber's intended value-free analysis.[59] Weber's use of ideal – typical analysis allows him to bracket together historically and structurally distant forms of bureaucratic organisation on the basis of their perceived common administrative features. His formal model of bureaucracy is, to borrow Gouldner's phrase, 'innocent of spatio-temporal cautions'.[60] Historical examples of bureaucracy cited by Weber include the system of rule in Egypt during the period of the New Kingdom, the later Roman Principate, the Roman Catholic hierarchy, the modern European state and the large-scale capitalist enterprise. He proposes that bureaucratic status incentives tend to be superior to physical coercion in that they are more likely to promote 'steadiness'. Nevertheless, degree of bureaucratisation and, for example, the expansionary power of a state need not of necessity correspond: the Roman and British Empires, Weber points out, had little in the way of bureaucratic organisation during their most expansive periods.

Weber argues that the decisive reason for the advance of bureaucracy is always its 'technical superiority over any other form of organization'. In particular, he points to its precision, speed and unambiguity, as well as the reduction of material and personal costs that it allows.[61] The more perfect it becomes, the more it is 'dehumanized' of personal, irrational and emotional elements. Weber observes a 'levelling' process in the development of bureaucratic administration, and argues that with its ascendancy it becomes increasingly necessary, progressively determining 'the material fate of the masses'; it brings the system of 'rational examinations for expertise' to the fore and promotes, he suggests, a 'rationalist way of life'.[62] Accordingly, it is epitomised by the presence of the 'specialist' rather than the 'cultivated man' of, for example, the traditional English administration of notables.

Despite the historical rootlessness of the formal model, Weber is suggesting a profound and significant relationship between the development of modern Western rationality on the one hand, and the growth of bureaucracy, a peculiarly Western phenomenon in its more developed and generalised forms. He defines bureaucratic administration as 'the exercise of control on the basis of knowledge' and, as such, it is distinguished as being 'formally the most rational known means of carrying out imperative control over human beings'.[63] Weber further, and more explicitly, identifies this form of social organisation with the principle of rationality by asserting that:

> The purest type of exercise of legal (or rational) authority is that which employs a bureaucratic administrative staff.[64]

This, it must be remembered, was written considerably prior to the bureaucratic ossification of the non-capitalist Eastern European states. The Weberian model of rational bureaucracy, to use Parsons' terminology, is characterised by the values of universalism, achievement, specificity and affective neutrality,[65] qualities which, in Weber's formal analysis, govern the modern, that is capitalist, world.

It is this perspective of bureaucracy which guides Weber's political analysis of the modern state. In *Economy and Society*, he contends that 'the large modern state is absolutely dependent upon a bureaucratic basis'.[66] The 'rational state', he elsewhere argues, is unique to the Western world.[67] On its organisational basis, the trained official makes decisions in accordance with a 'law which can be counted upon, like a machine: ritualistic-religious and magical considerations must be excluded'.[68] Weber counterposes this form of state to that of ancient China, where the mandarins played no important role in the way of political service, the view that their perfection in literary culture 'keeps things in order in normal times' being essentially a magical theory. Historically, he accounts for the creation of a body of rational law in terms of an alliance between the modern state and the jurists for the purpose of making good the former's claims to power. This alliance, Weber observes, was 'indirectly favourable to capitalism', and he identifies fourteenth-century English mercantilism as 'the first trace of a rational economic policy'.

Weber characterises mercantilism as the carrying of the point of view of capitalist industry into politics: the state is handled 'as if it consisted exclusively of capitalist entrepreneurs'.[69] Noting that few of the industries created by mercantilist policies survived that period, he proposes that capitalism proper developed not as an outgrowth of national mercantilism, but rather alongside it: a stratum of entrepreneurs, which had developed independently of the political administration, secured the support of decisive sectors of parliament in the eighteenth century. In this way, 'rational' and 'irrational' capitalism faced each other in a relationship of conflict, the former type progressively gaining ground as the latter lost it.[70]

For Weber, the rational state thus emerged in eighteenth-century Britain as the embodiment and political expression of the emerging form of rational capitalist activity. He lists the primary formal characteristics of the modern state as the presence of an administrative and legal order subject to change by (bureaucratic) legislation, the possession of legitimate powers of coercion on a territorial base, and the monopoly of legitimate force.[71] Weber's recognition of the coercive dimension of state authority is consistent with and occupies an important position within his model of the class structure of capitalist society. In the first place, he notes that law, expressed through the political organ of the State, acts as a guarantor of a wide variety of particular interests, both economic and otherwise:

> Law (in the sociological sense) guarantees by no means only economic interests but rather the most diverse interests ranging from the most elementary one of protection of personal security to such purely ideal goods as personal honor or the honor of the divine powers.[72]

At the same time, however, economic interests are the most powerful single factor contributing to the. creation of legal systems:

For, any authority guaranteeing a legal order depends, in some way, upon the consensual action of the constitutive groups, and the formation of social groups depends, to a large extent, upon constellations of material interests.[73]

Weber lists the major functions of the contemporary State as those of law enactment, protection of public order and personal safety, protection of vested rights and cultural interests, and defence against outside attack.[74] He relates these functions directly to his conception of the capitalist class structure by indicating how the actions of the State benefit certain classes more than others, especially in the modern period when the expansion of the market has cut away the basis for a 'community of interests'. Thus, the State

> obtains a powerful and decisive support from all those groups which have a direct or indirect economic interest in the expansion of the market community, as well as from the religious authorities. These latter are best able to control the masses under conditions of increasing pacification. Economically, however, the groups most interested in pacification are those guided by market interests, especially the burghers of the towns, as well as those who are interested in river, road, or bridge tolls and in the tax-paying capacity of their tenants and subjects. These interested groups expand with an expanding money economy.[75]

The rational state is thus, for Weber, both an expression of and vehicle for the particular rationality of capitalist society. Weber's conception of the modern state, in other words, is in the last analysis bound to his account of the class relations of capitalism which, it will be remembered, are primarily market-oriented: the market, in turn, is seen to embody and provide the stage for economic activity of a specifically capitalist, rational and calculable character. The State is a central expression or dimension of this system of class relations and, consequently, both reflects and promotes the formal rationality of economic action that it embodies. There is no suggestion, as in Marx's analysis, that extended capital reproduction has a dynamic of its own which imposes direct imperatives on the actors who, at the level of direct production and at the other necessary stages within the total circuit of capital, fulfil the tasks vital for that reproduction to take place.

Certainly, Weber was aware that imbalances and disproportions may enter into the functioning of the formally rational, capitalist economy. Such developments, however, are attributed to the substantive rationality or irrationality of certain economic practices: for example, speculation and the struggle for job control on the part of workers, both of which have figured prominently in the history of capitalism, are accounted for as respectively a major cause of economic crises and a symptom of the absence of 'a rational system of provision for wants'.[76] Neither crises nor the struggle for workplace control, in other words, are inherent in the capitalist mode of production, despite Weber's acknowledgement of the basic conflictual nature of employment relations; these are seen by him to be expressive of the non-presence of the full, formally rational, economic system.

Whereas Marx set out to discover the law of motion of capitalist society on the basis of the production of commodities within historically grounded and specific structures of class relations (defined primarily at the level of relations of production),[77] Weber constructs an ideal type of rational, capitalist economic activity and via a conceptual transposition reproduces the formal rationality he finds there at the level of the system itself. The principal mediating concepts in this theoretical structure are the definition of classes at the point of market interaction and the assumption that, in its most rational form, capitalist production will correspond closely to 'mass demand' and 'mass needs'. That these aspects of Weber's analysis are mutually reinforcing is expressed perhaps most concisely in the following passage from *Economy and Society*:

> Above all, it [rational bureaucratic administration – D. B.] was influenced by the rise of the bourgeoisie in the towns which had an organization peculiar to Europe. It was in addition aided by the competition for power by means of rational – that is bureaucratic – administration among the different states. This led, from fiscal motives, to a crucially important alliance with capitalistic interests.[78]

Class, the state and capitalism as a system are thus theoretically reconstructed in terms of the guiding Weberian concept of rationality, a concept which in turn is grounded in the methodology of Verstehen. The contradiction identified by Marx between the dual nature of the commodity as use value and exchange value, with its implications of an inherent tendency in capitalism towards crisis, is circumvented in Weber's inductivist systems analysis. The realisation of the rationality of capitalist economic calculation at the level of the system is rendered conditional upon the presence of certain substantive conditions. Principally, these are market struggles, capital accounting and 'effective demand'.[79] On examination, these conditions are, in fact, no more than aspects of the capitalist environment itself, in so far as it is formally rational in the Weberian sense. The nature of his neo-Kantian methodology means that for Weber, as for Hegel, the rational becomes the actual. Capitalism is, for Weber, rational.[80]

CONCLUSION

If, in summary, a single feature may be identified as the overriding theme which permeates Weber's analysis of the class structure of capitalist society, it is the displacement of the concept of rationality and its transposition into other sectors of the social world, in particular those of the determination of classes and the overall functioning of the economy. His inductivist methodology in this way produces a model of capitalism which serves to mystify both its characteristic class structure and the *modus operandi* of the system as a whole.

In the following chapters we shall look at some of the influences that this approach to class structuration has exerted on subsequent sociology, especially that of the last two decades. In the course of this exposition certain key themes will inevitably recur. We do not, of course, claim to offer the definitive exposition and critique of the Weberian tradition in sociology. This will have to wait until a hypothetical time when the social conditions which Weber sought to portray have become a historical curiosity and, with them, interest in the many possible variations on and permutations of his sociological themes a retrospective form of leisure activity. Nevertheless, as things stand, the spirit of Weber is very much with us, and if our book serves to foster a critical approach to its many and varied manifestations, both academic and commonsensical, it will have performed at least a minimal contribution to the critique of a major strand of contemporary ideological thought. And this, it should be stressed, is our primary intention.

2

Max Weber and the Legacy of Political Economy

Weber approached the analysis of class within capitalist society primarily from the point of view of distributive and market-interactive processes. While the particularity of Weber's sociology, especially in so far as it derives from his neo-Kantian epistemology, should not be minimised, it is also important to stress that his account of class structure has precedents within and is, like much sociological work in this area, inseparable from a wider background of economic thought.

At the heart of this tradition is the development of and subsequent reaction against the labour theory of value. A common theme in the various pre-Marxian labour-value doctrines was the recognition that workers do not receive the full economic value of what they produce. Thus posed, the basis of class divisions unequivocally appears as the ownership of property and its effective control, and it was in these terms that the classical theorists examined the physiology of social and economic structure. Adam Smith thus opposes a hypothetical pre-accumulation stage of social development, in which the entire produce of labour belonged to the labourer, to the emergence of private property, where both landlord and employing farmer intervene in order to charge a deduction from the labourer's product. Similarly, in industrial manufacture the master advances to the worker both materials of work and wages for maintenance, in return for a share in the produce of his labour.

Smith, writing in a period when capital was expanding rapidly as a social and economic force, was optimistic that the division of labour, based on the human propensity to barter and exchange, was synonymous with a general improvement in material living standards and the quality of civilisation as a whole.[1] His general optimism, however, did not completely obscure the conflictual implications of a systematic division between classes along the lines of property:

> The workmen desire to get as much, the masters to give as little as possible. The former are disposed to combine in order to raise, the latter in order to lower the wages of labour.[2]

Expanding riches for society as a whole broadly correspond to the most comfortable conditions for the labouring classes, and vice versa. Fluctuations notwithstanding, however, the different classes together stand to commonly benefit or suffer by changes in the general fortunes of social production.[3]

While Smith viewed the possibilities of class conflict and economic stagnation with some concern, these themes were in the main overshadowed in his work by an optimistic belief in the principles of reason and harmony. A different tone is apparent in the writings of Ricardo where the landed, industrial and labouring classes more obviously and more fundamentally embody conflicting interests. The natural price of labour is that which enables the labourer to subsist and reproduce on a numerically static basis; but its actual market price represents a variable factor, diminishing the rate of profit as it rises. Conversely, profits rise in the event of a fall in wages.[4]

Strongly influenced by Malthus' pessimistic theory of population, Ricardo identified a progressive rise in rent, especially on the more fertile lands, as a consequence of increasing population pressures. But since rent of land represents the compensation paid to the owner for the use of 'its original and indestructible powers',[5] the landlord stands to benefit from the disadvantage of the other classes in so far as his real rent rises together with the exchangeable value of 'his' produce in times of low productivity.[6] For Ricardo, the long-term tendency for industrial profits to fall results from growing population pressure on scarce land resources, above all on the supply of corn. Wages may temporarily rise when the agricultural yield is abundant, but the resulting stimulus to population undermines the newly-increased living standards and 'will speedily reduce the labourers to their usual consumption'. The same process then occurs on the poorer lands,

a greater proportion of total produce going to the labourers,
though usually on a smaller per capita ratio, while profits receive
a share which is yet smaller in absolute terms.[7]

It has recently been suggested by David Yaffe that the most
fundamental problem for the Ricardian framework is that of
'how the income generated by production is shared between
capitalists and workers'.[8] Such an interpretation implies that the
principal Ricardian problematic concerns the account of distributional struggles between classes, the most basic contradiction
of capitalist society being, as Yaffe suggests, 'the antagonism for
the share of the net product'.[9] Now Ricardo did suggest that the
natural price of labour, estimated in terms of food and other
necessities, is a relative and variable phenomenon, essentially
depending upon 'the habits and customs of the people'.[10]
Marshall made much of this observation in his polemic against
the socialists who, he claims, erroneously interpreted Ricardo's
theory of wages as an 'iron' law.[11] But in fact, Ricardo's account
of the tendency for industrial profits to decline has a law-like
character which is irreducible to the outcome of particular
distributional struggles and market movements. Profits, as we
have seen, are pressured by the dual squeeze from landowners
and labourers; moreover, the absolute limits imposed by nature
on agricultural productivity ensure that this tendency is cumulative and irreversible.[12]

It is not of immediate importance that Ricardo may have
underestimated the potential of scientific techniques to increase
agricultural yield or that he drew over-pessimistic conclusions
concerning the propensity of the working class to reproduce at
the most rapid possible rate. More fundamentally, Ricardo
deduced a *distributional* movement to the disadvantage of industrial capital from what he perceived to be a long-term trend in
the sphere of *social production*. In this, he maintained the classical
view of economic process, seeing property rather than distribution relations as the basic determinant of class divisions and
relations. Broadly speaking, distributional patterns are a function of the accumulation and reproduction processes. It was left
to later political economists to attribute an independent role and
mode of causality to the forms of distribution within the total
economic structure.

The analytical distinction between the spheres of production and distribution had been sharply drawn in the writings of the leading classical economists. Smith observed that both productive and unproductive labourers, as well as those who do not labour at all, are equally maintained by the annual produce of the land and labour of their country. The latter two sectors are maintained by revenue, a deduction from the total produce available for replacing and expanding capital and for supporting those productive workers whose labour alone 'adds to the value of the subject upon which it is bestowed'.[13] Smith saw the portions of national wealth thus distributed to be variable both between countries and over time in the same society. In particular, the share destined to replace a capital and that which constitutes revenue, either as rent or as profit, typically differ between rich and poor countries, a larger portion replacing capital in the former.[14] As with Ricardo's theory of rent, the social division of total produce into its component parts has a law-like character, the direction of which derives from the accumulation of capital as a progressive function of inter-class relations in production. Smith writes of the determination of distribution in general:

> . . . the whole produce of the land undoubtedly belongs to him who can dispose of the labour and service of all those whom it maintains.[15]

In 'the opulent countries of Europe', capital is relatively highly concentrated in trade and manufactures and, in consequence, its replacement and the maintenance of its productive labourers account for an increasing part of the total economic product.

While criticising the ambiguities in Smith's theory of productive labour,[16] Marx recognised that his emphasis on socially determined human labour as an essential source of value was a crucial scientific principle. An important step in the development of political economy had been taken by the eighteenth-century physiocrats, led by Quesnay, who conceived of economic structure in terms of the physiological forms of society emerging as material laws from the natural necessity of production itself. A number of scattered earlier attempts had been made to establish political economy on an objective and scientific basis. Petty and Benjamin Franklin had come close to seeing the value of a commodity as determined by the quantity of labour necessary to produce it. Again, Cantillon's conception of a 'natural price', whereby commodities tend to sell at their costs of production plus profit at a 'natural rate', suggested a law-like basis for market-price determination, as against the prevalent indeterminate notion of 'supply and demand'.[17] It was the physiocrats, however, who made the important contribution of systematically deriving value and surplus value from the sphere of production rather than circulation, although they confined the concept of productive labour to that performed in agriculture and depicted capital in terms of its narrowly material forms of existence.[18]

Smith's major achievement was to generalise the physiocratic thesis into a theory of labour in a wider sense as value-producing. As early as 1844, Marx referred to Smith's acknowledgement of labour as the subject of private property as 'this enlightened political economy'.[19] But while Smith saw that a commodity acquires value because it is a product of social labour, he did not deduce that the magnitude of its value is determined by the quantity of labour worked up in it. The measure of value lies in the conditions of a commodity's exchange rather than in production: it is equal to the quantity of labour which it enables the producer to purchase or command. Commandable labour, and not the quantity of labour embodied in commodities, is the 'real measure' of value in Smith's theory.[20]

Ricardo, Marx observes, even more clearly than Smith understood that the exchange value of commodities is in fact no more than an expression, a particular social form, of human productive activity, 'an objectively expressed relation of the productive activity of men'.[21] Scholars such as Pilling have argued that the essential difference between Marx's understanding of the law of value and that of his predecessors, especially Ricardo, centres on the methodological procedure which Marx used in his analysis of capitalist society. Whereas Ricardo sought to reconcile the apparently inconsistent phenomena of bourgeois society in an immediate and direct manner, Marx proceeded by carefully depicting the interconnections between the underlying social relations of production, the reflection of which is to be found in the category 'value', and the other phenomena within the system, including the transformation of values into prices.[22] But despite the qualitative advance that Marx's treatment of the law of value represented, his praise of the Classical school's attempts to uncover the laws which govern the production and distribution of wealth in capitalist society is indicative of the progress they made in the development of an objective science of political economy.

With the increasing rejection of the labour theory of value during the nineteenth century, however, the Ricardian system was undermined even by economists who, like McCulloch, were nominally concerned to correct its weaknesses and bring it to completion. It has often been suggested that Ricardo's system represented the highest stage of development of classical political economy prior to Marx's reformulation of the law of value.

Subsequent to Ricardo, McCulloch represented the optimistic strand of non-Marxist economic theory, still viewing classes as in fundamental harmony, despite the prevalence of often intense class conflict. In this, McCulloch was restating what had been a dominant notion from the earliest days of political economy, that of a natural harmony between classes. In the early seventeenth century, Antoyne de Monchrétien proposed an intrinsic communality of interests between the three great classes: ecclesiastical, noble and popular. As with all natural-harmony theories, acquistive activity, here in the form of merchants' trade, 'makes and causes a good part of the public good'.[23] The view that self-seeking activity can produce a more general social benefit was to re-emerge in Adam Smith's work, and was well fitted to reconcile the new individualism of a developing capitalist society to the classical ethical problem of social order.

The immediate impulse for McCulloch's theory, however, was the attribution to capital of the power to create value. Ricardo, especially in his last writings, had come close to identifying the source of absolute value in embodied labour. A perfect measure of value, Ricardo observed, must both have a value itself and, in order to provide a measure which is commensurable between all other commodities, should be invariable.[24] While not a perfect measure, the quantity of labour required to produce commodities is identified by Ricardo as the best criterion available. He therefore recommends the uniform measure of labour as 'eminently well qualified to measure the value of all other things', while noting its imperfection on the grounds of the heterogeneity of the wages and profits proportions into which different commodities are divided.[25]

Ricardo felt unable to resolve the disproportion between embodied labour ratios and exchange ratios, and never fully overcame the view that values are partly determined by factors independent of labour time. Embodied labour, for Ricardo, was essentially the measure rather than the substance of value. Nevertheless, he consistently maintained that purely technical innovation, while raising the material output of industry, does not of itself increase the value of its output.[26] Exchangeable value varies with both the quantity of labour required to produce a commodity and the durability of capital. The influence of the latter, however, serves only to modify rather than to replace the labour standard of value; the labour measure itself provides the essential rationale for this modification. Thus, two instruments, each requiring the same quantity of labour in their manufacture but of unequal durability, will transfer correspondingly different proportions of their own embodied labour to the commodity over the same period of production.[27]

With McCulloch, by contrast, the meaning of labour was diluted to encompass the 'activity' of any agent, human, mechanical or natural, in so far as it effects an intended instrumental alteration in production.[28] Technical change was thus able to provide the value-producing basis to counteract an otherwise falling rate of profit, and McCulloch envisaged a more optimistic scenario for the development of the social economy than that implied by Ricardo's theory of population and rent. Harmony is reconstructed on the foundations of McCulloch's sweeping definition of labour, according to which profit on capital represents 'the wages of accumulated labour', another term for Nassau Senior's 'wages of superintendence'.[29]

An important turning point was reached with Ricardo's confusion over the relation between embodied labour ratios and actual exchange ratios.[30] The decisive period for the subsequent shift of approach in economic theory was the years immediately following the crisis in the British cotton industry in the early 1830s. The change of fortune in this important industry led to the increasing acceptance of radical criticism of property institutions within the labour movement.[31] At the same time, and through a complex chain of explanations, additions, criticisms and counter-criticisms, a series of economists, including McCulloch, James Mill, J. B. Say, Torrens, Bailey and Wakefield, steadily chipped away at the classical problematic of accumulation as a labour-centred process, and developed what Marx termed the 'most complete fetish' of 'interest bearing capital'.[32]

There were a number of important aspects of this development in economic theory.[33] Its most fundamental effect, however, was to sever the causal link between production and distribution as understood by the classical political economists, a departure which had been anticipated by the social and economic writings of J. S. Mill. Social reform, in fact, is a direct corollary of Mill's conception of liberty and the appropriate conditions for its cultivation. His central conviction was that individuals should be allowed to carry their opinions into practice at their own cost in matters which do not restrict the liberty of others; a mature person's proper mode of living is to interpret and use his own experience in his own way.[34]

The limits of Mill's libertarian outlook are marked by his modified Benthamite utilitarian conception of morality and social life. Actions, according to this doctrine, are evaluated as right 'in proportion as they tend to promote happiness, wrong as they tend to produce the reverse of happiness'.[35] Pleasure and freedom from pain are thus the fundamental ends deemed desirable in Mill's moral philosophy. Nevertheless, he proposes a hierarchy of pleasures, some being more valuable than others. The principal criterion for grading is the unanimous or near-unanimous preference of those who have experienced two pleasures for the higher, a preference which Mill attributes to the sense of 'pride' or dignity that is common to all men.[36]

The radical democratic implications of this view of human nature — all mature people are capable of making morally rational choices — are reinforced by Mill's insistence that the utilitarian princile has as its primary referent the general resultant social happiness rather than the exclusive happiness of a particular individual. The principle of the intended maximum happiness of humanity in general is, for Mill, 'the end of human action', 'the standard of morality'.[37] It is this social or universal content of Mill's utilitarianism that underlies his acceptance of the desirability of some forms of collective social reform. The problem he considers is that of how the ideal of socially-directed activity can be best approximated. Mill, very much a child of the Enlightenment, proposes that education can and should attempt to establish the impartiality of a 'disinterested and benevolent observer' in the mind of every individual, a project greatly facilitated by the objective ordering of social arrangements so as to correlate the attainment of personal happiness and the interests of society as a whole as closely as is possible.[38] Such a programme for social reform would both reinforce and derive support from the natural basis of sentiment for utilitarian morality in the 'social feelings' of mankind, a conception which had figured prominently in the social and ethical writings of Locke, Cumberland, Shaftesbury, Hume and many others. The desire for unity with others, the 'contagion of sympathy', is, Mill believed, steadily growing with the advance of civilisation, and with it grow the chances for the implementation of positive and informed social reform.

Mill did not fail to notice the large and persistent inequalities of reward that had become crystallised within the class structure of nineteenth-century Britain: 'The more revolting the occupation,' he wrote, 'the more certain it is to receive the minimum renumeration.'[39] In this particular instance, as in his general philosophy of utilitarianism, Mill advocated social reform with the condition that it did not contradict the basic principle of free competition. His support of competition went so far as to allow him to suggest that only in relation to it can political economy claim the status of a science.[40] The tension between Mill's *laissez-faire* economic instincts and his support for progressive reforms in a variety of social and economic areas led him to envisage a schematic differentiation of the scope for conscious social intervention in the production and distribution spheres respectively. He proposed that 'The laws and conditions of the production of wealth partake of the character of physical truths', whereas its distribution 'depends on the laws and customs of society'.[41]

The material forms of production have an eternal quality, but those of distribution are amenable to adjustment in the direction of greater welfare and equity. Distribution, in other words, is attributed a distinct set of potential determinants, and therefore has an autonomous capacity for change. With this formulation, the classical assumption that distribution patterns are, with minor variations, a function of the accumulation process is decisively abandoned and, at the risk of doing injustice to what was in fact a complex chain of development, the stage is set for the fully-fledged neo-classical theory of distribution to be elaborated. Marginal propensities to save, to invest, or even to write economics textbooks could be calmly discussed without contemplating the horrors of falling rates of profit, surging populations, stagnating investment, and the other sombre vistas that the classical writers had opened up for general view.

The celebrated Marginal Revolution, consolidated around the 1870s by the independent work of Walras, Jevons and Menger, decreed that the value of a product or service is due not to the quantity of labour embodied in it, but rather to the usefulness of the last unit purchased. The marginalists were by no means the first to raise substantive and theoretical questions concerning the distributional aspects of economic activity. Their ideas to a considerable extent simply represented the culmination and systematisation of a number of earlier tendencies within economic thought.[42] In addition, doubts had been expressed during the heyday of classical theory about the ability of prevailing distribution and consumption patterns to keep pace with the productive potential of the developing capitalist economy. Perhaps most influential was Sismondi's explanation of industrial depressions in terms of the tendency of capital investment to raise the level of production above the capacity of society to purchase its output.[43] Spence, again, had suggested that the accumulation of savings could reduce general purchasing power and consequently undermine the prosperity that the new production techniques had allowed.[44] Malthus also argued that falling prices and an ensuing reluctance to invest would be the likely outcome of the inability of wages to purchase the entire output of industry.[45]

The orthodox reply to arguments of this type derived from Say's proposition that while sectoral and largely self-correcting imbalances may well occur in particular branches of industry, the ability of supply to create its own demand excludes the possibility of a general glut of unconsumed commodities. Ricardo replied to Malthus essentially along these lines, suggesting that the increased savings placed in the hands of capitalists in times of low agricultural activity allow both a higher level of personal expenditure and the payment of additional taxes, if required. Whatever the initial distribution of national income, Ricardo suggested, neither its total amount nor the overall ability to pay taxes and 'purchase enjoyments' are diminished by short-term shifts in its pattern of allocation.[46]

Economic crises of under-consumption have in fact been endemic throughout the known history of class society. V. Gordon Childe, for example, admirably documents the social and economic consequences of a restricted internal market for consumer goods in classical Greece, where the institution of slavery both curbed the development of the productive forces and contributed to the general state of impoverishment by limiting the purchasing power of society.[47] Under-consumptionist theories received a special stimulus from the uneven development of the expanding capitalist system and have even found a reflection in a number of recent Marxian-influenced studies of contemporary capitalism.[48] The early nineteenth-century doubters, nevertheless, in the main elaborated their theories from an essentially unchanged classical perspective. Malthus argued for the inability of wages to purchase the full output of industry on the grounds that they represent less than the total costs of production. His starting point remained the classical paradigm of production and its effects on consumption, although he emphasised the limitations imposed on production itself by the prevailing forms of commodity distribution.[49]

The later marginalists, by contrast, systematised a qualitatively different approach to the study of economic phenomena by proposing the determining priority of subjective utility. Each factor of production is seen to be rewarded according to its marginal productivity, or that change in productivity brought about by employing an additional unit of the particular factor at a given level of output. There has, however, been little in the way of agreement concerning the precise meaning of the basic concepts 'factor' and 'production' themselves. E. H. Chamberlin distinguishes three interpretations of the increments in productivity, obtained through the application of additional factor units, as referring to the physical output itself, its value, and the ensuing increase in company revenue.[50] The latter interpretation is adopted in a recent study by D. H. Heathfield, who assesses the risk-taking dimension of entrepreneurial activity in terms of the relation between the marginal revenue product of each factor and its marginal cost.[51] Heathfield's orientation does not represent an orthodoxy, however, and the exact object of marginal analysis is still an issue of lively controversy.[52]

Equally diverse have been the applications of marginal productivity theory. Oscar Lange has developed Schumpeter's analysis of the economic role of innovation in a Marxian-tinged variant of marginal theory: innovation, Lange proposes, constitutes a change in the production function, or the relation between the input of factors of production and the output level, which allows a firm to maximise profits in given market conditions.[53] Cassels, by contrast, has used marginal theory in an attempt to clarify the economic law of diminishing returns.[54] Whatever the particular factor object or field of application, the marginal productivity theory embodies a distinctive conception of economic structure and process; it provides the general basis for a homogeneous theory of distribution, all shares of the total product being governed by the common principle of *rational* consumer choices. Menger's proposition that the consumer weighs the relative advantages of different possible courses of action and always chooses that which offers him the greatest increment in welfare reflects this orientation, as does the view of Walras that the entire economic system is keyed to consumers' spending decisions.[55]

The marginalists' conception of the sphere of production is of a process in which, as Rowthorn's important critique observes, 'inputs of labour, land and means of production . . . are mysteriously transformed into outputs of material and non-material goods'.[56] Jevons, for example, formulates 'The problem of economics' as that of employing a certain population, with various needs and powers of production, in such a way as to maximise the utility of the produce.[57] With capital representing the material aggregate of commodities required for sustaining labourers engaged in work, *social* relations are relegated to the sector of distribution, the typical focus of the marginalists' concern.[58] Their characteristic preoccupation with distribution as a structure of subjective market orientations effectively autonomous from the expenditure, control and appropriation of the labour effort which produces goods destined for use is epitomised by Jevons' seminal proposition that 'the scientific basis of economics is in a theory of consumption'.[59]

In accordance with Jevons' dictum, Marshall, perhaps the greatest populariser of marginal doctrine, describes the basic law of distribution in the following terms:

> The net aggregate of all the commodities purchased . . . is divided up into earnings of labour; interest of capital; and lastly the producers' surplus, or rent, of land. . . . It is distributed among them, speaking generally, in proportion to the need which people have for their several services — i.e. not the *total* need but the marginal *need*.[60]

The social structure of distribution thus viewed harmoniously, little logical room is allowed for the concept of exploitation. When considered by the marginalists, exploitation is conceived in an idiosyncratic form: Chamberlin, for example, suggests that in a situation of monopolistic competition, where individual producers have a recognised or legitimate control over their own economic resources, 'all factors are necessarily "exploited" '.[61] The rationale of Chamberlin's proposition is that, under these conditions, all factors cannot be paid the full value of their marginal product without exceeding the total amount available for distribution: for technical reasons, the sum of incomes computed on the basis of marginal productivity is greater than the total product.[62] Exploitation is perceived as a phenomenon of marginal methodology rather than as a structured relation among economic classes.

Marginal productivity theory has been the object of criticism from a number of directions, especially since the 1950s. Prominent among its critics are Joan Robinson and John Eatwell, members of the Cambridge School of Economics.[63] In addition, some erstwhile proponents of marginal theory have more recently expressed objections to its assumptions, particularly those relating to the theory of distribution. Champernowne, critically assessing his own theoretical study of income distribution originally published in 1936, points to its 'crudest marginalist' perspective. In weighing the relative values of different 'qualifications for obtaining income', he suggests, normative and power-oriented facts are of greater significance than marginal productivity and the pure functioning of the market-price mechanism.[64]

Champernowne's comments reinforce Therborn's demonstration that many leading proponents of marginal theory, including Alfred Marshall, have been outspoken critics of trade unionism and the working-class movement in general.[65] More fundamental is the marginal premise of a schematic division between the branches of production and distribution. Mill, as we have seen, expressly used this division in order to establish the theoretical basis for progressive social reforms and, in his *Principles of Political Economy*, anticipates a future 'utopia' in which voluntary associations of workers will exercise control over production.[66] As A. Bhaduri points out, the concept 'production function' purports to depict the pure production aspect of an economy in terms of material inputs and outputs. Risk-bearing or profit-maximising behaviour gauged by marginal calculations, on the other hand, leads directly to a marginal theory of distribution.[67] Thus bracketed off from the socially-structured relations of production, the marginal theory of distribution rests on a narrowly technical model of 'factor' components. The ensuing proposition that the various factors receive rewards corresponding to their respective contribution to the joint product incorporates the macro dimension of economy as a deductive and teleological component of the model as a whole. It is deductive in that an *a priori* community of interests within the productive enterprise is assumed, and teleological in so far as social relations are introduced in the mystified form of relations between persons and things, located at the point where production, abstracted from its concrete social conditions, affects individuals or 'factors' through the distribution of rewards. The marginal harmony model represents the perfected rejection of the classical postulate that distributional patterns derive from and are grounded in a production complex itself expressing a systematic structure of social relations.

WEBER AND UTILITY

Gunnar Myrdal suggests that Weber, while challenging the economic theories of both Marxism and the German Historical School, did not attempt to systematically examine the classical and neo-classical doctrines.[68] Weber's relative silence concerning the latter should not be taken to indicate a lack of familiarity, since in fact he incorporates, though not without modification, some of the central tenets of the neo-classical approach into his general theory of economic organisation. Weber is critical of all attempts to conflate economic analysis into the study of 'wants' and 'satisfaction'. Since a valid definition of economic action must be formulated in such a way as to take account of the complex modern market economy, the orientations of consumers can not, Weber says, constitute the point of departure.[69] Nevertheless, his ultimate grounding of social interactive processes in actors' meaning complexes determines the form of, for example, his discussion of the role of technology in economic life. Weber observes that the rapid development of technology in recent times has been largely oriented to the goal of profit-making. The modern factory, distinguished by the simultaneous presence of an organised workshop with internally differentiated functions, the appropriation of all non-human means of production, and a high degree of mechanisation of the work process, is a unique category of the developed capitalist economy.[70] As such it embodies and reflects the concrete objectivity of a determinate historical epoch.

In accordance with his definition of economically-oriented action as that action which in its subjective meaning is concerned with the satisfaction of a desire for utilities,[71] Weber accounts for the specific determination of modern technology in terms of the meaning orientations which are inseparable from the forms of economic activity to which it corresponds:

> Had not rational calculation formed the basis of economic activity, had there not been certain very particular conditions in its economic background, rational technology could never have come into existence.[72]

Utilities are accordingly designated the status of means towards the ends of economic action.[73] Drawing on the theories of Böhm-Bawerk, Weber proposes that the utility of particular goods does not derive from their physical properties as material objects, but from the specific ways in which they can be put to 'desirable and practical uses'.[74] Weber, in fact, explicitly endorses marginal utility theory in relation to the determination of prices both in the budgetary unit and in the profit-seeking of the entrepreneur in so far as it approximates to the ideal type of formally rational activity. The capital accounting and calculation of the capitalist are 'in the last analysis dependent on the income of consumption units and, through this, on the marginal utility of the available income of the final consumers of consumption goods'.[75]

Weber insists, however, that the determination of the direction of production by the marginal consumer is applicable only 'for purposes of economic theory'.[76] The sociologist also wishes to know how 'this supposed relation of marginal utilities' affects human action in such a way that actors are able and willing to make differences in preferences a basis for the payment of interest, a form of activity unique to profit-making economies. The formal rationality of money calculation is dependent upon the presence of certain substantive conditions, important among which is the regulation of the production of goods by consumers' 'effective' demand for utilities; formally rational capitalist economy is determined by the structure of marginal utilities in those income groups which actually purchase a given utility. Weber notes the considerable influence exerted on the demand functions of consumers in the modern economy and suggests that in developed capitalist society even the dominant types of food and housing provisions are importantly determined by producers' interests.[77] The formal rationality of money calculation, in other words, of itself has no implications for the actual distribution of goods, and it is only with a knowledge of the latter that the criteria of formal rationality can be of explanatory value in relation to the satisfaction of real wants.

Now profit-making, for Weber, corresponds to that activity which is oriented to opportunities for seeking new powers of control over goods.[78] In capitalist society, the services of labour are subject to a contractual relation which is formally free on both sides and which entails the absence of the forms of appropriation present in, for example, the unfree labour of serfdom and slavery proper.[79] The formal equality of power posited for the wage – labour relationship is likely, however, to be disturbed by actual inequalities of market influence. Thus, an important condition for obtaining a maximum of formal rationality of capital accounting is the presence of substantive freedom of contract, or 'complete absence of substantive regulation of consumption, production, and prices, or of other forms of regulation which limit freedom of contract or specify conditions of exchange'.[80]

Weber emphasises the importance of a legal guarantee of control over the means of production and the functions of labour. The present exchange economy is sustained by a network of contractual relations, each originating in a consciously planned process of acquisition of powers of control and disposal. Alternative principles for the distribution of such powers are conceivable, in particular the socialist and anarchist types, both with a distinct form of control over the necessary services of labour and the means of production. The mode of control in any particular instance may be guaranteed either by law and convention or by non-external sanctions such as legitimate expectations in terms of self-interest. Ultimately, Weber stresses the necessity of legal compulsion as a fundamental guarantor of 'the modern economic order':

> It is by no means true that only the legal assurance of powers of disposal is decisive, either for the concept or in fact. It is, however, today empirically an indispensable basis for control of the material means of production.[81]

For Weber, the means of production appropriated by the capitalist entrepreneur and guaranteed by the legal order are the non-human elements of the production process. They may hypothetically be owned by capitalists, by the workers themselves, or by a regulating group in the form of a third party.[82] In their specifically capitalist form, however, entrepreneurial control over the material means of production allows for a higher level of technical utilisation as well as the exercise of managerial coordination in such a way as to impose a stringent discipline on the speed and quality of labour. The improved orientation towards market advantages resulting from this control has in fact been an important factor favouring the expropriation of the means of producion from the labour force.[83]

The formal rationality of capitalist economic activity, however, depends for its maximum realisation upon the presence of formally free labour and the free negotiation of employment contracts. Weber's account of economic relations thus opposes the private appropriation of the material means of production to the total non-appropriation of labour services under capitalist conditions of ownership. His related definition of 'capital' as a sum of money in terms of which the enterprise's means of profit are valued[84] corresponds to the fetishised marginalist view of capital as a 'thing' rather than a social relation. This conception is reinforced by Weber's distinction between non-human objects which are a potential source of utilities and those derived from human sources as 'goods' and 'services' respectively, linked only by their common basis of value in 'desirable and practical use'.[85]

Despite his concern to 'sociologise' the economic theory of marginal utility by adding substantive distributional and political flesh to the bones of formal capitalistic rationality, Weber adopts its central tenets. He posits a sharp conflict between two types of socialism, oriented to the problems of production and distribution respectively; he indicates an awareness of the tension between the classical and neo-classical problematics in the specific case of socialist theory.[86] Again, when he discusses the distinguishing features of the orientation towards profit-making in the modern world, Weber singles out activity directed to the exploitation of market advantages, as against the various forms of 'politically oriented' capitalism, as being of special significance. Yet he does not attempt to establish the relative determining weight of production and market exchange within this far from precise category of activity. Both, quite simply, may be pursued, either singly or together, in relation to the market structures.[87]

Weber's general analysis of economic action and class structuration is, as we have seen,[88] oriented to the sphere of market encounter and distribution and, as such, it reflects the neo-classical problematic. Thus, the principal aim of regulation in an economy is to influence the distribution of incomes. Acquisition of and control over future income is similarly presupposed in the economic orientations within a market economy.[89]

Moreover, in the market economy all rational capital accounting is oriented to expectations of prices and their changes 'as they are determined by the conflicts of interests in bargaining and competition and the resolution of these conflicts'.[90] Weber views exchange as a 'compromise of interests' on the part of the involved parties, in the course of which a resolution is effected over an agreed price. Competitive bidding is the typical method of resolving rivalry between aspirants to the exchange itself.[91] This account, of course, refers to the formal rationality of market-conflict resolution, and is subject to modification by the influence of monopolistic modes of appropriation of labour services and other sources of economic utilities. Weber characteristically sets down his methodology with admirable clarity:

> . . . the facts of the economic situation provide the flesh and blood for a genuine explanation of the process by which even a sociologically relevant development takes place. What can be done here is only to provide a scaffolding which is adequate to enable the analysis to work with relatively clear and definite concepts.[92]

In particular, Weber's version of marginal utility theory has the character of an ideal-typical model of economic structure and process, the special task of the sociologist being to augment the basic paradigm by a consideration of the relevant political and other social relations. Pure economic theory utilises ideal-type concepts constructed on the basis of assumptions concerning exclusively economic factors in order to ask how men would act under certain conditions if their actions were entirely rational. But the causal explanation of actual economic phenomena is inseparable from the reciprocal influence of other, non-economic social events, in particular political actions and structures.[93]

The substantive power inequalities and conflicts that Weber perceives allow a sociological perspective of conflict to be built on the basis of underlying marginalist distributional assumptions. Honigsheim, sensitive to the variety of nuances within and influences upon Weber's theory, notes the essential role of marginal utility in his thought.[94] What is just as important is the role of Weber in transmitting the basic market paradigm, plus an added conflictual edge, from marginal-utility theory to the emerging science of social relations to which he contributed so much.

CLASS AND OCCUPATION

Once the processes of market encounter and the corresponding distributional structures have been granted a fully autonomous role in the economic process, the theoretical framework has been established within which accounts of class structuration as determined by a heterogeneous range of independent principles of apparently equal causal weight may be developed. This, broadly speaking, is the theoretical basis for all sociological accounts which adopt an eclectic view of class structure, stressing here the role of property ownership, there that of market capacity, status, prestige, authority or whatever. Pareto once likened history to 'a graveyard of aristocracies'.[95] It would perhaps be fruitful to extend the analogy to the history of elite theory itself. Social theory of the last century in particular is littered with more or less impressionistic, more or less rigorous, models of class structure based on the accentuation of particular aspects of social differentiation and their reification into primary or at least major determinants of political or economic rule. Burnham's thesis of an emerging, global, managerial ruling class is one of the most popularised and widely read studies of this type.[96]

A related, more diffuse, current in sociological theory is the tendency to fragment the concept of class into its supposed constituent parts. Marshall suggests that the extension of citizenship rights in society has had the consequence of limiting the economic determinants of class, so that whatever inequalities survive have primarily other than economic functions.[97] The idea of 'other than economic' bases of class structuration typically accompanies a merging of class with a more broadly, if not loosely, defined conception of stratification. An extreme illustration of this approach is Gross's terse equation of social hierarchy with the presence of 'groups that stand in a superior — subordinate relationship to other groups or to organized publics'.[98] If, as is the case with Gross, class is initially subsumed into a statically conceived general phenomenon of hierarchy, it is a short step to see its appropriate method of analysis as a symptomatic description of the visible associational forms of inter-group relations and, possibly, conflicts. Not untypical is the work of Lipset and Bendix, whose comparative study of social mobility in industrial societies assumes a multiplicity of partly overlapping and partly conflicting hierarchies, each determined by a different 'factor'. Family background, services rendered, consumption patterns and education are all autonomous within their own rank-orders. Further differentiation is provided by ethnic, religious and other divisions within these principal hierarchies.[99] Stratification becomes as potentially elusive as social interaction itself; now you see it, now you don't.

Rather more provocative is Geiger's analysis of changing patterns of stratification in developed societies. Geiger notes a number of emerging 'post-Marxian' social trends, including the increasing political independence of the middle strata, the rise of consumer status, conflict between consumers and the agents of production, and the growing power of 'experts'.[100] It is significant that at least three of these trends concern patterns of market interaction rather than classical production relations on the one hand, or purely subjective status differences on the other. A distinct sub-genre of multi-factorial theories of stratification, in fact, assume that the bedrock of social differentiation is the economic order, typically analysed from a distributive or market point of view. Despite the bewildering ambiguity of their formal model, Lipset and Bendix conclude that mobility patterns in Western industrialised societies are determined primarily by trends within the occupational structure.[101] Parkin, not unsimilarly, views class structure as a system of unequal rewards, the roots of which lie in the occupational order and the political arrangements which reinforce it.[102] Property ownership, however, is clumsily appendaged as an auxiliary determinant of rewards.[103] Property and occupation assume the form of independent determinants related only through their effects on the reward hierarchy, thus reproducing the eclecticism that Parkin criticises at the level of the *elements* of stratification (age, sex etc.) in the context of its *sources*. Parkin's exposition is often awkward,[104] but its distributive orientation bears the clear mark of Weber's influence, regardless of his intended anti-Weberian stance.[105]

The Lipset–Parkin thesis represents a response to very real developments which have taken place in the occupational structure of the advanced capitalist societies.[106] Partly as a result of concern with changing patterns of social mobility, a number of sociological studies have drawn attention to the expansion of white collar and professional groups, broadly termed the tertiary sector, and the parallel contraction of the manual occupational category.[107] In Britain, this trend is apparent from the relatively rapid rate of growth since the early twentieth century in industries such as engineering and shipbuilding, vehicles and, above all, chemicals, with a high proportion of administrative, technical and clerical staff to industrial employees.[108] The proportion of manpower in 'services' as against 'goods' rose in Britain from 48 to 52 per cent between 1924–38, and again continued to rise in the post-war years, although from a lower level due to the industrial reorganisation of the war economy.[109] The trend is even more pronounced and regular in the United States, the share of persons employed in the services sector there rising from 47 per cent in 1929 to 51 per cent in 1947 and 58 per cent in 1965.[110]

The increased social differentiation that the growth of the 'middle classes' implies occurs primarily as a function of the developing occupational division of labour. Adam Smith's famous example of the fragmentation of work tasks in the manufacture of pins underlines the economies that are opened up by the increasingly scientific application of the division of labour. But alongside the specialisation of technical skills that occurs in this process, there also develops an oppositional movement in the direction of de-skilling in the labour force. The gearing of the mechanised factory to mass production represents an extreme case of the de-qualification of the majority of industrial workers while, simultaneously, new skilled manpower needs arise in the fields of programming and control, trained maintenance personnel and electronics. The regularity of individual advancement in skilled and semi-skilled occupations, moreover, should not be exaggerated. Changing technology, as well as the vicissitudes of corporate profitability, mean that skills are continually being created, diluted, modified and made redundant. The progress of the organisation man's career is probably rarely as smooth and orderly as the sequence of functions and status positions portrayed by both his friends and critics alike.[111]

The theoretical problem concerns not the fact of growth in the tertiary and skilled sectors, but its significance for the overall functioning of the capitalist economy. Marx distinguished between the division of labour in society and that in manufacture: while the former originates in the exchange of commodities between distinct spheres of production in society at large, the latter is a relatively recent development, brought about by the sale of different labour powers to a single capitalist who employs them as a combined form of labour power, or a collective worker. In the former, competition between independent commodity producers is the principal external authority; in the latter, authority resides in the hands of the employer, and is a particular historical form of the authority inherent in property ownership.[112]

Marx thus saw the division of labour in society to historically precede that in manufacture. The division of labour in society is a general consequence of commodity production, a necessary but not sufficient condition for the division of labour in manufacture, which requires the specifically capitalistic organisation of the labour process. Weber, by contrast, examines the technical forms within which the division of labour may vary in an essentially ahistorical ideal – typical account of human and non-human productive variables. Variations concern the differentiation and combination of work services, the way in which fixed plant facilities and implements of work are used, and other strictly technical aspects of the production process.[113] The social classification of the types of division of labour, by contrast, embraces Weber's typology of historically concrete forms of joint production. Here, variations take the form of differences in either the mode by which qualitatively distinct functions are divided between more or less autonomous economic units, or that by which economic advantages are appropriated (by the individual worker, by the owner of 'unfree' labour, by associations of workers, or not at all in the case of contractual, formally free labour).[114] A further source of variation is the form of appropriation of the non-human means of production.

Now while Weber's studies in economic history are rich in empirical observations concerning developments in the historical forms of labour organisation, his conception of class structure at the particular stage of capitalist industry is, as we have seen, articulated in terms of the centrality of income sources and the marketability of goods and services. Weber does not, either methodologically or substantively, reconcile his typology of forms of joint production to his wider orientation towards the phenomena of the market. Surely, for example, his claim that the expropriation of workers from the means of production is due to the higher level of technical efficiency and the greater access of a capitalistic management to credit thus allowed[115] is a shallow historical observation when viewed against his account of the actual, compulsive social and economic conditions of the institution of 'free labour'.[116]

Yet it is precisely the technical—occupational aspect of Weber's work that has been taken up by the Lipset—Parkin school of stratification. Their general problematic is the observable fact of economic inequalities that do not appear to derive from or even correspond to the divisions based on property ownership. Now, occupational differentiation may be irreducible *in its details* to the capitalist mode of production and the forms of labour organisation that it historically develops. Nevertheless, the existence of a steadily growing strata of employees who do not take part in directly productive economic activity is inconceivable without the presence of structural conditions which have been created in the course of development of the capitalist system: in particular, the need to consume a growing economic surplus and the increasing technical necessity of unproductive workers in the service and related sectors.

To merely state this, however, is, as John Ure points out, to propose a thoroughly functionalist explanation for the growth of the 'middle' strata.[117] The technical, service and adminstrative economic categories, while far from homogeneous,[118] are a *technical* necessity in developed capitalist society, but are *structurally* sustained by the increasing mass of surplus value that it historically generates. As Dahrendorf suggests,[119] both status and material differentials characteristically preoccupy the incumbents of these positions, as well as the sectors of productive labour whose market scarcity allows for a relatively high degree of bargaining power and, consequently, at least a potential material advantage.[120] A major perceived obstacle to the success of contemporary wage-restraint policies, in fact, is the very real opposition of relatively well-positioned sectors of the labour force to the threat of eroding differentials under the joint impact of inflation and wage controls.

Nevertheless, variations in relative wage rates have not historically been as wide as would be expected if, as the Parkin thesis implies, the scarcity-value of occupational skills in the market place were the chief determinant of the distributional structure. Routh's study of occupation and pay in Britain reports a remarkably stable structure of income distribution. The years 1911–58 saw a narrowing in dispersion for males, but this was largely offset by a widened dispersion for women employees. Routh concludes: 'The outstanding characteristic of the national pay structure is the rigidity of its relationships.'[121] In the short term, ratios between occupational class averages fluctuate, but over a longer period they 'seem to have the capacity to regain previous shapes'. Coalminers and agricultural workers, for example, suffered a relative decline after the First World War, but returned to their earlier position within the national pay structure after the Second.[122] Rees similarly reports that even during the transformative years of 1899–1914 only a very slight tendency for earnings to narrow could be detected among the thirteen U.S. industries studied.[123] Wage differentials, it appears, tend to preserve their relative levels over time.

As against the relative constancy of earnings among different sectors within the working class, significant empirical variations in the overall distribution of income between classes do take place. The 1960s, for example, saw a substantial decline in the real share of total national income going to wages and salaries in Britain.[124] Such variations concern adjustments within an enduring structure of distribution, the character and limits of which are circumscribed by the prevailing form of property ownership.

In capitalist society, the means of subsistence accrue to labour in the form of wages, profits being initially distributed among industrial capitalists, financiers and landlords. Without the wages system and the private ownership of productive property on which it rests, the general framework of distribution between labour and the various factions of the owning class would be inconceivable. As Baldamus points out, the concept of wage disparity describes the phenomenon of non-parallel movements in effort intensity and wage payments, the two principal components of the employment contract. Work obligations in the organisation of industry, as presently constituted, centre on the administrative control of employees' effort, where the worker's 'sacrifices are greater than his gains':[125] a quantity of labour power is surrendered gratis to the employer. Even if empirical shifts in the distributional flow of inter-sector rewards were quantitatively more significant than they are at present, they would not justify the elevation of occupational skills and their market scarcity into the primary determinants of class structure. For, as Baldamus observes,

> . . . the conditions that create wage disparity – limited upward mobility and institutionalized work obligations – are part of the larger social system.[126]

3

Market Sociology Today: Anthony Giddens

In the case of Anthony Giddens, a different aspect of the market is abstracted from the total process of economic production and reproduction. Like Parkin, Giddens attaches considerable importance, for the emergence of common class situations, to the scarcity-value of the various attributes that social actors bring to the market encounter. He does not, however, follow Parkin in viewing class primarily in terms of the resultant structure of unequal rewards. Rather, he is more directly and more consistently concerned with actual social relationships in the sphere of market interaction. Giddens' analysis of class structuration is of particular interest, both for its relative rigour and because his debt to Weber is explicitly acknowledged.[1] His work is also instructive in that it directly challenges the Marxist theory of class and capitalism and, in doing so, makes explicit many of the assumptions that are more or less hidden in less sophisticated versions of market sociology.

Giddens initially sets himself the ambitious task of analysing 'the problem in sociology: the question of classes and class conflict'.[2] In explicating the process of class structuration, he adopts Weber's concept of 'social class', which he reformulates as

> a cluster of class situations which are linked together by virtue of the fact that they involve common mobility chances, either within the career of individuals or across generations.[3]

Giddens' concern with 'class situation' leads him to focus attention on the market capacity of members of different social classes as they struggle for 'scarce returns' within the market structure of competitive capitalism. His model of the structuration of class relations distinguishes between its *mediate* and *proximate* aspects. The former refer to the 'overall connecting links' between particular market capacities on the one hand and the formation of identifiable classes on the other; the latter concern more 'localized' factors, in particular the distribution of mobility chances.[4]

Concerning mediate structuration, Giddens identifies three types of market capacity that are of particular determining significance: ownership of productive property; possession of educational or technical qualifications; and possession of manual-labour power. He relates these three factors to the upper, middle and lower or working classes of the 'basic three class system in capitalist society'. Further, he locates three sources of proximate structuration in the division of labour in the productive enterprise, its authority relations, and the influence of distributive groupings relating to the consumption of economic goods.

At one point, he posits that the 'central focus of class relations' is 'founded in production',[5] yet it is apparent that Giddens' principal concern is the definition and analysis of class at the level of market encounter. Individuals confront one another on the market with diverse attributes which have a greater or lesser degree of scarcity-value. The possession or non-possession of these attributes, along with the proximate factors mentioned above, determines the way in which common class situations emerge. The structuration of classes and their relations thus becomes contingent upon a number of unevenly located determinants, as is clear from Giddens' claim that structuration is 'facilitated to the degree to which mobility closure exists in relation to any specified form of market capacity'.[6] As with Parkin, Giddens is eclectic in his account of the sources of class structure.

Through this market model, Giddens systematically shifts his focus away from the Marxist view of class as rooted in the social relations of production, a view to which he pays formal lipservice. This shift becomes explicit when he asserts that Marx

> . . . failed to recognize the potential significance of differentiations of market capacity which do not derive directly from the factor of property ownership.[7]

Market capacity, in Giddens' usage, refers to 'all forms of relevant attributes which individuals may bring to the bargaining encounter'.

In fact, Marx was well aware of the importance of explaining how the different elements or moments of the production cycle, including the various aspects of exchange, are related to one another; his view was that their relationship is of an essentially unitary nature. Thus, in the *Grundrisse* he writes:

> The conclusion we reach is not that production, distribution, exchange and consumption are identical, but that they all form the members of a totality, distinctions within a unity.[8]

But while maintaining the relative determining power of the other moments, Marx drew consistent conclusions from his identification of the source of the whole cycle and, consequently, the roots of classes in production:

> Production predominates not only over itself, in the antithetical definition of production, but over the other moments as well. The process always returns to production to begin anew.[9]

For Marx, industrial capital is the primary determining moment of the total process because it is only at this point (as against the stages corresponding to the forms of money-capital and commodity-capital) that not only the appropriation but also, and simultaneously, the creation of surplus value is a function of capital.[10] Only in production are the elements, both in terms of materiality and of value, actually generated for further rounds of the whole cycle of extended reproduction. And it is on this productive function that the other moments of the cycle are absolutely dependent.

Specifically concerning the type of market attributes with which Giddens is concerned, Marx wrote:

> It is clear that the exchange of activities and abilities which takes place within production itself belongs directly to production and essentially constitutes it.[11]

Given the primacy of production in the total cycle, particular skills and attributes should be viewed as aspects of the labour power of their 'owners' within specific historical modes of production. To take Giddens' example of the formal qualifications of the middle class, Marx prophetically, it may be said, located their source of material support in the rising mass of profits that he saw to accompany extended capital accumulation and the growth of social productivity.[12]

The conditions necessary for the support of the middle classes and for their characteristic mode of involvement in the capitalist market, in other words, are dependent upon and, in the last analysis, determined by the degree of development of society's productive potential. The 'recognized skills' which Giddens correctly sees to be important in influencing market capacity are aspects of labour power, which in turn draws its particular social character from its relation to production. Giddens' market-encounter orientation towards class structuration is indicative of a confusion concerning the question of determination in society. Its roots may be detected in his earlier 'non-applied' study, *Capitalism and Modern Social Theory*, which should be considered as a companion or at least preparatory work to his *Class Structure*.

In *Capitalism and Modern Social Theory*, Giddens correctly stresses the importance that Marx attributed to market forces of supply and demand in the determination of prices.[13] In the later work, however, he contends that Marx underestimated the significance of economic actors' market capacity in the bargaining encounter. This capacity, central to the structuration of class relations, is seen as used to secure economic returns on the basis of individuals' 'attributes' for which there is a demand. The logic of Giddens' argument is that the price of, for example, labour power, the attribute of the worker, is determined by its scarcity-value, thus understood, as he brings it to the market at a given level of demand.

Yet this, in fact, is precisely what Marx contended. On commodities generally, his view was that 'Supply and demand create the market-price'.[14] The fluctuations of the price of labour power around its value are, as with any other commodity, determined in this way:

> Supply and demand create nothing but the temporary fluctuations of market prices. They will explain to you why the market price of a commodity rises above or sinks below its value. . . . The same holds true of wages and of the prices of all other commodities.[15]

Yet Giddens, in his later work, claims to be correcting an underestimation of the importance of this aspect of the working of capitalism on Marx's part.

A key to Giddens' inconsistency can be found in his discussion of Marx's theory of alienation. Here Giddens, albeit cautiously, distinguishes between alienation in the labour process and that of the worker from his product as two sources of alienation in capitalist society; he terms them 'technological' and 'market' alienation, respectively.[16] While locating the source of both in the capitalistic division of labour, he suggests that for Marx it was only through the overcoming of the latter that the former would be abolished.

Now this distinction in fact corresponds to Marx's own distinction, developed in *Capital*, between the division of labour in manufacture and that in society.[17] In Giddens' *Class Structure*, 'technological alienation', seen in the earlier work as associated with occupational specialisation and work fragmentation, and as essentially dependent upon and subordinate to 'market alienation', assumes an autonomous role in the determination of the capitalist class structure. We will attempt to identify the basic assumptions in Giddens' work which structure this effective bifurcation of Marx's concept of alienation.

In the *Economic and Philosophic Manuscripts*, Marx identifies four aspects of alienation: the alienation of the worker from his product, from the act or process of labour itself, from his species-being, and from other men.[18] All four aspects are, for Marx, expressions of 'the act of estranging practical human activity, labour'. Alienation is the process whereby man objectifies himself through practice in the world in conditions under which his products become external powers in relation to himself; it is a unitary phenomenon, deriving its unity from the determinate social conditions of commodity production:

> We took our departure from a fact of political economy – the estrangement of the worker and his production. We have formulated this fact in conceptual terms as estranged, alienated labour. We have analyzed this concept – hence analyzing merely a fact of political economy.[19]

Alienation is, in this way, conceived in terms of Marx's materialist ontological model of human essence and practice, the elements of which are succinctly expressed in his *Theses on Feuerbach*. People make history, but not in conditions of their own choosing.

Giddens, by contrast, endorses Mumford's view of man as a 'mind-making, self-mastering and self-designing animal'.[20] In order to illustrate this voluntaristic, consciousness-centred characterisation of man's social being, Giddens, echoing Weber's interpretive analysis of capitalism, defines 'industrialism' as the application of calculative rationality to production. Counterposing this interpretation to Marx's supposed view of 'tool-using and production' as the basic component of human life, he rejects the 'myth' that 'industrial man was made by the machine'.

It is at this point that Giddens seriously misrepresents Marx's analysis. Marx was not primarily concerned with 'industrial man', nor with any other non-relational abstraction *per se*; his theoretical concern was to lay bare the social relations of production, the relations of ownership and exploitation, together with the laws of motion that characterise specifically capitalist industrial society.

Now Giddens offers a definition of 'industrial society' (a social order in which 'industrialism', or the transfer of inanimate energy sources to production through the agency of factory organisation, predominates in the production of marketable goods) which is neutral as regards social relations of production.[21] His accompanying definition of capitalism, on the other hand, incorporates some of the key features of Marx's analysis, in particular the pursuit of profit, private ownership of the means of production, and the presence of a market.[22] His idiosyncratic characterisation of contemporary Western society as 'post-Marxist', but neither 'post-capitalist' nor 'post-industrial', when unravelled, is particularly revealing.[23] Giddens' claim is that the Marxist association of the exploitation of wage labour and its potential for revolution no longer holds. He suggests that:

> The revolutionary potential of the working class depends on the initial encounter with capitalism, not upon the maturity of the capitalist mode of production.[24]

While Giddens holds open the possibility of a renewal of class conflict in a political form,[25] he considers that the development of social democracy, oligopoly and long-range state planning together constitute changes far-reaching enough to speak of the present period as one of 'neo-capitalism'.[26] Keynesian-type state intervention, he suggests, is able to transform capitalism's tendency towards crisis into a relatively minor series of economic fluctuations, while a whole range of inter- and cross-class 'tensions' undermine the potential for a transition from working-class economism to overt revolutionary confrontation.[27]

Again, however, we are brought back to the static, abstracted interpretation of capitalism that we found in Giddens' analysis of class structuration. The pursuit of profit, correctly seen by him as inseparable from capitalism, is conceptualised in total isolation from the obstacles it encounters in the actual historical development of that system. The present global recession attendant on a now well-documented international profitability crisis, the demise of the post-war system of liberal trade, the collapse of fixed exchange rates in the monetary sphere, and the last decade's experience of an intensification of the wages struggle in the capitalist heartlands as well as of successful national liberation wars in Asia and Africa, tell a tale quite different from the relative stability of Giddens' neo-capitalism. What is absent from that model is precisely the uneven mode of functioning of capitalist society which, if ignored, leaves the present condition of the Western world quite inexplicable. Profits are not simply an 'essential trait' of capitalism, as Giddens suggests: they are specifically the life-blood of extended capital accumulation and are increasingly under pressure on an international scale. The qualitative political transformation of class struggle from merely economic struggle is not, as Giddens correctly points out, unproblematic. What is problematic is his utopian characterisation of late capitalism as inherently more stable than its earlier forms.

We will conclude our assessment of Giddens' thesis with a suggestion that two closely related sources of mystification converge in his discussion of 'industrial' and 'capitalist' society. Firstly, an over-voluntaristic and consequently indeterminate conception of humanity, reflecting an exaggerated concern with the Weberian problematic of consciousness in social action. Secondly, an interpretation of capitalism which, while formally conceptualising some key characteristics of capitalist social structure, views it statically as stable, rather than historically as the developing, conflict-ridden system that it actually is.

The connection we see between these two aspects of Giddens' work is as follows. His market model of class structure, in the first place, is essentially individualistic, the totality of incumbents of a 'class situation' being a numerical aggregate rather than a socio-economic category. In this context, Giddens' identification of labour power as a commodity[28] is undermined by a cross-cutting characterisation of 'social class' as a cluster of class situations with common mobility chances. The implication of this position is that from the point of view of general social and economic organis-ation, *every* class is, to borrow Marx's image, essentially like 'a sack of potatoes'.[29] This aggregative–individualistic view of class structuration is clearly consistent with Giddens' image of man, his basic categories of 'mind', 'self' etc. being individual proper-ties, albeit socially located and determined (or, as Giddens has it, 'governed').[30]

Furthermore, his Keynesian-influenced model of neo-capitalist stability assumes the triumph of the rationality of private property at the level of systems-management. Man's 'self-mastering' includes the peaceful conquest of his social environ-ment despite the continued hegemony of essentially unplanned, capitalist, property relations. A primarily voluntaristic image of man can thus be seen to underpin and direct Giddens' market-oriented analysis of capitalist society, both in his general account of its class structuration and in the specific instance of con-temporary tendencies. His particular version of market sociology precludes the possibility of a systematic analysis of what is happening in the world now which, after all, is ironically 'where the action is'.

4

Consciousness and Society: Weber, Schutz, Ethnomethodology and Rex

WEBER: UNDERSTANDING SOCIETY

Weber's methodological writings can be viewed as the starting point for much of the twentieth-century debate on the nature, forms and determination of social consciousness. The aspect of Weber's theory which has placed him at the centre of subsequent developments in this area is the tension in his work between the acceptance of the general principle of causality in social life, and its removal from the sphere of exclusively external relations. In particular, he opposed what he saw to be the 'more naive' historical materialist thesis that 'ideas originate as a reflection or superstructure of economic situations'.[1] Causality, for Weber, is a function of the interactive, motivated plans of individual social actors working in a necessarily social environment and deriving the content of their action orientations from the resources available within it. The task of sociology is to formulate law-like generalisations in which motives have a causal role.

Social conditions are recognised by Weber as having a coercive form in relation to the individual. This is how he depicts the 'objectivity' of capitalist economic relations against the motivations of social actors:

> The capitalistic economy of the present day is an immense cosmos into which the individual is born, and which presents itself to him, at least as an individual, as an unalterable order of

things in which he must live. It forces the individual, in so far as he is involved in the system of market relationships, to conform to capitalistic rules of action.[2]

Nevertheless, there is a countervailing current in Weber's writings which emphasises the plasticity of social structures in the face of determined and consistent motivational strategies, a theme especially apparent in his political writings. Here we find that, contrary to the myth of representative democracy, politicians undertake the mobilisation and direction of masses in a creative synthesis of problem-solving and innovation. Even – or perhaps especially – the struggle for democracy entails the cultivation of a dynamic and committed leadership within definite social conditions. Roth thus cites Weber's remark: 'We individualists and partisans of democratic institutions are swimming against the stream of material constellations.'[3] The 'stream' of which Weber wrote was the 'developmental tendency' of bureaucratisation and unfreedom, against which he defended the 'weak' principles of liberal democracy. Neither in sociology nor in politics did Weber recognise the category of total inexorability.

More fundamentally, we showed in an earlier chapter[4] how Weber's insistence upon the indispensability of empathic interpretation in sociology colours his writings on the methodology of the social sciences. His famous proposition that sociological interpretation should be adequate at the levels of both meaning and causality, expresses not a radical separation of these two dimensions of analysis, but more the incorporation of interpretable meaning orientations into the conception of social causality itself. Not only the subject matter of sociology, but also its distinctive forms of procedure, are bounded by the possibilities of socially constituted consciousness. Weber's methodological writings are significant not least in so far as they represent a reaction against the pervasive influence of irrationalism in social theory around the turn of the twentieth century. Rationality in motivation, indeed, is one of the central issues in Weber's critique of Eduard Meyer, whom he charged with equating freedom of the will with 'irrationality' of action.[5] Human action, for Weber, invariably has a subjective aspect which distinguishes it from the phenomena of the natural world. It is the task of the sociologist to confront the subjective dimension of human behaviour objectively and offer a causal explanation of human conduct in terms of the analysis of understandable relations of motivation. Weber distinguishes between direct observational understanding, as when anger is deduced from facial expressions, and explanatory understanding, or understanding the meaning of a particular action or course of actions in terms of motivation. The latter form of understanding entails the explanation of why somebody does a certain thing at a particular point in time and under particular circumstances.[6] 'Motive' here refers to a complex of subjective meaning which seems to the actor to constitute an adequate reason for a certain item of conduct.[7]

In approaching the analysis of motivation in this way, Weber was not reproducing the classical utilitarian conception of rationality in human behaviour. Most action, in fact, is acknowledged to be only partly conscious.[8] Weber stresses the absence of a sharp empirical line between meaningful action on the one hand and 'merely reactive behaviour' on the other.[9] Nevertheless, his sociology derives its unity and distinguishing features from the notion of social action, or subjectively meaningful behaviour in which the actor takes into account and is oriented by the behaviour of others. In March 1920, Weber wrote to Liefmann affirming his intention as a sociologist to 'put an end to the mischievous enterprise which still operates with collectivist notions'.[10] This declaration of intention upon taking up the chair of sociology at Munich well expresses Weber's self-imposed labours against the reification of the products and effects of social action. As he was to write in *Economy and Society*:

> It is customary to designate various sociological generalizations . . . as 'laws'. These are in fact typical probabilities confirmed by observation to the effect that under certain given conditions an expected course of social action will occur, which is understandable in terms of the typical motives and typical subjective intentions of the actors.[11]

Whatever valid laws the sociologist may formulate must, given the nature of social action, be based upon the motives and intentions of the relevant social actors.

SCHUTZ: MEANING AS A PROBLEM

When considering the influence of Weber's social-action theory it is convenient to distinguish between the micro- and the macro-perspectives which derive from his methodological writings. In the former, the work of Schutz on the thought structures of everyday life has, as Lassman points out,[12] been instrumental in effecting a shift in the orientation of the sociology of knowledge towards the analysis of micro-phenomena. Schutz criticised Weber's approach to the sphere of subjectivity on the grounds that he erroneously perceived meaningful action to be the irreducible base line of sociological analysis. This, for Schutz, resulted in a questionable framework for the interpretation of social behaviour, since the concept of 'meaningful' is itself problematic and requires clarification.

A fundamental task for the social sciences, according to Schutz, is to develop a methodology which can deal with the subjective meaning of human action in an objective way.[13] The source of the difficulties that face the sociologist attempting to accomplish a scientific mastery of social reality is the underlying nature of the 'so-called concrete facts of common-sense perception' as highly complex abstractions constructed within the 'natural attitude' of daily life. The social scientist seeks to develop 'constructs of the second degree', based upon the primary constructs of people, whose behaviour the scientist explains in accordance with the procedural rules of his discipline. Whereas the natural scientist deals with phenomena which are 'just facts', the 'thought objects' of social science refer to and are founded upon the commonsense constructs of people living their everyday life in society.[14] This everyday contextualised signification of the social world has a history and includes the 'purpose at hand' of actors, their possibilities of practical or theoretical activities.

Schutz emphasises the personalised character of the individual's biographically determined situation, being 'the sedimentation of all his previous subjective experiences' and experienced as a unique temporal and spatial reality.[15] But far from constituting the substance of a private realm, biography and social typification are developed within an 'intersubjective world of culture', where the individual lives as a social being among others within a shared 'texture of meanings'.[16] The interpersonal nexus of subjectivity is instituted by a vast range of human actions, past and present, and is identified by Schutz as the basis of the postulate of subjective interpretation.

Knowledge thus has an inherently social character. Transmitted principally through the vocabulary and syntax of everyday language, the stock of knowledge-at-hand of individuals is structured in accordance with their system of prevailing relevances and is therefore biographically determined. This process of individualisation within the socialised structures of knowledge raises the possibility that the objects of the world may assume different meanings for different actors with varied biographical situations and histories. In principle, the 'experienceability' of the objects of the life-world by others is similar to one's own. But differences between individuals' spatial arrangement of the life-world, their respective zones of operation, and the structures of their biographical articulation, result in the 'same' object or event revealing different aspects of itself to different persons. In the fully social, natural attitude of everyday life, modifications of the fundamentally similar field of experience are set aside through the pragmatically motivated idealisations of the 'interchangeability of standpoints' and the 'congruence of relevance systems', which together form the 'general thesis of the reciprocity of perspectives'.[17] In other words, it is taken for granted in everyday life that the same life-world is fundamentally assumed by everyone, and that whatever differences may exist between actors' standpoints are irrelevant for their purposes at hand.[18]

In this way, everyday concepts come to be viewed as objective and anonymous, independent of the unique definition of the situation of any individual and presumed as known in common by all who comprise the particular in-group. The postulate of the *reciprocity of perspectives* is the source of socially-shared means for coming to terms with typified social situations of diverse types. As such it is, for Schutz, the basis of the perceived 'typicalness' and objectivity of the social environment.[19]

SCHUTZ AND ETHNOMETHODOLOGY

Schutz is notoriously ambiguous concerning the precise nature of the differences between commonsense and scientific constructs,[20] but it is apparent that he views the scientific and practical attitudes towards the social world as intrinsically distinct. In contrast to the biographically determined situation of the everyday actor, the social scientist has no 'Here' in the sense that one considers one's own social position as irrelevant for any chosen scientific undertaking.[21] The stock of knowledge, derived from his attitude as a 'disinterested observer' of the social world, has a quite different structure to that of people in everyday life.[22] Again, the clarity and distinctness of scientific-thought objects and their compatibility with the principles of formal logic are important in differentiating them from the constructs of commonsense thinking.[23]

But if all hope of grasping social reality is not to be abandoned, the social scientist must interpret interactive patterns with reference to their subjective-meaning structure.[24] This involves the creation of a model of an actor gifted with consciousness, but the elements of which are restricted to those attributes relevant to the scientist's 'problem under scrutiny'. These theoretical 'actors' are no more than 'puppets' constructed by social scientists for their own purposes rather than full representations of actual people with biographical situations in the social world of everyday life; they are, essentially, ideal types of subjective orientation.

Two major aspects of Schutz's work have been of importance for the development of recent phenomenological sociology. Firstly, it is apparent that his painstaking dissection of the motivational aspects of social action represents a major methodological challenge to the structural orientation that has dominated sociological theory, at least since Durkheim affirmed the ontological existence of a sphere of supra-individual social facts. By proceeding in this direction Schutz developed, in a non-transcendental context, Husserl's critique of what Bauman describes as the intrinsically tautological 'obviousness of objectivity'.[25] And secondly, the dictum that scientific constructs should be grounded in the primary constructs of actors introduces a two-step removal of the researcher from the actual social world which he wishes to investigate. These two 'problematics' are related through the inbuilt individualism of Schutz's writings on methodology. He occasionally referred to the presence of structural dimensions of society, including the division of labour,[26] but did not account for their formation and temporal reproduction. Knowledge is seen as intersubjective, but this very intersubjectivity centres on the motivational elements of human action rather than features of the societal framework. In particular, the social world is built up in experience through certain structured forms of direct and indirect interaction. The face-to-face 'encounter' is the only social situation in which the orientation of consciousness is characterised by spatial and temporal immediacy. This, the turning of attention to the other, is what Schutz terms the 'thou orientation', where the individual experiences the other 'in-person'. If the direct form of apprehension is reciprocal between partners in a social relation there exists a 'we-orientation', involving the mutual apprehension of specific personal characteristics through which is realised 'the joint flow of *our* experiences'.[27]

But alongside the immediacy of certain experiences, individuals bring their stock of knowledge to the concrete situations in which they encounter others. This stock of knowledge includes a network of typifications of people, their motivations, patterns of action and hierarchies of plans, as well as knowledge of prevailing social sign systems, including language.[28] A characteristic way of acquiring knowledge of 'contemporaries', or persons who live in the same present span of world time but are not partners to a we-relation, is through the 'they relation' where experiences are interpreted as more or less anonymous events on the basis of typified knowledge of the social world. The they-relation is built upon the expectation that certain behaviour is probable on the part of contemporaries, or types of contemporaries, towards whom the actor has an orientation. The assumed typicality among classes of others and their forms of motivation is, for Schutz, a constituent feature of everyday life in a wider range of experiences than are included in the formal category of they-relations: 'In the routine of everyday life we unite both our own conduct and that of other men in meaning contexts which are relatively independent of the *hic et nunc* of actual experience.'[29] Furthermore, we-relationships can be transformed into they-relationships through the process of typification, especially in the case of institutionalised acts such as transactions between buyers and sellers. Schutz suggests that the world of contemporaries is essentially stratified according to levels of anonymity, that is according to degree of experiential immediacy.[30]

Schutz does not proceed to examine the social regularities represented by institutionalised forms of interaction in terms of their properties, histories and structures as constituted objectifications. The methodological individualism that pervades his writings may be illustrated with reference to his discussion of contemporaries and predecessors.[31] It is possible, Schutz suggests, to obscure the dividing line between these two categories of others by viewing memories of past experiences as a special form of experience of social reality. In a narrower sense, the world of predecessors is definitively concluded: their experiences are ended, they can no longer act. Reciprocal social relations with ancestors are impossible, and the present individual's experience of their world is restricted to the indirect mode. Predecessors are futher distanced from the experience of living social actors by important differences between 'the world views of different generations': since they lived within different meaning-contexts, it must be assumed that the 'content' of their we-relationships was at least in some respects divergent from that of the present actor. The 'same' experience cannot be assumed to have the same meaning to actors in different contexts of social typification.

Nevertheless, as human experiences the experiences of predecessors must have had 'some kind' of subjective meaning which is in principle testable through a complex structure of 'internal' assumptions and interpretations.[32] Schutz identifies a class of 'so-called social collectivities' (such as the State, social classes, the economy) which are typified at an exceptionally high level of anonymity and are completely unamenable to 'conversion into the living reality of a fellow-man'.[33] But the fundamental task of a phenomenology of the social world is, for Schutz, precisely to effect such a translation of 'anonymous' into 'living' typifications. He considers that even the abstract conceptual models of economic theory are a form of 'intellectual shorthand' through which the underlying subjective elements of human actions are either taken for granted or deemed irrelevant for the scientific purposes at hand.[34] It is in the sphere of immediate we-relations that the biographically determined stock of social knowledge is subject to verification and development: 'In the course of the we-relation I use my knowledge, test it, modify it, and acquire new experiences.'[35] Through the immediacy of face-to-face encounters the construction of the social world becomes possible, and 'the intersubjectivity of the life-world is developed and continually confirmed'.[36]

Schutz's handling of the primary world of common experience is a distinctive and seminal attempted resolution of the motivational problem of social behaviour as indicated by Weber. In the remainder of the present section our concern will be with the theory and practice of ethnomethodology as the most extreme significant expression of the phenomenological approach in recent sociology. Our intention is not to provide an exhaustive account of ethnomethodology, since more or less detailed histories, both critical and appreciative, are already available.[37] We will instead consider the influential work of Garfinkel as in important ways typical of the ethnomethodological endeavour, and indicate the implications of its behind-the-scenes assumptions concerning the nature of social organisation.

Turner has identified the concern with 'practical reasoning' as a central theme in ethnomethodological writing.[38] Ethnomethodology's solution to the problem of the status of everyday activities in social life can be thrown into high relief by contrasting its attitude towards routine social activities with that of psychoanalysis. Freud believed that in everyday life 'certain seemingly unintentional performances prove, if psychoanalytic methods of investigation are applied to them, to have valid motives and to be determined by motives unknown to consciousness'.[39] He was especially concerned with word slips, memory lapses and other idiosyncratic gestures and actions. Consciousness, the realm of the ego, takes a less than decisive role in the determination of these 'faulty and chance actions'. As in Freud's account of dream formation, 'the phenomena can be traced back to incompletely suppressed psychical material which, although pushed away by consciousness, has nevertheless not been robbed of all capacity for expressing itself'.[40] Their origin lies in the repressed instinctual structures of ontogenic formation, within which process the determining significance of the ego is 'superficial'.[41]

Ethnomethodology, by contrast, is concerned with the methods by which everyday life is organised, with how the actor makes his routine activities accountable in their setting. Its focus is precisely those fields of social behaviour which may appear to more orthodox sociological perspectives as either obvious or irrelevant. Thus, Garfinkel states his intention as to treat 'practical activities, practical circumstances, and practical sociological reasoning as topics of empirical study, and by paying to the most commonplace activities of daily life the attention usually accorded extraordinary events, seek to learn about them as phenomena in their own right'.[42] When examining everyday life, he suggests, orthodox sociologists typically leave unexamined its socially standardised, 'seen but unnoticed' background expectancies, those features of society which come into view only under conditions of estrangement. Terming this shared culture 'common sense knowledge of social structures',[43] he denies that strictly rational discourse is implied by the typical practices of daily life. On the contrary, for the purposes of conducting their everyday affairs, members systematically refuse to permit each other to understand what they are 'really' talking about. 'Specific vagueness' is a quality of typical discourse, and departures from assumed but unspoken usages result in immediate attempts to restore the 'right state of affairs'.[44]

In his discussion of objective and indexical expressions, Garfinkel adopts, indeed clarifies, Schutz's distinction between the scientific and practical attitudes towards the social world. The primary feature of indexical expressions is their relativity to the speaker and his context: 'Their use depends upon the relation of the user to the object with which the word is concerned.'[45] While it is the goal of science to rid itself of such usages, the substitution of indexical by objective expressions is problematic in the social sciences, for scientific rationalities are neither stable features nor sanctionable ideals in everyday routines. Attempts to make everyday conduct conform to them 'will magnify the senseless character of a person's behavioural environment and multiply the disorganized features of the system of interaction'.[46] Indexical expressions have rational properties of their own in reference to, for example, the rules of procedure in terms of which the individual assesses the correctness of judgements and inferences.[47] Nevertheless, daily life lacks the objective rationality associated with the principles of formal logic, the attainment of clarity and distinctness 'for their own sake', and the congruence of a definition of the situation with scientific knowledge. The gulf between indexical and objective expressions, and the practical difficulties associated with making the transition from the former to the latter in the social sciences, lead Garfinkel to criticise the common sociological practice of substituting scientific rationalities for the actual rationalities of members' behaviour;[48] a related criticism is his objection to the view of the social actor as a 'judgemental dope' of a cultural or scientific type. The central theme of his studies is 'the rational accountability of practical actions as an ongoing, practical accomplishment',[49] against which activity the properties of scientific rationality should be treated as 'empirically problematical material' rather than 'a methodological principle for interpreting activity'.[50]

On this basis, Garfinkel seeks to enlarge the scope of valid sociological enquiry: human activities of every kind, from divination to theoretical physics, 'claim our interest as socially organized artful practices'.[51] This impulse to scrutinise the routine has stimulated ethnomethodologists to examine areas of practical activity including conversation closures, the methodic procedures of walking, and the decision-making of jurors. Conspicuous among Garfinkel's own documentations is the case of Agnes, supposedly born a boy with apparently normal genitalia, yet with an abiding preoccupation to attain competent female sexuality. He describes at length how Agnes idealised her biography so as to secure the status of an adult female, an accomplishment which required resourcefulness, vigilance and ingenious dealing in 'good reasons' or adequate justifications. Euphemism, the adoption of an impersonal tone, feigned ignorance and 'casing situations' are among the manipulative techniques and adaptive-cum-learning strategies she would adopt. Many of her strategies satisfy Goffman's criteria for gamelike action, but Garfinkel points out that other occasions in her 'passing' were very ungamelike. In particular she would, unknown to them, use (other) women's examples to learn conventionally female behavioural patterns. In addition, she undertook prolonged and continuous developmental passing strategies, for example during her school years. Agnes was, in Garfinkel's phrase, a 'practical methodologist', making observable both that and how normal sexuality is accomplished through witnessable displays of talk and conduct against a 'seen but unnoticed' background of commonplace events. She strove consciously and continually to make her assumed sexuality 'visible and reportable – accountable – for all practical purposes'.[52]

STRATEGIES AND STRUCTURES

What, then, is the overall import of Garfinkel's approach to practical and accounting activities (the two being considered identical) for more conventional, institution-oriented forms of sociological analysis? First of all, it should be noted that when Garfinkel himself attempts to account for wider structures of social relations, his characterisation is at the same time amorphous and discursive. Indexical expressions and actions have 'ordered properties', but little is said of the structural dimensions of this ordering of practical accomplishments. The searchlight instead falls upon the artful actions whereby 'scenes' are constructed, maintained and – as in the case of Garfinkel's famous, or notorious, 'demonstrations' – disorganised. Indexical procedures, furthermore, are depicted in a quasi-Cartesian form, with the precarious social cogito undertaking, often with much improvisation, what are stunningly dextrous and even devious manoeuvres. For Garfinkel, social interaction appears as little more than verbally and otherwise symbolically managed practical accomplishments. Members encounter and know the 'moral order' as a complex of perceivedly normal courses of everyday action.[53] The substance of these assumed usages, however, is conflated into the strategic and 'self-organizing' undertakings of Garfinkel's solitary social conspirators. Society, thus viewed, often presents itself as 'all talk'.

The often unstated ethnomethodological view of the 'social whole' is one of a collectivity sustained and integrated through members' routine practices against a background of taken-for-granted expectancies. The rational properties of these practical activities, Garfinkel considers, cannot be assessed by using an externally-derived rule or standard. Rather, all instances of 'social organization' are the contextual achievements of reciprocal artful actions, 'contingent accomplishments of socially organized common practices'.[54] A highly consensual image of societal organisation is consistent with this conception of sociality. Cicourel, for example, proposes that in everyday life a common scheme of interpretation ('the basic rules') is assumed by participants in social interaction and in terms of which they supply meanings and impute motives. The basic interpretive rules 'govern the sequencing of social interaction (the basis for social order)'.[55]

It should be emphasised that from an early date ethnomethodology has been the object of a number of more or less serious internal disagreements and schisms, not least on the long-term significance of its phenomenological orientation. The Epilogue to the 1968 Purdue Symposium on Ethnomethodology, attended by among others Sacks, Garfinkel, Cicourel and Becker, admits to 'differences . . . as to strategy, emphasis and method'.[56] The common critical ground of the ethnomethodologists, however, is the dereification of perceivedly unjustified imputations in orthodox sociological theories. This is at the heart of Garfinkel's objections to the attribution of scientific rationality to the indexical expressions of members' accounts, as it is of Douglas's assertion that 'objective facts' are often problematic in so far as the data they purport to refer to is the result of subjective interpretation and social construction.[57]

But beyond the useful task of subjecting ascribed qualities and beliefs to the criteria of demonstrability, ethnomethodology faces an insuperable obstacle when it attempts to account for the wider social environment within which the practical activities and utterances of group members are articulated. No notable ethnomethodologist has questioned the existence of structural properties of society and their significance for members' practices. Garfinkel, for example, adopts Parsons' conception of the social actor as a collectivity member[58] and, although he insists that the decisions of jurors-as-jurors are not substantially different from those in their everyday life, he acknowledges the former to be consistent with 'the juror line'. This means that the situation is treated as an object of 'theoretic interest', with the criteria of 'legality' overruling those of 'fairness' or any other everyday occasion.[59]

Yet the very language of 'legal' discourse is historically bound up with certain social institutions and forms of relationships, in particular those concerning the emergence, development and protection of property. Historical and structural factors thus 'give meaning' to the indexical decisions of jurors in a society based on the private ownership of property. Wagner suggests that Schutz's notion of the intersubjective constitution of social knowledge evidences the relevance of phenomenological sociology to other than small-scale contexts of social action.[60] But if members' everyday practices are taken as the principal *and introductory* object of sociological analysis, how is the researcher to move towards an examination of the structural features which comprise the totality of social relations in a given instance or type of society? That this transition can only be arbitrary may be demonstrated 'internally' by considering the implications of Sacks's discussion of the 'etcetera clause'.[61] For Sacks, concern with the etcetera problem is the single methodological consideration which distinguishes the theorising of the sociologist from that of any other member of society. Literal description is a scientific requirement, but the possibility that any description can be indefinitely extended compels the researcher to add an etcetera clause to his account, no matter how exhaustive it may be, in order to bring it to a close. Sacks views the 'discovery' of the commonsense world as an important theoretical development. If sociology is to emerge as a science, it must free itself from the commonsense perspective, for example from such partisan assumptions as the desirability of reducing crime. But Sacks remains sceptical that such a development can in fact take place. The inability of sociologists to handle the full extension of a description by means of a formula without abusing the phenomenon in question means that any description can be read as complete or as incomplete as any other. Even if, then, the sociologist claims to be undertaking a qualitatively different task from that of any other social member, it is uncertain that his activity can be justified as 'more scientific'.

But is it true that the goal of science is to produce a 'literal description' of its subject matter? Sacks suggests that the differences between sociologies reside in the different 'resolutions' that are effected to the etcetera problem, the different ways in which the act of extending description is concluded. Yet if we look at comparable theoretical treatments of, for example, class conflict, we find that the most important differences are inexplicable in terms of the strictly quantitative extension of empirical procedure which is implied by Sacks's account of sociological enquiry. The difference between the approaches to class conflict explored by Weber and Pareto centres on the perception of enduring divisions around the phenomena of the market, on the one hand, and the generalisation of conflict to encompass all antagonisms between socially-perceived interests, on the other.[62] Such widely differing models of the 'same' phenomenon are neither identical at any stage of their alleged 'descriptive' extension, nor in either case logically deducible from an initial account of members' indexical practices. An empiricist documentation of individuals' strategies, moreover, could not hope to systematically arrive at an adequate conception of the structural dimensions of any society, or type of social organisation. As D. and J. Willer summarise the fatal logical flaw in empiricism:

> A generalization does not explain the particulars which make it up because it is defined by them and does not explain or predict other particulars because those particulars are not included in the scope of the generalization and might indeed contradict it.[63]

Given the problematic of 'literal description' and the assumed primacy of members' practical accounting, the movement from 'micro' to 'macro' analysis can only be arbitrary, with the augmented image of societal structure typically deriving from an otherwise established model of the social totality (as is the case with Garfinkel's resort to Parsonian systems theory for the definition of the collectivity member). To suggest that phenomenological sociology can proceed otherwise from its preoccupation with the literal description of the phenomena of consciousness is to ignore the complexity of theoretical construction in the representation of system properties. It is no more true to say that Durkheim did — or could have — constructed his model of organic solidarity from the consciousness of its members than it would be to suggest that Marx deduced the law of motion of capitalist society from the 'practical' activities of individual capitalists. In both cases, a theory of social structure-in-change is attained through a process of abstraction, the character of which is in turn inseparable from a particular conception of the relation between the theory and the practices of both its object and its creator (Durkheim's reformist conception of the reorientation of social facts, and Marx's opposition of the needs of humanity to their alienation and possibilities of reappropriation in determinate historical conditions).

Garfinkel assumes a literal identity between social being and consciousness in his account of indexical expressions. The activities whereby members produce and manage settings of organised everyday knowledge, he proposes, are identical with members' procedures for making these settings 'account-able'.[64] The rules of everyday social action come from 'the occasions of their use', that is, from the contextual settings which members 'know' and take for granted in their social operations.

Thus far, Garfinkel's account of social action and meaning closely resembles Winch's notion of social action as 'following a rule'. For Winch, as for Garfinkel and Sacks, language is the source of members' ideas of what counts as belonging to the world. Language is by definition publicly accessible, allowing the possibility that a particular judgement may be verified by criteria independent of the will of any individual.[65] Winch follows the phenomenologists in criticising the traditional refusal by social psychologists to analyse the dimension of meaning and its constitution within linguistic usages: 'What is missed is that those very categories of meaning, etc., are *logically* dependent for their sense on social interaction between men.'[66] Winch rejects Durkheim's view that social life should be explained in terms of 'more profound causes which are unperceived by consciousness'.[67] Rather, if one is not to commit the error of misplaced 'externalization', social relations must be considered as 'a species of internal relation'. As against a causal relation, an internal relation presupposes the concept of following a rule and exists in reference to certain definite established conventions. As with Garfinkel, Winch suggests that to give an account of a word is to describe how it is used, and to describe its usage is to account for the social relationships into which it enters. He goes on to identify these social relations with the concepts formulated by actors *prior to* their realisation in social practice: 'social relations are expressions of ideas about reality'.[68] With this assumption, Winch abandons the search for social causation for the explanation of regularities in social life through the understanding of 'meaningful' internal relations of concepts. 'Social interaction', according to this view, 'can more profitably be compared to the exchange of ideas in a conversation than to the interaction of forces in a physical system.'[69]

The thorough-going relativism that is implied by Winch's redirection of interest to the contextual constitution of meaning in social interaction[70] is the logical corollary of Garfinkel's ethnomethodology when shorn of its Parsonian additions. It is a theoretical position which has been opposed by Goldthorpe on the grounds that there exists a social world which has an autonomous, *an-sich* existence, and which cannot be understood through interpretive procedures alone. This world contains objects for enquiry which, while still the products of social action, exist 'in their own right', that is apart from their interpretation by social members.[71] This, of course, is implicit in the ethnomethodologists' recognition of relatively enduring patterns of background expectancies and assumptions in everyday life, but their own theoretical efforts have failed to account for these regularities in social life in anything but reductionist terms.

Garfinkel's sociology of practical and accounting activities directs attention away from those social relations whose attainment, as against their effects, are neither constituted nor experienced within the sphere of consciousness. To take an example: few sociologists, whatever their other views on the theories of Marx, would deny that the employment contract in capitalist society is a social relation based on the sale of labouring time in return for a monetary payment which, if the enterprise is to remain viable, must result in a profit for the employer. Yet there is no particular reason why the sale of labour power should automatically appear thus to the parties involved. The worker, as well as the employer, is likely to perceive the employment relation precisely as it *appears*, as a relation of things rather than social powers. Certainly, many economists have viewed the wage-labour relation in this way: Lipsey's standard economics text book, for example, classifies fork-lift operators along with the 'literally hundreds of factors of production' which enter into the process of car production.[72] But here we have an order of structural and historical social relations which is inexplicable in terms of the phenomenological reduction. Garfinkel's arbitrary resort to Parsonian systems theory is only one extreme illustration of the impossibility of deducing a theory of social structure directly from phenomenological premises.

JOHN REX: STRUCTURAL PHENOMENOLOGY

One contemporary sociologist who has attempted to develop a theory sensitive to the structural dimensions of society from the interpretive procedures pioneered by Weber is John Rex. Whereas Giddens approaches the particular problem of class structuration from a neo-Weberian viewpoint, Rex has been concerned in a series of works to develop a more general theoretical framework based on a modified social-action perspective through which to examine social structure. Rex, like Gouldner,[73] is concerned to affirm the emancipatory role of sociology as an instrument of social and self understanding.[74] By adopting this position, he at once sets himself the dual task of developing a critique of erroneous sociological perspectives and clarifying the liberatory basis that is obscured by them. Two particular types of sociological mystification are criticised:

(i) Functionalism and other anti-voluntarist theories.
(ii) Intuitionist and astructural micro-perspectives.

Firstly, Rex objects to the 'finality' and 'form of closure' in the functionalism of Malinowski and Radcliffe-Brown. The consensualist form of their functionalism, he suggests, is of limited value, since the integration that it proposes is not concerned with the detail of social action, but rather the framework within which men may act.[75] More fundamentally, Rex expresses serious doubts as to whether the 'needs of the system' as understood by the functionalists are in fact really needs at all.[76] Even Merton's notion of 'dysfunction', which avoids the idea of consensus in its more simplistic forms, still has for its basic referent the needs of the system, and therefore rejects the insights of the action framework.[77] Similarly, Althusser's structuralism is basically anti-humanist, being concerned primarily with systems, their properties and dynamics.[78] Rex considers that in these and similarly uncompromising systematic theories there is no place for a 'real voluntarism' in social life: as such, they betray the emancipatory promise that a humanistic sociology holds out.

Rex is no more sympathetic towards unaugmented inter-personal and micro-sociological perspectives. Ethnomethod-ology and the labelling deviance theorists are charged with turning away from the structural axes of society and exaggerating the fluidity of meaning imputation in social interaction.[79] Again, Mead's emphasis on the dimensions of personality and role-playing does not in itself qualify as sociology as it explains nothing about social structure, which 'requires action' in its constitution but is irreducible to it. Far from elucidating the forms and processes of social action, symbolic interactionism portrays individuals as trapped within the defensive posture of devising strategies for 'preserving selfhood in the face of soci-ety'.[80]

Rex's critical comments on Mead indicate the essentials of his own position. Sociology, he proposes, is concerned with struc-tures of social relations which are based upon shared meanings or, possibly, confusions. Rex's attempt to outline the foundations of a systematic and valid sociology has its roots in Weber, but he criticises Weber's methodological writings as incomplete and ambiguous. While correct in claiming that explanations ad-equate at the level of meaning are verifiable by reference to actual events, Weber was unclear as to the cognitive basis of the sociologist's alleged privileged status in accounting for social action. In particular, he vascillated between a view of ideal types as relatively contentless constructs, and the notion of meaning as adequate from the point of view of the actor.[81] Rex seeks to resolve Weber's inconsistency by asserting the non-identity of sociologists' ideal types and actors' own accounts of their social actions. Whereas the latter are open-ended, situation-bound and often inconsistent, the former may be used to subject the interpretations of actors to scientific testing. Sociologists, in other words, do not merely offer another account, 'no better than that of any ideologist or of the actor himself'. As a question of 'moral integrity', their value judgements are kept to a minimum, an ideal which is facilitated by the testing of propositions among a group of observers with the intention of attaining verified agreement.[82]

Actors' own theories do nevertheless have a part to play in the formulation of ideal types. Much of the sociologist's work, Rex explains, consists of systematising the language of commonsense by developing a meaningful set of ideal types for the analysis of 'recurrent bits of historical social structures'.[83] Rex's project, then, is to develop the Weberian foundations of action theory in a manner which is sensitive to aspects of the modern social structure. He is especially concerned to establish that Weber's 'methodological individualism' is not merely a procedure for the study of sociation between individuals: rather, implicit in the notion of the ideal type is the view that courses of action may be imputed to a collectivity, or a multi-person structure. Class, for example, refers to more than members' mental constructs concerning the nature of society: it is a social reality in terms of membership and regulatory effects, and is often a primary determinant in the sphere of political organisation. Classes typically possess a distinctive 'culture' with regional connections, and are partly bounded by a linguistic code which unites members and generates, for example, the 'we-feeling' that allows the working class to exist as a sociological category.[84]

In his *Key Problems of Sociological Theory*, Rex specifies the basis of social conflict as the presence of two groups with conflicting interests or claims. Most basic conflicts involve the question of access to the means of life, and can usually be located along a continuum between contract and violence or the threat of violence.[85] Weber's conception of class, Rex proposes, is wider in scope than that of Marx, concerning as it does the typical chance for a supply of goods, external living conditions, and personal life experiences, in so far as this chance is determined by the type and amount of power to dispose of goods and skills for income within a given economic order.[86] In addition to conflicts centred on the ownership of property, conflicts may develop over the control of legitimate power, or the control of ideas; there may be either one or a number of cross-cutting conflicts in any given situation. Rex discusses, for example, the class structure of housing opportunities in the context of inter-ethnic residential patterns.[87] His intention in such studies is, as he says elsewhere, to 'do justice' to the industrial sociology of Marx and Weber;[88] his study of residential patterns is conducted with reference to Weber's theory of domestic property as a basis for class, and his many comments on the bureaucratisation of the modern world reveal the unmistakeable influence of Weber's sociology.

In effect, however, Rex develops an empiricist and culturological approach to class. Class analysis is viewed as the interpretation of *visible* social relations and actions, with the structures which underlie these actions appendaged as their (necessarily potentially shifting and variable) *effects*. The capitalist productive enterprise, for example, is that 'collective actor' which constitutes the central, structural and institutional fact of the developed Western world.[89] The historical absence of both socialist revolution and capitalist military coups, except in the special conditions of relative economic underdevelopment (Spain, Greece, the Soviet Union) or general social crisis (Germany), leads Rex to reconsider the categories of ruling class and working class through the use of ideal types. The types that he formulates define the principal classes of capitalist society in terms of their existent forms of typical practices. Typical working-class behaviour thus expresses the dual influence of political reformism and disruptive trade-union activity. Organised labour, Rex insists, is typically integrated into the wider social and economic system through the institutions of collective bargaining.[90] More generally, the transformation of a class-in-itself into a class-for-itself is dependent upon members' perceptions and individual needs. Whereas Marx examined the origins, structural role within capitalist society and, above all, historical potentiality of the working class, the traits emphasised by Rex's ideal type are bounded and defined by his perception, impassioned but imprisoned, of the present.

Rex's combination of a structurally-informed action perspective and ideal typical analysis produces a view of society which is at the same time manipulative in the Marcusean sense and over-voluntaristic. The rationality of actors is confused with that of modes of production, with the unintended consequence of emphasising the 'irrationality' of specifically working-class practices. Rex suggests, for example, that the 'rationalities' of the ruling class are imposed upon the system as a whole by the oligarchies' ensurance that effective power is not 'dangerously diffused', and by their exploitation of the 'impotence and irrationality' of the masses.[91] It should be stressed that these impotent masses are in the same work correctly portrayed as developing effective and significant trade-union and political strategies in their relations with the ruling class.[92] For Rex, the rationalities of the ruling class are the same as particular actors' perceptions of their needs and strategies: 'The bourgeoisie and their allies became a class through their capacity to think in terms of free economic enterprise for themselves, and through élite education.'[93] These rationalities in turn become the rationalities of society as a whole by virtue of the manipulative abilities of the dominant interests which they express.

It is at this point that serious confusions, which go to the heart of Rex's sociology, begin to be apparent: 'moral nihilism', the deliberate self-displacement of the investigator from the 'sacred values' of his society, is proclaimed as an essential condition for the practising sociologist. Thus ostracised from the key institutions and values of their respective societies, sociologists are able to perform a valuable service to humanity by developing an international community of the enlightened ('the wise') as the basis for informed action on a wider scale.[94] One possible avenue of change that Rex considers is the transformation of capitalism through the substitution of machinery for people at work and the imposition of the rationality of the 'welfare' sector on society at large.[95] But the economic nature of the recently expanded state sector of developed capitalist society is, as Rex himself observes, precisely that of a necessary and subsidised support for free enterprise.[96] Despite his 'realism' on the question of the political limits of working-class reformism,[97] Rex proposes that one 'collective actor' (the incumbents, beneficiaries and victims of the public-welfare sector) can oust or dominate another (the interests of private capitalism) without the agency of a major struggle for power between the ruling and subordinate classes.[98] The peaceful transition to some form of socialism is the other side of Rex's conception of a crisis-free capitalism in which unemployment generates 'private troubles' only as a marginal and sectoral problem.[99] In both cases, the rationalities of collective actors, be they classes or whole societies, are little more than large-scale transcriptions of the rationalities of typical actors. Rex's social structures, as much as Giddens' social classes, are generalisations of the specific social properties of actors' consciousness. Such a literal socialisation of members' rationalities represents one particular resolution to the structural impasse of phenomenological sociology, but its inbuilt myopia as regards extra-individual social obstacles to the realisation of members' strategies conceals a logic in the development of society which cannot be explored within the movement from micro- to macro-analysis.

While he formally discerns a universal struggle of humanity against the antagonistic social forms that have been created, Rex's sociology of rationalities reproduces at a 'higher', allegedly structural, level the reductionism which is performed directly by the social phenomenologists. In the following chapters we will consider the theories of a number of sociologists who have attempted to develop Weber in the direction of a non-reductionist sociology of structures. We pay particular attention to the writings of Dahrendorf, C. Wright Mills and Parsons. Then in our final chapter we will attempt to locate classical sociology, including Weber, within the development of certain themes in Western thought and tendencies in Western society.

5

Ralf Dahrendorf: Conflict and the Dimension of Authority

INTRODUCTION

Inseparable from Weber's sociology is the fatalistic assumption of the necessity of domination. At the same time, his analysis of the class structure of capitalist society is articulated specifically in terms of and at a particular level of economic action. Ralf Dahrendorf, by contrast, has abstracted the concept of authority from the totality of Weber's work and elaborated a comprehensive theory of class structuration wholly in terms of it. It will be our contention that Dahrendorf's social theory, while having superficially responded to the massive social changes in the capitalist world during the last two decades, as a corpus of work is flawed by its metaphysical assumptions concerning the primacy of authority relations in the dynamics of conflict group formation.

Central to Dahrendorf's account of social reality is his persistent failure to examine the class formations which emerge from the interaction of man with nature through particular historical modes of social production. In order to demonstrate this, we will identify the misleading and erroneous evaluation of Marx's work which pervades Dahrendorf's analysis, and the liberal ideological influences which structure it and divert attention from the actual sources of power and conflict in capitalist society. Finally, it will be argued that Dahrendorf's scheme cannot be adequately revised on the basis of his own initial assumptions, as has been suggested by J. H. Turner.[1] Rather, his contentions can only be critically assessed from a viewpoint which sees capitalism as a form of society in which the principal structural cleavage derives from the private ownership of productive property and not, as Dahrendorf holds, the possession of authority.

DAHRENDORF AND MARX: DEPARTURES INTO CONFLICT

In his influential *Class and Class Conflict in an Industrial Society*, Dahrendorf presents his theory of 'integration and values' on the one hand and 'coercion and interests' on the other as the embodiments of 'the two faces of society'.[2] He argues that two schools of sociological thought, each claiming for itself the ability to account for the problem of how societies cohere, have historically stood in conflict. Both the 'utopian' school, stressing value consensus, and the 'rationalist' school, stressing force, domination and constraint, 'advance claims for the primacy of their respective standpoints'.

Dahrendorf asserts that both models have equal explanatory validity for the solution of different sociological problems, but proceeds to argue that recent sociological thought has been excessively dominated by integration theory. In particular, he criticises Parsons for the essentially one-sided nature of his 'utopian' analysis. Citing the East Berlin revolt of 1953 as evidence of an aspect of society inexplicable in terms of such theory, Dahrendorf similarly challenges the universal explanatory power of coercion theory. The two models, he suggests, constitute complementary rather than mutually exclusive aspects of social structure. The notion of a 'Janus-headed' society, in other words, is Dahrendorf's methodological starting point.

His principal concern in *Class and Class Conflict* is to explain the aetiology of organised social conflict 'on the assumption of the coercive nature of social structure'.[3] Dahrendorf's intention is to account for a particular set of problematic social phenomena in terms of the constraint as opposed to the utopian or consensus model. His main thesis is that the coincidence of economic and political conflict, as stressed by Marx, is inapplicable to 'post-capitalist' societies, but his case rests largely on a confused and confusing interpretation of Marx's writings and, in consequence, Marx must be initially rescued from Dahrendorf if the latter's work is to be meaningfully evaluated.

Dahrendorf cites Marx as an exponent of the rationalist school of social theory: Marx assumed, he notes, 'the ubiquity of change and conflict as well as domination and subjection'.[4] But Dahrendorf completely misinterprets the essence of Marx's work, giving primacy to his political sociology, an aspect which in the context of Marx's work as a whole is predicated, though by no means in a mechanical way, upon his political economy. To examine Marx's formal statements on the formation of economic classes in capitalist society without serious consideration of his theories of commodity production, surplus-value and exploitation is, in a fundamental sense, to miss the central point of his life's work, but this is precisely what Dahrendorf does.

Dahrendorf lists the factors which he sees to be of particular importance in Marx's theory of class. He identifies the supposedly heuristic nature of the theory, its 'basis characteristic' of being an essentially two-class model, and the source of classes in the ownership and non-ownership of the means of production. In addition, he notes the identification of economic and political power, the realisation of classes as such when and only when they are organised in political conflict and, finally, an image of society and social change in which systematic conflict is 'an essential feature'.[5]

These factors, when examined, are primarily concerned with what may be termed the political sociology of Marx. While Dahrendorf correctly identifies Marx's view that classes derive their existence from the ownership or non-ownership of the means of production,[6] he avoids any detailed analysis of Marx's actual work on the production and market dynamics of capitalist society. A rare and formal reference to the way in which Marx emphasised the free sale of labour power, the production of surplus value, and the development of mechanised factory production 'along with private property and the existence of social classes as fundamental to capitalist society',[7] does little to alter or augment this absence of analysis. Neither does Dahrendorf's quotation from *Capital*, the essence of which is the equally formal proposition that:

The specific economic form in which unpaid surplus labour is pumped out of the immediate producers determines the relation of domination and subjection as it grows directly out of and in turn determines production.[8]

While adequately identifying Marx's *overall* assumptions concerning exploitative systems of social production *in general*, this selective quotation indicates only the theoretical starting point for his analysis of capitalism as a concrete mode of production with concrete and unique structural features. Dahrendorf's analysis at no point goes beyond this level of generality and abstraction.

Dahrendorf sees Marx's theory of class to be an essentially heuristic device. He ignores the fact that Marx also saw classes as historically bound, objective socio-economic formations arising from the social relations of production in definite material circumstances. Thus capital, essentially a social relation,

arises only where the owner of the means of production and the means of subsistence finds in the market a free worker who offers his labour power for sale.[9]

To view Marx's theory of class as primarily heuristic is, in fact, quite consistent with Dahrendorf's effective divorce of Marx's political economy on the one hand and his analysis of class formations on the other. Both, for Marx, were intimately related theoretical explanations of actual patterns of social relations. Dahrendorf, by effectively severing them, reduces Marx's notion of class to a speculative and unlocated sociological category, upon which the other 'features' of his work, such as the convergence of political and economic power, appear mechanically predicated. His almost exclusive concern with Marx as a political sociologist thus serves to shatter the internal consistency of Marx's theory. In addition, it diverts attention away from Marx's analysis of commodity production in capitalist society, the starting point of *Capital* and clear evidence of his concern to explain, in theoretical terms, *actual* as against purely conceptual social relations of production.

The same one-sidedness of interpretation is apparent in Dahrendorf's comments on the tendencies towards social change supposedly identified by Marx in his analysis of capitalist society.

The processes in question are primarily those of class polarisation, proletarian pauperisation, intra-class 'levelling' and the
tendency of capitalism towards revolutionary supersession.

In the first place, Dahrednorf quotes and comments on a
passage   from   *The   Communist   Manifesto*   which   refers
to the polarisation of capitalist society into the 'two great hostile
camps' of proletariat and bourgeoisie.[10] Dahrendorf then ignores
the evidence that in his later work, informed by a mature
political economy, Marx's model of the class structure of
advanced capitalism had developed radically to incorporate 'the
constant increase of the middle classes'.[11] This theoretical
advance derived from the labour theory of value as applied to
long-term tendencies in the development of the capitalist mode of
production. In particular, Marx predicted that with the growing
social productivity of labour there would be a simultaneous rise
in the mass and decline in the rate of profit. The rate of profit
tends to fall because, while labour power is the source of all new
value produced in the labour process, the competitive drive of
technical innovation generates a progressively rising proportion
of constant capital (value of machinery and raw materials) to
variable capital (value of wages), thus diminishing the relative
size of the value-producing component of the process as a whole.
It was on the basis of the rising mass of profit that the expanding
middle classes could, for Marx, be supported, but Dahrendorf's
brief remarks are untouched by such considerations. As such,
they are unable to consider, let alone challenge, Marx as a
political economist.

Dahrendorf quotes from *Capital* in order to attribute to Marx
the view that as the two 'great hostile camps' polarise their class
situations become 'increasingly extreme'. He deduces that,
according to the 'so-called theory' (*sic*) of pauperisation, 'the
poverty of the proletariat grows with the expansion of production
by virtue of a law postulated as inherent in a capitalist
economy'.[12]

But again, Dahrendorf's interpretation is invalidated by a
more careful examination of Marx's work. Marx's *Capital*
observes that:

> In manufacture the enrichment of the collective worker, and
> therefore of capital, in the matter of social productivity, is

dependent upon the impoverishment of the workers *in the matter of their individual* powers of production. [my emphasis, D.B.][13]

The context of this passage is Marx's analysis of large-scale industry, which detaches science from labour, making the former an independent force of production and 'pressing it into the service of capital'. He goes on to quote approvingly a passage from Ferguson, comparing the workshop to 'an engine, the parts of which are men'. What Marx is discussing thus emerges as the qualitative deterioration of the life-situation of the working class as, with scientific and technological development, it becomes increasingly subject to the specifically scientific exploitation of its labour power by capital.

Furthermore, Marx elsewhere speaks of a worker's wage as that part of the total product

required for the maintenance and reproduction of (his) labour power, *be the conditions of this maintenance and reproduction scanty or bountiful, favourable or unfavourable.*[14]

Even in the restricted sense of wages, then, pauperisation for Marx is relative rather than absolute. This formulation is consistent with and derives from Marx's materialist view that human needs are essentially historical products: to use Marx's own terminology, the value of labour power includes 'a historical and a moral factor'.[15] While the working class may, in certain conditions, suffer an absolute decline in its living standards,[16] this is not what 'pauperization' in its broadest sense meant for Marx. His concern was to depict the contradiction between the developed nature of the means of production and the increasing alienation of the direct producers in the face of them. This insight is quite different from Dahrendorf's mechanical and over-economistic interpretation.

Dahrendorf further attributes to Marx a remarkable prediction concerning 'the reduction of all workers to unskilled labourers by the technical development of production'.[17] Now what Marx did in fact predict was that with the development of the 'automatic factory' there is

a tendency towards the equalisation or levelling down of the work which the assistants of the machinery have to perform.[18]

But 'In so far as the division of labour reappears' in this situation, Marx locates it in the distribution of workers among the specialised machines. He identifies the main cleavage to be that between the minders of machines and their attendants; in addition, he speaks of a scientifically-trained 'superior class of workmen'. While specifying the emerging division of labour to be 'purely technical', Marx at no point postulates the general and all-embracing de-skilling of the working class incorrectly attributed to him by Dahrendorf. In the first place, 'equalization' is considered as a tendential development rather than a uni-directional or linear iron law and, furthermore, Marx never imagined that either capitalism or its historical successor would do away with technology, requiring skill and training, as vital to production. Dahrendorf, in short, attributes an unwarranted utopian dimension to Marx's analysis.

More recently, Dahrendorf has asserted that in Marx's work

> the terminology of economics serves above all to express disgust in a seemingly objective manner and thus to impress those other dreamers of a world without all the nasty realities of economic life, without capital and wage labour, without the alienated reality of money and the exchange value of human effort, without even a division of labour to speak of, the unpolluted world of non-economic man.[19]

To merely list some of the key concepts of Marxist analysis in this mechanical way, however, is not to examine their theoretical validity in relation to social reality, let alone to offer a systematic critique of them. As with his treatment of the question of the 'equalization' of labour, Dahrendorf unjustifiably accuses Marx of a fundamental utopianism. Marx, in fact, was concerned with the analysis of historical societies, capitalism in particular, on the basis of their structure and tendential movements as they derive from underlying patterns of socio-economic relations. To identify him with 'those other dreamers' is to ignore, for example, his comments in the 1870s on the Eisenacher socialist faction.

In the *Critique of the Gotha Programme*, Marx criticised their utopian demand that workers should directly receive the 'un-diminished proceeds' of their labour on the grounds that deductions are necessary to cover replacement costs for the means of production, expansion of production, and any unanticipated social expenses that may arise.[20] Perhaps one need only agree with Dahrendorf's comment on the passage quoted above, that 'This is a caricature, to be sure'.[21] The basis of this caricature is a view of Marx as primarily a political sociologist at the expense of any serious analysis of his political economy. Thus, Dahrendorf's formal allusion to the notion of a classless society[22] fails to examine Marx's claim to have discovered, on the basis of the labour theory of value, developments inherent in capitalism which determine its tendency towards crisis and the potential for qualitative supersession. Within this questionable focus of attention, moreover, Dahrendorf commits a number of serious misreadings and misunderstandings concerning key aspects of Marx's analysis. Particularly relevant are the distortions discussed above concerning the significance of class in Marx's work.

CLASS REVISITED

While offering a critique of Marx's usage of class, Dahrendorf seeks to preserve and develop the concept as such: he defines class as a category for the analysis of conflict-oriented formations with systematic roots in the structure of society.[23] Whereas Marx located the foundations of class conflict in the social relations of production, Dahrendorf's innovation is to view classes as aggregates of the incumbents of identical or similar positions within particular relations of authority.[24] For Dahrendorf, the identification of authority roles and their distinctive characteristics constitutes 'the basic task of conflict analysis'.[25] His unit of theoretical analysis is the Weberian 'imperatively co-ordinated association', characterised by internal relations of legitimate authority and within which the dominant and subjected groups have different and opposing interests.[26] Using a scheme incorporating 'quasi-groups' and 'interest groups', Dahrendorf constructs an elaborate model of the transition from 'latent' to 'manifest' interests which both augments and flows from the logic of his initial assumption concerning the primacy of legitimate relations of authority as a determinant of class interests and conflict. It is on this assumption that Dahrendorf's analysis of the class dynamics of 'industrial society' must stand or fall.

Giddens has recently challenged Dahrendorf's model in terms

of both its claims to account for the social reality of class conflict and its internal consistency.[27] Concerning the former, Giddens attacks both the dichotomous nature of Dahrendorf's model and its tendency to shift attention away from the problem of 'classlessness'. Giddens further points out that Dahrendorf's model neither implies that there is any necessary conflict of interest between dominant and subordinate conflict groups, nor that special attention should be paid (as it is in *Class and Class Conflict*) to the areas of the State and industry. These weaknesses in Dahrendorf's exposition share a common source in his initial attempt to substitute authority for property ownership as the key determinant of class structure; but they all raise substantive problems of sociological method and, as such, should be considered independently.

Giddens initially questions Dahrendorf's assumption that authority relations necessarily possess a dichotomous character. He seeks to correct what he perceives to be the theoretical crudity of Dahrendorf's inflexible polarity of possession and non-possession of authority by postulating 'a graded hierarchy of relationships'.[28] Now while this criticism is essentially correct, it should be pointed out that Dahrendorf does empirically recognise the widespread delegation of authority in many associations, including the State.[29] His comments remain at an empirical level, however, and leave his basically dichotomous model unaltered. What delegation may take place occurs, for Dahrendorf, within and subordinate to the essentially two-class paradigm.

Further, Dahrendorf's analysis of itself in no way implies the necessity of conflict over the question of authority which he posits.[30] Whereas for Marx the opposition of interest between classes derives from the generation and appropriation of surplus value, Dahrendorf's theory allows the sociological possibility of permanent, voluntary and consensual cooperation around a set of enduring shared purposes. His model of society as conflictual and his image of class as an aspect of an authority relationship are, in other words, mechanically paired and have no organic or intrinsic connection outside their strictly conceptual association.

Dahrendorf's formulation, moreover, implies and even posits an indeterminate plurality of classes, corresponding to the interest aggregates in each and every imperatively coordinated association.[31] His actual concern with 'the two great associations' of the State and the industrial enterprise[32] at the relative expense of all others is, in terms of his own theory, intuitive and arbitrary, and cannot be accounted for by reference to his most basic sociological assumptions.

Giddens points out that Dahrendorf's view of class 'directs attention away from the contrast between "class" and "classlessness" as conceived in Marxian theory'.[33] Dahrendorf's model of society assumes the *a priori* necessity of relations of authority and, since he defines classes in terms of such relations, the notion of classlessness becomes both a logical and a sociological impossibility. Giddens' ensuing claim that 'we do not make any significant theoretical gains by substituting "authority" for "class"' is an understatement.[34] Dahrendorf's shift of emphasis, we will argue, represents a mystification at the theoretical level rather than the mere absence of intellectual advance. His conceptual myopia as regards the question of classlessness follows directly from his understanding of class and is logically quite consistent with it.

POWER AND THE KANTIAN HERITAGE

While Giddens' remarks constitute a useful corrective to some aspects of Dahrendorf's theory, a more thorough-going critique requires a shift of attention to sectors of the social world not broached by Giddens' assessment. In particular, Dahrendorf's decision to sever his analysis of imperatively coordinated associations, especially when he considers the industrial enterprise, from the wider economic context in which they operate, results in a decontextualised portrayal of the constraints which typically operate on them.

Concerning the analysis of societies as totalities, Dahrendorf writes:

total societies can present the picture of a plurality of competing dominant (and, conversely, subjected) aggregates.[35]

But what, it must be asked, does this really mean? At its simplest, different associations may at certain times find themselves in competition or, by extension, in conflict with one another. To state this is to state a mere truism and what is lacking is an explanatory account of the concrete conditions and forces which make actual dominant groups compete with their equivalents in other associations at particular points in time. The increasing social prominence of economistic wages struggles in Britain since the mid-1960s, for example, is inexplicable outside the stagnation of workers' real incomes consequent upon a steady decline in corporate profitability.[36] Dahrendorf's indeterminate image of a plurality of competing élites is quite irrelevant to the structural imperatives imposed by capitalism, the general scenario of productive activity in societies where ownership of the means of production rests in private hands. Capitalism and the distinctive social relations that derive from it are left unexplored.

A key problematic in Dahrendorf's theory is thus his treatment of the phenomenon of power. His own view is that scientific research is characterised by what he terms 'problem consciousness': 'at the outset of every scientific investigation there has to be a fact or set of facts that is puzzling the investigator'.[37] At no point, however, does Dahrendorf systematically approach power as a problem to be examined by scientific methods. Throughout his work he repeatedly refers to the divergent interests to be found in contemporary societies. After *Class and Class Conflict*, he came to argue increasingly for the essential superiority of the coercion or conflict model.[38] This important shift of emphasis itself reflects the increasing militancy of workers both in the developed capitalist world and the bureaucratic states of Eastern Europe during the 1960s and, to an even greater extent, the early 1970s. In this context, the fall of Gomulka in Poland is just as significant as the re-emergence of the effective strike in West Germany.

The notion of a 'plurality of interests in society and their contradictory character' is, then, a recurrent theme in Dahrendorf's work. A different element of finality and *sociological absolutism* is introduced, however, when he posits an inherent inequality in social life: in *On the Origin of Inequality among Men* he argues that the inevitable operation of norms and social expectations implies that

> there must always be at least that inequality of rank which results from the necessity of sanctioning behaviour according

to whether it does or does not conform to established norms.[39]

Social norms and sanctions are thus the basis not only of 'ephemeral individual rankings' but also of 'lasting structures of social positions'. This, in its bare outlines, constitutes Dahrendorf's explanation of the empirically correct observation that:

> Even in the most affluent society it remains a stubborn and remarkable fact that men are unequally placed.[40]

The enduring nature of the particular inequalities of capitalist society is inexplicable in terms of this theory. In the first place, Dahrendorf's account of normative sanctioning is incorrect: it is in fact *behaviour* that is subject to sanctions, although all human behaviour takes place within and is mediated by a system of more or less visibly coercive social relations which find their expression in '*positions*'. The irony of Dahrendorf's view that norms constitute, in the last analysis, the basis of ranking emerges when it is remembered that he attacks Parsons for offering an almost identical explanation. Even within his own assumptions, there is a profound and unresolved inconsistency concerning the relationship between norms and social ranking.

The fundamental weakness of Dahrendorf's stratification theory becomes apparent when he identifies power and its social consequences as the primary obstacle to the realization of the 'pure' market model of society.[41] Nowhere, however, does he attempt to explicate in theoretical terms the source of power itself. Power is defined as

> the ability, by virtue of social roles, to make and enforce norms influencing the life chances of others.[42]

But on the question of how and why such structured relations of legitimate authority emerge, Dahrendorf is persistently silent. A circular and tautologous argument accounts for power in terms of the authority relations which it was introduced to explain. It is defined in terms of Dahrendorf's assumption of the nature of social institutions as imperatively coordinated associations and introduced, in a mysterious and enigmatic manner, seemingly above and beyond theoretical analysis.

When, perhaps aware of the circular nature of his explanation, Dahrendorf does offer a solution to the problem of power-as-a-problem, the result is unconvincing and, in terms of its sociological content, arbitrary:

> Perhaps we must indeed assume something like Kant's 'unsociable sociability' in order to find a convincing argument for the universality of ruling and serving.[43]

This 'explanation' is inadequate for at least two reasons. In the first place, it is ahistorical. Any analysis of power which fails to account both for different modes of rule (in terms of the social composition of the dominant and subject groups) and forms of rule (for example, relying mainly on accepted authority, or on a more or less widespread exercise of open violence) is neither of operational use nor explanatory power. Secondly, it is metaphysical in so far as it seeks to define the 'essence' of man in an abstract concept which relates concretely to neither features of his social nor of his natural environment.

Dahrendorf, in fact, defends his analysis of power and social stratification on the grounds that its presuppositions, the existence of norms and the necessity of sanctions, 'may be regarded as axiomatic'.[44] But Dahrendorf himself implies that norms cannot be thus viewed if they are to have any genuine *explanatory* as opposed to purely *definitional* and *dogmatic* content when he asserts that:

> In the last analysis, established norms are nothing but ruling norms, that is norms defended by the sanctioning agencies of society and those who control them.[45]

How, one may ask, does this differ from Marx's view that the ruling ideas in any society are those of the ruling class? Since, for Dahrendorf, conflict between different ruling groups within the same society is a feasible development, 'the expression "ruling class" is, in the singular, quite misleading'.[46] In the same work, however, he actually identifies a national, political ruling class in the form of the State administrative staff, the governmental élites at its head, and those 'interested parties' represented by them.[47]

This schema cannot account for the 'most general authority' from which it is claimed that bureaucracies borrow or are delegated their authority. Dahrendorf suggests that the governments of Western societies are often 'mere switchboards of authority; decisions are made not by them but through them'.[48]

The logic of this problematic of personnel leads him to conclude that the ruling class is fundamentally a changing body of interest groups and individuals assuming power on a transient and typically electoral basis.

What Dahrendorf's argument misses is the basic fact that in capitalist society the principal interest groups generally preserve their overall positions of relative strength or weakness over time, no matter which party or 'veto group' is in power. Table 1,

TABLE 1

Changes in the distribution of wealth in Britain, 1911–13 to 1960[49]

Year	Proportion of wealth owned by the top		
	1%	5%	10%
1911–13	69	87	93
1924–30	62	84	91
1936–38	56	79	88
1954	43	71	79
1960	42	75	83

spanning almost half a century, demonstrates this continuity as expressed in the distribution of wealth in the case of Britain. The figures indicate a persistent but small decline in the proportion of reported wealth of the top 1 per cent and, to a lesser extent, the top 5 per cent of the population over the period in question, although the tendency is less conclusive when the top 10 per cent is considered. A closer look at relative variations in the level of real wages in Britain under the Labour government of 1966–70 and the Conservative government of 1970–3 (Table 2) similarly

TABLE 2

Real yearly wage rise (adjusted to retail price index)[50]

Labour (%)	Conservative (%)	Sector
2	1.7	Lowest paid manual
2.6	3	Top industrial management

shows that a mere change of ruling party had little redistributive effect. The variations, it is clear, are small, and the overall pattern indicates the marginal impact of social democratic rule on the distribution of wealth within capitalist society. The owl of wisdom may well fly after sunset, but it certainly has not flown yet.

Renner has demonstrated how, after the decline of feudalism, the transition from simple commodity production to the accumulation of capital as such was accompanied by a change in the social function of property, even while the laws of ownership underwent no corresponding change. As the social process of production increasingly derived its unity from capital, the legal detention of the means of production was progressively transferred to the private employing class. These employers, at the same time, eventually ceased to perform any productive labour themselves.[51]

Social organisation increasingly assumes a systematic form with the labour–capital relationship as the basis of the new synthesis. In particular, the private owners of productive property preserve their structural position as an exploiting class as long as that property remains in private hands. Such minor shifts in the pattern as do take place occur *within* the context of enduring capitalist property relations and as such represent no change in the overall structure of production relations, in the structured relations between individual social actors 'in so far as they are personifications of economic categories, representatives of special class relations and class interests'.[52] The sanctity of private property is maintained by the law and its agencies, and is ideologically reinforced through a variety of channels, private and state-owned, formal and informal. Quite in contradiction to Dahrendorf's view, authority is in this way derived from factual relations of production. In his celebrated discussion of *Homo Sociologicus*, Dahrendorf at no point attempts to explain the *genesis* of roles, the general theory of which he elaborates at some length.[53] On a rather more concrete level, he asserts that:

> For the industrial worker, the labour contract implies acceptance of a role which is, inter alia, defined by the obligation to comply with the commands of given persons.[54]

To, admittedly bluntly, demystify this proposition, Dahrendorf breaks his analysis before the point at which an explanation of the way in which an employer (capitalist) buys on the market the labour power of a worker (property-less labourer) and of how this economic relationship determines their mutual role expectations, becomes necessary. Dahrendorf's analytical halt is consistent with and derives from his conception of class, which is myopic to the way in which the authority relationships he examines are circumscribed and, in the last analysis, determined by wider socio-economic patterns of structured influence and constraint. By abandoning the analysis of the range of *types* of authority which reinforce and legitimise *modes* of production relations,[55] Dahrendorf abandons the theoretical problem of the roots of authority in social power and, as a consequence, the source of that power itself. The key to this mystification is the reification of *authority* as a sociological category. The consequence is an image of society as a structure of mutual and reciprocal legitimate expectations for which no origin or source is indicated. Nor could such an origin be formulated, for Dahrendorf's dualistic Kantian conception of man and his historical potential is, in a literal sense, timeless.

DAHRENDORF, LIBERALISM, AND THE GHOST IN THE MARKET PLACE (IN WHICH KANT MAKES A SECOND APPEARANCE)

Parallel to Dahrendorf's failure to systematically examine power are the liberal philosophical and political assumptions which permeate and, in a vital sense, structure his work. The essence of the liberal world outlook is the fundamental right of the individual to develop his own personality and potentialities with the minimum of repressive interference from outside agencies. Or, as J. S. Mill formulated this leading idea:

> To give any fair play to the nature of each, it is essential that different persons should be allowed to lead different lives.[56]

This principle is taken up by Dahrendorf in his discussion of forms of economic rationality:

> Only one thing remains certain: that if the new rationality is to be compatible with human freedom, it must be market rationality.[57]

Since Dahrendorf has already specified the 'market' or 'liberal' option to be that which seeks 'a maximum yield at a minimum cost – for example, a maximum of individual happiness with a minimum of political decision',[58] the liberal basis of his proposition is apparent. His example draws directly on the ethics of political liberalism and reiterates a theme which has figured prominently in recent Western political philosophy, embracing for example Isaiah Berlin's notion of 'negative freedom' and Maitland's definition of freedom as the absence of 'external restraints on human action which are themselves the results of human action'.[59]

Now while such an ethic may ideally (under a set of hypothetical 'ideal' social relationships) be a liberating principle, its value as a methodological tool in sociological analysis is marginal. In particular, it is oblivious to the asymmetrical exchange and distribution relations characteristic of the capitalist mode of production. Dahrendorf posits the fundamentally uncertain nature of human knowledge and draws the corollary that 'Freedom for conflict' is a necessary precondition of 'the just society'.[60] But while he formally accepts that science concerns the realm of the true and stresses, à la Popper, that it is a verifiable procedure developing through open and mutual criticism,[61] his analysis fails in key areas to operationalise his dictum of the desired objectivity of sociological explanation. Most notably, his theoretical categories do not account for observable regularities in the social relations of production. Dahrendorf's notion of 'freedom for conflict' neither recognises nor explains the labour–capital relationship which directly and materially reveals the central conflict of bourgeois society.

Similarly, he suggests that the rules of conflict regulation can only 'serve their function' when the two sides are able to compete 'on an equal footing'.[62] The outstanding structural feature of capitalist society, however, is that the two major classes, property owners and the property-less, do *not* and *cannot* compete equally so long as the sanction of property rests in private hands. Some of the leading founding fathers of contemporary liberalism, in fact, envisaged an antithesis between the conceptions of freedom and equality. Echoing similar formulations by Bagehot and Acton, Lecky held that democracy, or equality of political power, 'may often prove the direct opposite of liberty . . . it destroys the balance of classes'.[63] The more consciously conservative Edmund Burke writing under the impact of the French Revolution and its aftermath, similarly identified the struggle of the individual to preserve his possessions as 'one of the securities against injustice and despotism implanted in our nature'.[64] De Tocqueville's observation that countries lacking a stabilising aristocracy are especially prone to despotic forms of government, and Mill's fears of the 'tyranny of the majority' fall broadly within the same tradition. Dahrendorf typically avoids an explicit view of liberty and equality as mutually irreconcilable. He approaches such a position in *The New Liberty*, the concern of our Appendix to the present chapter, when he asserts that 'the equality party has had its day, and the task today is to develop the full potential of a new liberty'.[65] Nevertheless, his account of conflict regulation develops in accordance with a particular line of logic which in effect serves to endorse prevailing forms of class relations: he proceeds by constructing an ideal–typical model of equal conflicting groups and then formally – virtually in parentheses – suggests that in some instances it may not correspond to empirical reality. A more transparent example of ideological exposition would be difficult to find in Dahrendorf's work. The objective social bases of inequality are systematically displaced by what is essentially a normative liberal paradigm of political organisation.

Dahrendorf's liberalism shows itself in a quite different way in his influential critique of role theory. Having outlined the recurrent themes of this sociological approach, he proposes that man is 'not merely the sum of his characters';[66] he polemically raises the philosophical issue of free will versus determinism and posits the Kantian solution that both views are

> simply different ways of comprehending the same subject, ways that derive from different sources of knowledge.[67]

Now, implied by Kant's analytical dualism of noumenal and phenomenal spheres is the proposition that as 'phenomenon' the individual is imprisoned in the subjective world of appearance, governed by and subject to the phenomenal laws of nature; only his rational or noumenal essence allows him to transcend the dictates of those laws.[68] Kant was well aware of the significance of commodity exchange relationships for his philosophical system:

commodity exchange, in fact, is crucial to his conception of the relation between the noumenal and the phenomenal. Thus, he wrote:

> That which is related to general human inclinations and needs has a market price. That which, without presupposing any need, accords with a certain taste, i.e. with pleasure in the mere purposeless play of our facilities, has an affective price. But that which constitutes the condition under which alone something can be an end in itself does not have mere relative worth, i.e. a price, but an intrinsic worth, i.e. dignity.[69]

'Dignity' and the realm of morality supplement the classical distinction between use value and exchange value in order to explain how individual commodity-owners can be 'ends in themselves', related to and acting in accordance with universal rational laws. The realm of the market, its clash of exchange and its objective relationship to human needs and practice are theoretically transcended through the influence of 'goodwill'.[70] The freedom of the individual is realised only in this proposed noumenal autonomy from social relations. Human essence thus posed, Kant does not consider the division of labour of commodity society as an obstacle to freedom: it is, in fact, endorsed as an unequivocally progressive dimension of social development.[71] Such a position is consistent with Kant's philosophical portrayal of the ideological abstract individual of bourgeois society, and is a conception that finds expression in Dahrendorf's anthropological dualism.

But in appealing to Kant, Dahrendorf introduces into his analysis a speculative and highly intuitive philosophical assumption, the implications of which he himself handles with caution. Why, we may ask, does he do this? The answer is implied in his suggestion that sociology, with its typically deterministic image of man, may have become

> a promoter, or at least an unprotesting supporter, of unfreedom and inhumanity.[72]

Dahrendorf's uncomfortable reiteration of the Kantian view of human nature provides a theoretical framework with which to rescue the idea of human freedom, without which he would be left with only 'the horrible phantom of the totalitarian society'.[73]

Kant's now rather dusty philosophical anthropology, appropriate enough for an epistemology seeking to come to terms with the revolutionary formative stage of capitalist development, is introduced by Dahrendorf in the form of a *deus ex machina*, an ontological assumption quite unrelated to his structural analysis of society on the one hand and his authority-oriented image of social man on the other. It is both compatible with and evidence of his underlying liberal values; values which are, as we have seen, an effective normative counterweight to his dogmatic approach to stratification. As such, it is directly analogous to his acceptance of the uncertainty principle and his preference for the market type of rationality, and is expressive of the same fundamental weakness: an inadequate account of power in society.

Critically assessing the 'hypostatized regularities' of sociological theory, Dahrendorf concludes:

> This is why an image of man may be developed that stresses man's inexhaustible capacity for overcoming all the forces of alienation that are inherent in the conception and reality of society.[74]

The basic problem with this plea for human liberation is that it is predicated on a fundamentally unsatisfactory explanation of the social conditions which produce the assumed condition of alienation in the first place. To posit, as Dahrendorf does, that differential 'rudimentary inequality' has its source in differential social sanctioning is merely to *describe* one aspect of social reality at the expense of scientifically examining its *nature* as a system of social production. Thus he can write:

> I am making an arbitrary decision here when I distinguish the distributive area of stratification – the explicandum of our theoretical discussion – from non-distributive inequalities such as those of power. According to this distinction, wealth and prestige belong to the area of stratification, even if they are assembled to a considerable extent by one person; property and charisma, by contrast, are non-distributive.[75]

In this short but vital passage, Dahrendorf specifies his concern to give an essentially descriptive account of the distributive sector, rather than the analysis of the dynamics of the social relations of production which underlie it. In the process of doing this he somewhat arbitrarily associates property with charisma. The essential problem is Dahrendorf's failure to deal adequately with social stratification, which derives from his substitution of metaphysical assumptions concerning authority relations for historically grounded *causes* of stratification.[76] Marx identified the genesis of specifically capitalist stratification in the process of primary capital accumulation: on the basis of this accumulation, capitalism developed into a system of social production with its own historical laws of motion and distinctive forms of social relations. Dahrendorf's account, by contrast, hangs on a transparently metaphysical reification of authority as the key determinant, and it is this feature that, in the last analysis, gives his work as a whole its mystified character.

APPENDIX TO RALF DAHRENDORF: CONFLICT AND THE DIMENSION OF AUTHORITY: NEW LIBERTY AND OLD IDEAS

Since the original writing of this chapter, Dahrendorf has delivered and published a series of Reith Lectures under the striking title *The New Liberty*. We will not attempt an exhaustive account of the many issues that he raises in this latest work because such a project would entail no less than a detailed counter-analysis of the present crisis of Western society, indeed of the world system as a whole. Our intention is rather the more limited purpose of identifying the roots of Dahrendorf's 'new liberty' in the assumptions and themes of his earlier work, as examined in the previous chapter.

In the relatively innocent days of 1960, Dahrendorf formally tackled the perennial question of the significance and role of values in social science. His position was that while Weber's ideal of a value-free science may be desirable, the sociologist must in fact always be morally committed if he is to protect himself and others from the unintended consequences of his actions. Far from ending with the completion of scientific enquiry, the political and moral responsibility of sociologists 'commits us . . . to professing our value convictions in our writings and in the lecture hall as well'.[77] Concerning the traditional division of labour between the researcher and the man of political action, Dahrendorf endorsed Weber's dual proposition that while the values of the latter can in no sense be said to be implicit in or derived from the findings of the former, the politician can make use of available scientific knowledge in his pursuit of technical means to attain otherwise formulated goals.[78]

It is apparent that Dahrendorf never envisaged the working out of the sociologist's moral commitments to be legitimately confined to the mere affirmation of personal value positions on the one hand, or the servile and mercenary subordination of theory to the purposes of a – any – value- or interest-motivated politician on the other. His own remarkable political career, spanning the German Bundestag and the Commission of the European Communities, excludes such simplistic conceptions of the desired relation between theory and practice, one expression of which is a recent discussion paper on the state of Britain where he advocates the establishment of an open-ended 'think tank' in which 'research is conducted, people are brought together, and ideas are disseminated'.[79] Presumably what Dahrendorf has in mind is a kind of latter-day, Anglicised *Verein fur Sozial politik*. Whatever form his think tank takes, however, it is against a varied background of professorial-cum-political activity that Dahrendorf wrote *The New Liberty*, and it would be unreasonable to expect its themes to predominantly reflect other milieux than those in which he has elected to work.

From the outset, Dahrendorf establishes the theme of 'the new liberty' to be the political economy of freedom in a changing socio-economic climate.[80] The assumptions of linear growth and indefinite quantitative expansion which have dominated Western social and political thought for centuries, and which have now been adopted as obsessive goals in the non-capitalist world, have become exhausted under the pressure of global and historically unprecedented events. Dahrendorf discerns in the blows delivered to growth expectations by the 1973 energy crisis and the onrush of inflation since the late 1960s, symptoms of a wider process of social change. Some twenty years earlier, a more optimistic, and presumably happier, Dahrendorf had speculated on the institutionalisation of class conflict in the post-war Western world, and it is of considerable interest to recall his diagnosis in the light of ensuing developments:

> My thesis is that in post-capitalist society industrial conflict has become less violent because its existence has been accepted and the manifestations have been socially regulated.[81]

Certainly, 'countertrends' were still at work. No serious writer on the development of capitalism has been able to avoid broaching the theme of countervailing factors since Marx wrote his celebrated account of the tendency for the rate of profit to fall. Nevertheless, Dahrendorf saw the general drift to be, for better or worse, towards a progressive decline in the incidence and intensity of industrial conflict.

As Dahrendorf must be the first to acknowledge, even the most well-considered plans and predictions may come amiss. After having remained more or less static for some two decades, the incidence of industrial strikes rose rapidly across most of Western Europe during the late 1960s: in Britain the number of days lost per year more than trebled in the five years leading up to 1970.[82] Rising labour militancy intensified this trend, both in Britain and in the developed capitalist world as a whole, throughout the early 1970s.

The New Liberty is Dahrendorf's attempt to account for this and related developments as indicative of a general crisis in Western society. He has no time for the facile optimism of politicians, be they in Washington, London or Bonn, who blandly predict an imminent 'upturn' in either economic activity or consensus politics. Indeed, his tone always avoids the complacent and at times borders on the apocalyptic: inflation 'undermines the foundations of free societies'; the escalating violence of a largely concealed redistribution struggle bodes ill for more peaceful forms of economic relations and 'includes the danger of a return of variants of fascism'.[83] Pollution, the decay of cities, the threat of world war, all announce the end of a phase of relatively orderly if *ad hoc* expansion, and Dahrendorf conceives the options favouring a progressive reorientation to lie in a rejection of the single-minded pursuit of quantitative growth. The keynote of the new liberty is not 'more of the same', but rather a novel and critical approach to the restructuring of social relations and the processes of collective decision-making.

The motive force of the political economy of liberty in the 1970s is no longer expansion but what I shall call improvement, qualitative rather than quantitative development.[84]

Following the precedent of his earlier writings, Dahrendorf links both his diagnosis and his proposals for social policy to the Weberian analysis of authority and bureaucracy. The pursuit of socialist goals has increased the general level of social security but at the same time reduced the chances for individual freedom, culminating in the 'ossification of justice' where an enslaving bureaucracy constitutes a paralysing buffer zone between leaders and voters, rulers and citizens. The dilemma is that of 'the alienation of enlightened progress'.[85] Tied to restrictive rules of procedure, individuals are allowed scope for participation yet denied room for manoeuvre and genuine purposive involvement in the determination and execution of their life affairs. Denied the opportunity to act outside of these structural constraints, their social existence approximates the conceptual atrophy glimpsed in Dahrendorf's earlier *Homo Sociologicus*. The condition he describes is a curious amalgam of themes which recall the deepest moods of cultural pessimism in the writings of Weber and Marcuse.

Bleak as his portrayal is, Dahrendorf does not abandon the possibility of cultural and social renewal. Writing initially for a spoken context, Dahrendorf in fact allows a more intimate and personal note to enter into his plea for liberal initiative than is to be found in any of his earlier academic works. He introduces his first lecture with a brief but carefully weighed account of his juvenile experience at the hands of the German SS State, and affirms a subsequent 'almost claustrophobic yearning for freedom . . . a visceral desire not to be hemmed in, neither by the personal power of men nor by the anonymous power of organizations';[86] which is the recurrent leitmotif of *The New Liberty*. Institutional arrangements are of course a necessary precondition of any viable and ongoing liberal form of social life, but they must be constructed and used in ways which respect the integrity and value of the individual and his chances for self-development in a potentially hostile environment. Authoritarian solutions to contemporary social problems, such as those advocated by Robert Heilbroner, anticipate a barren and stultifying prospect of pure, unmediated leadership and obedience. Positive and creative social reconstruction must avoid illiberal scenarios by channelling and asserting the great force of individuals, which above all means resisting 'the new bondage of organization'.[87]

On a rather more concrete level, Dahrendorf advocates a series of possible ameliorative measures which, if pursued, would be indicative of a positive step towards the process of social renewal. The recovery of the cities for people, the construction of precincts for pedestrians, the restoration rather than demolition of old buildings, all are mentioned and all are familiar issues in the field of liberal campaigning and protest politics. But behind this enumeration of 'causes' stands a more fundamental glimpse of social — even of societal — restructuring which derives from Dahrendorf's concern at the potential demise of liberal options, yet at the same time threatens the realisation of the very values that he is seeking to advance. We have already discussed Dahrendorf's examination and rejection of the Marxist conception of class. In *The New Liberty* he returns to this perennial theme, but in such a way as to transform what was previously, at least in its formal presentation, an academic discussion into the basis of a systematic and far-reaching political programme.

Recalling his Popperian critique of 'grand designs' of history and social change, Dahrendorf charges Marx with underestimating the capacity of societies to 'change without drama'.[88] Dahrendorf's own account of the dynamics of class conflict in the 1970s is a development of his Weberian analysis of 'imperatively coordinated associations'. Legitimate government is now in danger of becoming paralysed by a chaos of criss-crossing 'autonomous' and 'power' groups, functioning through 'impersonal violence' and dissociating themselves from 'the legal norms which bind all citizens by defining a separate world of rules'.[89] Dahrendorf again denies the relevance of Marx's analysis of class to the present situation: despite the existence of tough wage disputes, capital and organised labour frequently find themselves 'on the same side of the fence'. With an expanding economy, both are able to materially keep pace with the prevailing rate of growth and maintain their real position. Similarly, when economic growth is threatened, a convergence of interests may be detected in such areas as attitudes towards law enforcement. It is on this supposed common ground that Dahrendorf sees the basis of a new and thorough-going social contract to combat the dangers of uncontrolled inflation.[90] He is cautious to avoid potentially authoritarian implications in his advocacy of a general social contract: the central institutions of the 'improving society' must be public and open in order to ensure that their initiative and control 'ultimately derive their legitimacy from the common source of citizenship.'[91] As such, they guarantee rather than abuse the liberal opportunities posed by the radical changes that world society is going through; or, as he puts it:

> The new liberty then is the politics of regulated conflict, and the socio-economics of maximizing individual life-chances.[92]

Nevertheless, Dahrendorf's tentative programme for change raises possibilities which are anything but liberal in their implication. At a general level, he opposes empiricist and visionless forms of pragmatic political activity in favour of 'medium term perspectives', a kind of applied variant of Merton's advocated studies of the middle range. One familiar suggestion that he makes concerns the guaranteeing of essential public services by the provision of a universal public-service contract:

> This may well be a task to which everybody in a mature society should make a contribution; a contribution of time, not of money. Why should we not ask every citizen to devote one year of his or her life to public service?[93]

A subsequent denial that such a scheme would produce a militarised labour force does not alter its basic political character, the technical term for which is corporatism. The conflicts of civil society are to be subsumed within an embracing 'Council' which 'brings organisations into a structure of general responsibility and makes it therefore impossible to ignore them and un-necessary to fight them.'[94] Dahrendorf's proposals are far from new: Harold Laski, moving rapidly to the Right in British social democracy in the 1930s, advocated such schemes in the mining and other industries,[95] and the notion of workplace incorporation has figured prominently in social democratic thought ever since. The independent power of 'large organizations' is to be curbed by subordinating them to wider structures of legitimate social and political obligation. Dahrendorf is unquestionably sincere in his belief that such a development is not only compatible with but in fact essential for the furtherance of liberal rights and possibilities; his many appeals to the writings of J. S. Mill are far from mere rhetoric and flourish. But it is equally certain that there is a profound tension in his insistence on the need to reconcile 'the revolt of the individual' with 'the reality of organization'.[96]

Yet it is precisely the character of the 'organization' that most favours the development and fulfilment of social needs at present which is at issue. For example, is there not a definite class character in any attempt at formulating a 'social contract' for Britain, when the overwhelming majority of élite opinion and media sources advocate a redistribution of wealth towards 'industry', even though workers' living standards and share of G.D.P. have been falling both relatively and absolutely for a considerable period?[97] Dahrendorf is sensitive to the need to restructure the international system following the historic Nixon measures of 15 August 1970. Nevertheless, the seeds of the social contract that he detects in the united desire of workers and capitalists for subsidies and protection in the crisis-stricken textile industries of Western Europe are potentially a powerful in-gredient in the beggar-my-neighbour drift into trading, and perhaps eventually shooting, war that he understandably wishes to avoid.[98] Dahrendorf understands the increasingly in-ternational character of human society, but his most important substantive proposals for social reorganisation affirm the struc-tures of the nation state, however internally modified, and in doing so displace its domestic antagonisms and conflicts on to the level of international relations. Certainly, he advocates re-organisation in the international system, but this aspect of his work is confined largely to the task of diagnosis and is given neither the urgency nor the detailed consideration that his proposals for national change receive. As such, it represents at best a short-term holding measure, rather than a systematic attempt to find a remedy, against the re-emergence of manifest conflict at all levels, both analytical and territorial, of social life

The New Liberty is a provisional attempt to come to terms with a new and, for Dahrendorf, unanticipated world situation. The liberal outlook and Weberian perspectives of his earlier work are brought to bear on problems which in their implications transcend the scope of his strictly academic writings. In this sense, Dahrendorf's Reith Lectures evidence both continuity and innovation, although perhaps their most striking feature is the unresolved tension between liberal intentions and illiberal possibilities as we have described it. It may be objected that Dahrendorf's Popperian conception of both science and politics allows for such inconsistencies by the notion of a self- and mutually-correcting dialectic of critical exchange; but our own view is that his ambivalence over the desired limits of a libertarian impulse in social policy reflects an inability to convincingly relate his former academic analyses to the actuality of the contemporary world scene. For, despite the new substantive concerns, his liberal ethics and the Weberian sociological assumptions remain essentially unchanged.

6

C. Wright Mills: the Struggle to Make History

INTRODUCTION

During the two decades prior to the 1960s, C. Wright Mills stood out as the leading voice of radical opposition to the sociological establishment, its dominant assumptions and perspectives. As a pioneer of unorthodox ways of looking at the world in which he lived, his attempt to introduce an authentic radical note into the largely apologetic and conservative mainstream of American sociology earned him both recrimination and praise.[1] His work has a direct bearing on what are still central issues in the debate between socialist and more orthodox academic theorists of contemporary society, a debate recently brought into prominence by the writings of Gouldner, Giddens and others. A primary aim of these theorists is to effect a fusion or convergence of the perspectives of Marxism and sociology, both functionalist and Weberian.[2]

By the 1960s, Mills' writings had attained the status of at least nominal acceptance. Certainly, he would have been the first to suspect the motives behind this development: his account of 'the control of the insurgent by the agreements of academic gentlemen' was too well considered to allow him to take the appearance of formal political tolerance entirely at face value.[3] Nevertheless, the fact remains that Mills' distinctive contributions to themes and issues such as the power élite, the study of labour leaders and white-collar workers, and the 'sociological imagination' have entered into the vocabulary of the sociological community as tolerable and legitimate theoretical statements.

To this extent we see in Mills an example of how the academic social sciences can learn to live with and even draw a not inconsiderable strength from the frontier work of their wayward children.

One inescapable problem in assessing the work of C. Wright Mills is the sheer chronological distance between the period in which he made his most distinctive contributions – the 1940s to the early 1960s – and the post-Allende, post-Watergate, post-Vietnam and post-Bretton Woods world of our own times. It would be deceptively easy to abstract Mills' writings from their historical context and stress the pessimism that cuts across his anything but despairing attempts to politicise his often wretched fellow cultural workmen. Equally, it would be incorrect to minimise any substantive or methodological weaknesses on the grounds that they were somehow inevitable or unavoidable given the nature of the social and political constraints under which he wrote. Certainly, it was more difficult for a North American academic to consistently and rigorously assess the challenge of socialism in the cold-war-dominated climate of the 1950s than in our own period when Marxism, with however many disclaimers and however reluctantly, is generally recognised as a seminal influence on social theory, both radical and conservative. Nevertheless, Mills himself would have given little comfort to an apology for his work based on this line of reasoning. We can still learn from his sharp rejection of the notions of 'fate' and total individual moral helplessness often implied by the practitioners of grand theory.[4]

A serious critique of Mills must, rather, locate the corpus of his work not only within its immediate social and political environment, but also within the intellectual and philosophical traditions and perspectives from which it is developed. He wrote from the point of view of a committed radical, seeking ways to effectively influence the dominant and threatening social trends which he saw to be both a constraint and challenge to political action, both in his own country and in the world at large. As such, he inevitably encountered and sought to come to terms with the socialist alternative, but grounded in the tradition of pragmatism, Mills was unable to fully incorporate and develop the implications of this confrontation on the basis of his previous, challenging in itself, conception of social life, theory and their mutual relations.

On the question of how the 'Marxist edge' of Mills' writings would have further moulded the pragmatist attitudes which originally led to his interest in the problems of socialism, we can only speculate. Whatever our assessment of the work he did produce, Mills distinguished himself not least by being a man whose private troubles remained firmly grounded in the arena of public issues. This complete and authentic commitment to a radical re-working of his contemporary social world, is what distinguished him in his working and historical context.[5] While authenticity does not of itself make for theoretical adequacy, neither does a critical assessment of Wright Mills' work detract from what he did accomplish, with no fear of swimming against the prevailing conservative and reassuring stream. Not least among these accomplishments was his place as an intellectual rallying point for radical sociology in an otherwise largely uncommitted or complacent academic world.

SOCIOLOGY: TOWARDS THE UNITY OF THEORY AND PROGRAMME

Wright Mills' influence on recent sociology derives from the critique of and programme for social science elaborated in *The Sociological Imagination*. While this study is now generally accepted by the sociological community, its impact upon publication in 1959 cannot be overemphasised. Writing against a prevailing background of functionalist orthodoxy, Mills attempted to accomplish two closely related tasks: firstly, he offered a powerful and distinctive critique of some dominant trends in sociological thought; secondly, and more fundamentally, he sought to outline a perspective and programme for the social sciences which would be adequate to the major structural and institutional facts of contemporary social reality.

Mills saw the sociological imagination to be emerging as the distinctive reflective medium of the present intellectual age. He repeatedly drew attention to the heterogeneity of recent American sociology, which he characterised as 'a sort of Hellenistic amalgamation embodying elements and aims from the sociologies of the several Western societies'.[6] Mills' principal targets, however, are the practitioners of grand theory and abstracted empiricism. The grand theorists, he observes, typically work at such high levels of abstraction that their systems more often resemble an exercise in strictly conceptual gamesmanship than a serious attempt to examine and indicate possible solutions to problems of sociological substance; he pays particular attention to the theories of Talcott Parsons, attacking both Parsons' transparent verbosity and his unsatisfactory treatment of the question of power in society. The grand theorists, generally, are charged with a refusal to 'get down from the higher generalities to problems in their historical and structural contexts'.[7] Central to this critique is Mills' insistence on the need for a proper use of historical materials, 'the shank of social study', for both interpretive and comparative purposes.[8]

Mills' criticisms of the abstracted empiricists are no less pointed. His objection is that the statistical and empiricist methods of procedure which dominate many social-science research projects typically, if not explicitly, adopt philosophies of natural science as working models of 'the' scientific method. Such methodological inhibition, Mills points out, is associated with neither any distinctive substantive theories or propositions, nor with an original conception of the nature of society. Its distinctive characteristics, rather, lie in the types of administrative milieux and intellectual workmen through which it finds expression, which, in turn, derive from the adoption of a particular method of natural science, the positivist methodological procedure advocated by Paul F. Lazarsfeld being Mills' par excellence example. Mills observes:

> Those in the grip of the methodological inhibition often refuse to say anything about modern society unless it has been through the fine little mill of the Statistical Ritual.[9]

Mills rejects the style of abstracted empiricism as being no less a hindrance to the working out of a serious and worthwhile social science than the conceptual fetishism of the grand theorists.

In many different contexts, Mills extended his critique of prevailing sociological theories into a radical indictment of what he termed the cultural default. Sensitive to the increasingly widespread use of social scientists as knowledge consultants to the centres of social power and control, he drew attention to the lowering of intellectual initiative and raising of opportunism among researchers, appealing for a reflective re-assessment of the political significance of social-sciences practices. Abstracted empiricism

> makes questions of the moral and political policy of the social studies all the more urgent.[10]

Mills spoke directly to and against the ideologists of the 1950s who proclaimed the end of ideology, which he rejected as 'a weary know-it-all justification – by tone of voice rather than by explicit argument – of the cultural and political default of the NATO intellectuals'.[11] Intellectuals and cultural workmen effectively withdraw from the arena of constructive politics by uncritically accepting official, propagandist definitions of world reality. Their withdrawal directly contributes to the general decline deeper into 'semi-organised irresponsibility':

> Every time intellectuals have the chance to speak out yet do not speak, they join the forces that train men not to be able to think and imagine and feel in morally and politically adequate ways.[12]

As a means to counter this default, Mills urged 'men of independent minds' to formulate, for intellectuals and other publics, alternative social and political programmes. Such programmes must proceed from the basis of a clear understanding of the major institutional facts of the contemporary world.[13] For Mills, a convinced rationalist, politically-directed intellectual work was inseparable from a complementary emphasis on the need for publics to achieve some degree of self-understanding. While distinguishing private troubles involving individuals and their immediate areas of social life, from issues concerned with transcending cultural and political milieux, Mills advocates the sociological imagination as an attitude through which the individual can come to understand his own experience by locating himself within a wider social and historical context. Sociology is at least in part concerned with the relations between history and biography and has a rationalist-liberating potential. A widespread experience of uneasiness and indifference adds urgency to the need for contextual clarification, and makes the sociological imagination 'our most needed quality of mind'.[14]

PRAGMATISM: THE PHILOSOPHICAL BACKGROUND

Mills' concern to examine the main drift . . . the underlying forms and tendencies of the range of society in the middle of the twentieth century'[15] found expression in a series of structural and descriptive studies. His principal areas of analysis include the American power élite, labour leaders, white-collar workers and, towards the end of his life, the threat of a Third World War. While using concepts and perspectives adopted from other philosophical and sociological schools, Mills analysed these themes primarily in terms of a pragmatist epistemology and model of man. Before considering his treatment of particular substantive issues, we will clarify the general character and significance of this underlying pragmatist influence.

Pragmatism has been given various meanings and emphases both in technical philosophical and in everyday discourse, but its original epistemological implications, as developed by C. S. Peirce, and its sociological elaboration, by Dewey and Mead, are of most direct relevance for an understanding of Mills' work. It was specifically as an epistemological principle, or 'a method of ascertaining the meaning of hard words and abstract conceptions', that Peirce introduced the philosophy of pragmatism. Seeking to clarify, if not reject, problems of traditional 'metaphysical' philosophy, Peirce emphasised the practical character of thought, rooting the criteria of meaning in the context of its effective consequences:

> Consider what effects, that might conceivably have practical bearings, we conceive the object of our conception to have. Then, our conception of these effects is the whole of our conception of the object.[16]

For Peirce, the significance of an abstract conception or formula is, in terms of meaning, reducible to the occasions of its use. A corollary of this proposition is the assumption that a symbol's meaning is conditional upon the presence of a corresponding experience or series of experiences, actual or assumed, which constitute its basis, environment and object. This is made explicit when Peirce defines experience as the factor or realm which constrains the activity of thought and obliges a 'forcible modification of our ways of thinking'.[17]

Thus far Peirce is endorsing, although in a quite different social and historical context, the empiricist proposition of Locke that knowledge is invariably founded on direct sense experience. What is of particular interest is the idea of a social dimension to thought. Peirce insists on the symbolic character of cognition, observing that 'all thought whatsoever is a sign, and is mostly of the nature of language'.[18] These 'signs' or symbols, seen by Peirce to include all communicative expressions, are viewed as essentially dialogic. The form of interpretation of a sign depends both upon the general criteria of practical life and, specifically in the case of human communication, the particular relational context of the communicants. It is here that Peirce's pragmatism, as against the psychologistic radical empiricism of William James, suggests the inter-subjective nature of experience as the basis of symbolic thought; it is above all ' "our" experience that has to be thought of'.[19]

It is this stress on the role of cultural symbols, especially language, in the construction and development of knowledge that constitutes the principal influence of Peirce's epistemology on Dewey and Mead. The guiding idea of Dewey and Mead's symbolic interactionist sociology is the notion of human interaction as mediated by the use of interpretive symbols, or by ascertaining ('defining') the meaning of another's actions.[20] Behaviour is constructed by the individual in the process of on-going activity through a mechanism of self-indication in consciousness. This constitutive process invariably occurs within a particular social context. The sequence of interpretative meaning imputation is described, in Mead's theory, by the familiar notion of 'taking the role' of the other, or the 'generalized other' where a collectivity is involved.

Whereas Peirce adopts a species-eclectic usage of the concept symbol, it becomes in Dewey's hands the cornerstone of a specifically human-oriented sociological perspective.[21] But this difference notwithstanding, pragmatism does represent a distinctive philosophical attitude towards the character of knowledge. Peirce, as we have seen, sought to reduce theoretical or abstract conceptions to the specific occasions of their use. James, far more selective and less eclectic than Peirce in his attempts to offer an alternative to nineteenth-century doctrines of mechanistic materialism, brought out this dimension of pragmatism most explicitly:

> What difference would it practically make to anyone if this notion rather than that notion were true? If no practical difference whatever can be traced, then the alternatives mean practically the same thing, and all dispute is idle.[22]

The status of theoretical propositions is to be assessed in terms of their consequences if true or otherwise for practical affairs. But what then is the status of 'the practical' itself? It is, quite literally, operational utility in the field of everyday experience. Thus James:

> You must bring out of each word its practical cash-value, set it at work within the stream of your experience.[23]

And Dewey:

> . . . the term 'pragmatic' means only the rule of referring all thinking, all reflective considerations, to *consequences* for final meaning and test. [emphasis in original][24]

One corollary of the pragmatist conception of verification is a sceptical attitude towards any attempt to resolve the ontological status of a proposition or theory by strictly objective criteria. Concerning theology, James writes:

> If theological ideas prove to have a value for concrete life, they will be true for pragmatism, in the sense of being good for so much.[25]

James indicates the individualistic anchoring of his pragmatism by classifying 'private and personal phenomena' alone as 'realities in the completest sense of the term'. As against science, which seeks to minimise the influence of experiential factors in its findings, religiosity attains the status of absolute ontological validity, understood in terms of personal reality:

> By being religious we establish ourselves in possession of ultimate reality at the only points at which reality is given us to guard. Our responsible concern is with our destiny after all.[26]

Dewey's position differed in so far as he sought to locate practical applicability as the criterion of value and truth within the social collectivity itself rather than in the experiences of individuals. Leszec Kolakowski, partly on the basis of this idea of a social subject, suggests that Dewey's pragmatism drew closer to a Marxist position than that of James.[27] This proposition appears questionable, however, when Dewey's conception of the social collectivity is examined in the wider context of his view of the relation between social forms and reflective activity. In his own detailed study of American pragmatism, Mills points out that, largely in revolt against more formalistic epistemological positions, Dewey laid primary emphasis on the experiential context of reflective processes as they occur in the sphere of 'practical life and science'.[28] Pervading this approach is an optimistic belief in the possibility of a successful application of intelligence in human progress, for the purposes of a socially-shared democratic and community-oriented social life.[29]

Dewey's notion of sociality involves both a view of collective life as such and a corresponding set of political inferences which stand out sharply against those of Marx, despite the former's location of the pragmatist problematic in a social subject. Dewey regards the modifiability of the human young as the source of a great potential human value, that value being the capactiy for independent individuality. The general mechanism of this liberatory potential is the active role of the individual in the production of ideas as a function of his cultural existence in a shared symbolic milieu. Individuals

> live in a cultural environment. Such living compels them to assume in their behaviour the standpoint of customs, beliefs, institutions, meanings, and projects which are at least relatively general and objective.[30]

Constituted within this process, intelligence assumes an instrumentalist form, the elements of which activity comprise the acting organism and its environment. Social events appear as interactions between components of human nature, understood in a non-static sense, on the one hand, and cultural conditions on the other.

As Mills points out, Dewey's instrumentalism is to a large extent a biological doctrine, grounded firmly in the theory of organic evolution. Resting on the Darwinian conception of adaption as a primary precondition of survival, it is the basis for both a reformist view of social progress as a cumulative, step-by-step procedure, and a theoretical understanding of community existence which minimises the importance for social change of systematic inequalities of power and influence.[31] Dewey proposes an educational problematic as the cornerstone of social change or reconstruction, conceptualised in terms of his extension of sociality to the parameters of community itself. The teacher's

aims are social aims; the development of individuals taking ever more responsible positions in a circle of social activities continually increasing in radius and in complexity.[32]

Dewey's sociology develops from a voluntaristic image of man which interprets the social collectivity in a formal way. He locates the primary interactional locus between organism and environment, and the pragmatist problematic of the unity of theory and action in the procedures of practical educational accomplishment. The question of systematically antagonistic social interests is, within this perspective, accordingly mooted. For Marx, the overriding form of historical change is the revolutionary leap; for Dewey, it is a gradual ameliorative or reformist process based, like the development of the individual, on 'the evolution of problems out of immediate experience'.[33] Marx sees a historical contradiction between the human transformation of nature (the scenario of the forces of production) and the internal division of society into classes (the relations of production) which can only be resolved through a conscious bringing of the latter into correspondence with the former.

Dewey sees a common emergent basis for social liberty and the creative cultivation of intelligence as a function of the organism—environment relationship.[34] Finally, and most fundamentally, Marx holds that in the last analysis, developments in society's economic base, incorporating both the forces and relations of production, determine the forms of cultural, ideological and other superstructural elements; Dewey, by contrast, adhering to a cultural interactionist perspective, advocates a procedure for social investigation which involves 'the relativistic and pluralistic position of considering a number of interacting factors—of which a very important one is undoubtedly the economic'.[35]

With these distinctions in mind, we can see how Dewey's

pragmatism, while based on á conception of sociality absent in that of James, shares the latter's underlying commitment to a unification of theory and practice on the basis of subjective experience. In place of overtly subjective idealism, a quasi-objective form is developed, locating the agent or reference of operationality in the social subject. It is not simply that Dewey fails to attribute adequate weight to the question of unequal power in society; rather that his whole methodological procedure, no less than that of James, assumes a rationalist conception of social action which systematically militates against both the analysis of structural aspects of social life and the notion of a hierarchy of determination. The intelligibility of Dewey's account ends when one class within the social collectivity is unable, for institutional reasons, to realise its particular practical goals on the existent ground of society as a whole. A strictly formal recognition of man's cultural environment and his necessarily shared world of symbols, meanings and activities is unable to adequately account for such a situation.

The logic of pragmatism, rather, points to the beneficently ameliorative impact of experientially grounded reflection on the collectivity as a whole and its members as individuals. In this way, the requirement for a law-like understanding of structural processes as a basis for the formulation of strategic policy in political life is avoided. Public life centres on the elaboration of means appropriate to the realisation of ends whose rationality is inherent or intrinsic in the triadic complex of intelligence, activity and environment.

Dewey accordingly emphasises the urgency of

effecting the needed integration [of knowing and doing – D.B.] in the wide field of collective human experience. Philosophy is called upon to be the theory of the practice, through ideas sufficiently definite to be operative in experimental endeavour, by which the integration may be made secure in actual experience.[36]

It is both within and against this philosophy of operationality and reconciliation that Mills developed his distinctive form of critical sociology.

MILLS' SOCIAL WORLD: MEANINGS AND STRUCTURES

Mills' writings on culture and the social character of meaning draw heavily upon the pragmatist view of social life. In his influential *Character and Social Structure*, co-written with Hans Gerth, Mills adopts Mead's conception of the 'looking glass self' as a cornerstone of his analysis of role performance.[37] In *Language, Logic and Culture*, he utilises Mead's 'generalized other' in order to indicate the relational and conversational interplay of meanings in the process of identity maintenance.[38] Again, Mills follows the pragmatists in attributing primary importance to the function of language for both biographical development and macro-social coordination:

> To understand how any given person strives, feels, and thinks we have to pay attention to the symbols he has internalized; but to understand these symbols we have to grasp the way in which they co-ordinate institutional actions. Symbols mediate entire institutional arrangements as well as the conduct and roles of persons.[39]

Originally trained in philosophy with the pragmatists as his mentors, Mills' approach to sociology cannot be understood apart from this background. The suggestion, in his doctoral dissertation, that a study of contemporary American pragmatism 'would offer the possibility of a fundamental understanding of the conditions for the future development of philosophy in the United States' indicates the intellectual weight he attributed to the pragmatist point of view.[40]

Mills was not a pragmatist pure and simple: his work is essentially an attempt to develop the assumptions of the pragmatist image of social man through the consideration of systematic structures of power, authority and inequality. Thus, while positively appraising Mead's social psychology in general, Mills reinterprets his notion of the 'generalized other' in terms of individuals' apprehension of particular segments of social reality rather than society as a whole. For the sociology of knowledge, this implies a cultural reality differentiated in terms of its significance for variously located social members:

> We try to locate the thinker with reference to his assimilated

portion of culture, to delineate the cultural influences (if any) of his thought upon cultural changes.[41]

Vocabularies of motives, the terms through which social actors impute and vocalise motives to themselves and others, function to link up actions to situations, thus integrating the practices of different actors and aligning diverse patterns of conduct with norms; they are functions of socially-situated action rather than the property of 'individuals as such'. Further, vocabularies of motives systematically, if not always precisely, vary between social groups, motivational patterns of purpose being 'relative to societal frames', especially those of occupation and class, within wider society. Co-terminous with and expressive of such socially-structured patterns of role relations, typical vocabularies with definite situational functions constitute a heterogeneous complex of cultural and linguistic inferences:

> Back of 'mixed motives' and 'motivational conflicts' are competing or discrepant situational patterns and their respective vocabularies of motive.[42]

Mills did not either formally or substantively reject pragmatism as a basis for sociological analysis. The substantive studies, rather, represent a series of social explorations which link up the basic pragmatist propositions concerning social action, motivation and culture to a critical structural analysis of the major social and political features of contemporary society. Language, for example, functions not only as a means of mediating human behaviour but also, in fact primarily, as a system of social control. Linguistic symbols, socially constructed and maintained, are not neutral from the point of view of political differentiation. Thought is experientially subject to the content and forms of language, which through the context and occasions of its use 'embodies implicit exhortations and social evaluations'.[43] The 'master symbols' within this evaluatory nexus function as key elements of social control, both sanctioning institutional authority and selectively motivating personal conduct in terms of 'moral symbols, sacred emblems, or legal formulae which are widely believed and deeply internalized'.[44] Cultural definitions of reality, values and tastes are, moreover, increasingly subject to official management backed, if necessary, by overt coercion, particularly in the twentieth century when the permitted range of ideas and cultural images is 'judged officially, sometimes bloodily; or judged commercially, often ruthlessly'.[45]

In developing his structuralised pragmatist analysis of social life, Mills frequently refers to the Marxist theory of class and class conflict. We will examine his interpretation and use of Marx at a later point, but it will be emphasised now that Mills' social psychology neither derives from nor is compatible with Marxism as a method of interpreting the world. Mills is explicitly agnostic concerning the determining relationship between social existence and consciousness. He writes:

> The consciousness of men does not determine their material existence; nor does their material existence determine their consciousness. Between consciousness and existence stand meanings and designs and communications which other men have passed on – first, in human speech itself, and later, by the management of symbols.[46]

Here and elsewhere, Mills counterposes his own radical pragmatist conception of the nature of language to an assumed vulgar or untestable Marxian model of economic determinism. Mills even charges Marxists with implicitly assuming 'traditional, individualistic theories of mind'.[47] While a detailed account of the Marxian theory of ideology is beyond the scope of this chapter, a careful reading of the most important relevant texts clearly absolves their authors from such a conception of social consciousness. It is, indeed, fundamental to Marxism that social existence determines consciousness, since the real process of production, starting from the material production of life itself, is the context or 'ground' of human history. On the basis of the production and reproduction of their material existence, men enter into definite forms of social relationships which comprise a mode of cooperation. Marx opposes this materialist view of social life to the idealist exclusion of the relationship of man to nature, with its corresponding conception of an antithesis between nature and history. From the viewpoint of historical materialism, consciousness, including its linguistic forms, has a determinate historical existence which is inseparable from the development of material production and the corresponding forms of human intercourse.[48]

Marxists have never sought to reduce the superstructural sphere of social life to a purely passive status. Rather, while the economic structure of society is, in the last analysis, the determining ground of the forms of legal, political and conscious life, there is also at work the 'reciprocal action of these various sides on one another'.[49] A well-known series of letters written by Engels in the early 1890s explicitly elaborate on the determining autonomy of elements in the superstructure, while Plekhanov's distinction between the 'psychology of man in society' and the various ideologies which reflect it repudiates the notion of an automatic or unidirectional and unmediated influence of economic factors on consciousness.[50]

It is largely against such a vulgar interpretation that Mills develops his model of culture and consciousness. He does attempt to socially locate particular idea systems, as when he identifies liberalism as the specific ideology of the urban entrepreneurial middle classes in the pre-corporate period of capitalism,[51] but his general theory of 'symbol spheres' is elaborated in terms of classical pragmatist criteria. He suggests, for example, that the concurrence of rapid social change and a relatively static legitimating symbolic order is conducive to the alienation of men from the master symbols and their abandonment for a competing set of 'counter symbols'.[52] This formal depiction of a crisis of legitimacy constitutes a portrayal of the consequences of a given idea system's decreasing operationality in non-specified conditions. Following the pragmatists, symbolic reflection functions situationally in response to the practical applicability or pay-off potential of experientially-grounded sign complexes. Actors and symbols mutually adjust in a quasi-cybernetic, if perhaps not always harmonious, way:

> Whole populations may become alienated from one set of symbols and shift allegiance to other symbols which make more sense in terms of actual or expected practices.[53]

Mills insists that the determining capacity of symbols is limited by the extent to which they correspond to features of character structure and role performance, themselves largely shaped by institutional arrangements. Nevertheless, his formal account of situated motivation centres on a pragmatist view of the inter-mentalist processes of meaning imputation. From this perspective symbolic communication is assumed to be at its most rational and meaningful at the point of highest mutual-sign recognition:

> A block in social actions, e.g., a class conflict, carries a reflex back into our communicative medium and hence into our thought. We then talk past one another. We interpret the same symbol differently. Because the coordinated social actions sustaining the meaning of a given symbol have broken down, the symbol does not call out the same response in members of one group that it does in another, *and there is no genuine communication*. [my emphasis – D.B.][54]

The consensualist model of meaningful symbolic discourse that this culturological portrayal of class conflict expresses is due less to Mills' attempt to radically interpret the class structure of contemporary society than the anchoring of his theorisation in pragmatist epistemology. For Marxism, the social disjunctures and discontinuities associated with a heightened level of class conflict constitute a conscious clarification rather than essential breakdown in the structures of inter-class understanding. Mills, by contrast, maintains a weighty agnosticism on the significance of discrepancies between the objective position of various social strata and the political content and direction of their 'mentalities':

> If political mentalities are not in line with objectively defined strata, that lack of correspondence is a problem to be explained; in fact, it is the grand problem of the psychology of social strata.[55]

Mills sees the absence of a spontaneous unified political posture on the part of property-less employees as a basis for rejecting the view of absence of property as the only or even a crucial factor determining political will. Yet his pragmatist conception of symbolic breakdown undermines the basis of an alternative perspective which views 'false consciousness' as a political task requiring resolution in terms of the social relations which it ideologically conceals. As with Dewey, intelligence appears as an operational function mediating the relations between consciousness and environment.

Unable to break out of this instrumentalist orientation through his analysis of social structure, Mills can only portray, in sensitive and pained prose, the agony of actors whose motivations can find no field for expression within the existent parameters of experiential space. Mills describes the experio-reflective response to situations of non-renewing institutional and symbolic breakdown in the following terms:

> In such periods sensitive minds usually experience stress and strain, and formulate problems long before broad masses of men experience them consciously or act collectively in response to the mounting tensions accompanying . . . a state of normlessness. Then occurs in intellectual circles trial and error, criticism and countercriticism, self-searching and doubt, scepticism and enlightenement, desperate attempts to revive and to reaffirm what proves in the end to be outlived and hollow. Words and deeds fail to jibe, and boredom overcomes many who feel weary of uninspiring days.[56]

This passage, perhaps more than any other in Mills' writings, offers a glimpse into the aetiology of a disintegrating symbolic universe. The emphasis is on the subjective response to encountering a hiatus in the structured imputations of social meaning, where creative symbolic renewal on the basis of previous vocabularies of motives is no longer viable. Mills is trapped in a contradictory position in that he adopts the consensualist, pragmatist model of symbolic discourse at the same time as he rejects its macro-sociological counterpart, the gradualist conception of social process as elaborated by Cooley.[57] He rejects the processual view of social change, yet restricts the range of meaningful social vocabularies to the limits of existent social life. Consequently, his work reflects back the indecision and uncertainty of his sociological subjects rather than a consistent programme for political reconstruction. To do the latter would require a total abandonment of the pragmatist problematic, but it is from the point of view of a Weberian-influenced pragmatism that Mills encountered both the world he lived in and Marxism.

LIBERALISM AND THE LEGACY OF WEBER

Mills was committed to developing an account of the contemporary world which would draw on and continue 'the classical sociological tradition'. Developing many of his leading ideas under the influence of Weber, Mills saw his world as distinguished by the rising significance for individuals' experience of a pervasive trend of bureaucratisation:

> Great and rational organizations – in brief, bureaucracies – have indeed increased, but the substantive reason of the individual at large has not. Caught in the limited milieux of their everyday lives, ordinary men often cannot reason about the great structures – rational and irrational – of which their milieux are subordinate parts.[58]

Within this historical drift, the struggle for status and the managed fetishes of production and consumption 'possess', and are increasingly the focus for, the organisation of individuals' life, labour and leisure. This trend applies, with certain modifications, to both American society and the Soviet Union. Mills locates the new middle strata of white-collar employees, the major occupational change of the twentieth century, broadly within the Weberian, substantively rational, bureaucratic structure:[59]

> At the centre of the picture is the business bureaucracy with its trained managerial staff and its tamed white-collar mass.[60]

What remnants of the older forms of competition do survive are to be found in the 'new entrepreneur', whose activities consist of 'fixing things' between bureaucracies, and between bureaucracies and government departments. An agent of the employing bureaucracy, he works in the business-services sectors of communication, research, public relations, advertising and other congenial environments; but the milieu remains the bureaucratic structure whose interests he represents, and even here existence is precarious, an issue for careful and always risky management. The new entrepreneur competes not, like his nineteenth-century forefather, for markets and commodities, but for 'the good will of the chieftain by means of personality'.[61] The underlying trend is the bureaucratisation of increasingly centralised organisations, within which most men's actions are typically inconsequential. People are increasingly 'the objects of history, adapting to structural changes within which they have little to do'.[62]

Faced by this prospect, Mills sought over a period of some two decades to articulate a linkage between sociological understanding and the imperative need for an effective form of political action adequate to the historical facts at hand. As early as 1942, he hoped that Franz Neumann's *Behemoth* would 'move us all into deeper levels of analysis and strategy. It had better. Behemoth is everywhere united.'[63] Such a strategy would fill the vacuum left by the default of the body of degraded and resigned cultural workmen, whose end-of-ideology 'stands for the refusal to work out an explicit political philosophy'[64] Understanding alone is likely to deepen the sense of helplessness, when the situation calls for informed and consequential action, the communication of strategy 'with political effectiveness'.

Mills' struggle to give a political direction to theory is, as much as his conception of sociality, developed from a pragmatist position. Basically, the politicisation of cultural work will drive into the impasse of intellectual rigidity a critical wedge to produce visible and consequential practical effects. Mills conceived of such a programme in terms of a radical, liberal interpretation of the prevailing relations between rulers and ruled. He contrasts the relative union of knowledge and power of the early nineteenth century with their present divorce, and seeks to locate the intellectual collapse of liberalism with the decline of a community of publics. While insistent that such a community, the structural mooring of liberalism, is hopelessly inappropriate to the conditions of mid-twentieth-century corporate capitalism, Mills persistently formulates his critiques and programmes in terms of it as a political norm. Thus, the challenge of liberal education is to 'keep us from being overwhelmed' by the bureaucratic drift of social life; it should be directed towards the explanation of private troubles as public issues and the building of a self-cultivating liberal public. Such a project provides a basis from which the community 'is to fight all those forces which are destroying genuine publics and creating an urban mass'.[65]

Mills wanted a world in which people's creative abilities would correspond to and find expression in a compatible and sympathetic social order:

Human society, in brief, ought to be built around craftsmanship as the central experience of the unalienated human being and the very root of free human development.[66]

But instead of this he found increasingly bureaucratic centres of irresponsible influence, against which the masses alienate through roles the practices which comprise their social existence. *The Power Elite* is a detailed study of this process in the United States, documenting both Mills' general view of the power structure and the associated devaluation of intellectual and political integrity:

> Public relations and the official secret, the trivializing campaign and the terrible fact clumsily accomplished, are replacing the reasoned debate of political ideas in the privately incorporated economy, the military ascendancy, and the political vacuum of modern America.'[67]

The rise of bureaucratic executive power lowers the effectivity of other 'voluntary' orders between the State and the economy. A parallel increase of scale and centralisation in the means of opinion-making provides opportunities for powerful vested interests to have ready and continual access to the mass media, weakening the chances for small-scale and elective discussion.[68] The democratic state itself is also threatened: 'The political structure of a democratic state assumes the public.'[69]

Liberalism was anchored in a world of independent entrepreneurs, small-scale communities, autonomous institutional orders, all embodying the principle of free choice, with the individual as the seat of substantive rationality. The concentration of power in bureaucratic structures and the progressive convergence of the economic, political and military élites have decisively weakened if not destroyed all these institutional forms, and with them the realistic chance of an authentic liberal revival:

> The root problem of any democratic or liberal — or even humanist — ideals is that they are in fact statements of hope or demands or preferences of an intellectual elite psychologically capable of individually fulfilling them, but they are projected for a population which in the twentieth century is not at present capable of fulfilling them.[70]

Yet despite the power of this assessment of liberalism's contemporary unviability as a constructive political creed, it remained the norm of Mills' programme for democratic recovery. The task of the left, with whom Mills identified himself, is to produce structural criticism, reportage and radical theories of society which, in reply to the right's celebration of the *status quo*, are 'focused politically as demands and programmes'. These critiques and programmes should be 'guided morally by the humanist and secular ideals of Western civilization – above all, reason and freedom and justice'.[71] In other words, by the ideals of classical liberalism, which for Mills represent 'the secular tradition of the West'.[72]

Mills thus sought a political direction for his sociology in terms of political ideals, the social foundations of which he saw to be as irrelevant to the present world as the economic model of *laissez-faire* capitalism. His demands centred increasingly upon the theme of the responsibility of national ruling circles and the decline of the public. In 1943, he warned against the trend towards the incorporation of trade unions into the structures of irresponsible government if they failed to take independent political action on the issues confronting them. At this time, he virtually identified the organised working class as the contemporary form of the classical liberal public, alone able to check the rise of centralised corporate influence:

The chief social power upon which a genuine democracy can rest today is labour.[73]

Within a decade of writing this, Mills' concern had shifted towards a general, that is non-class-specific, exhortation in favour of democratised and more informed relations between rulers and ruled:

Only where publics and leaders are responsive and responsible, are human affairs in democratic order, and only when knowledge has public relevance is this order possible.[74]

Even when Mills notes the absence of such conditions in America, the ethos of his programme is clear: a nostalgic appeal to a historically distant epoch as the only viable basis for political reform. He believed that the centralisation of the means of power provides a framework within which the classical liberal ideals can, if democratic life is campaigned for publicly and consistently, be reconstituted. Thus, in *The Causes of World War Three*, he advises:

> We should take democracy literally and seriously. . . . The thing to do with civil liberties is to use them. The thing to do within a formal democracy is to act within it and so give it content.[75]

That Mills understands democracy in terms of a fundamental division between those who make decisions and those who are subject to them, a perspective grounded firmly in the Weberian tradition, is apparent from his general conception of the power élite. His analysis is unquestionably radical, but focuses specifically on the *abuse* of power and attempts to prepare the way for a strategy to rectify its deviations from the liberal norm. The keynote is thus a pluralistic critique of centralised irresponsibility and a corresponding set of political demands:

> It is now sociologically realistic, morally fair, and politically imperative to make demands upon the men of power and to hold them responsible for specific courses of events.[76]

Such a calling to account of the powerful would highlight and strive to overcome the prevailing divorce of knowledge from power, the situation in which men of knowledge work as little more than paid consultants to the ruling circles. It is on the question of power that Mills' theories diverge most conspicuously from those of Marx, and in the following section we will indicate the major areas of this divergence and locate their origins in Mills' underlying pragmatist outlook.

WRIGHT MILLS AND MARX: THE QUESTION OF LABOUR

In 1943, Mills identified organised labour as the sole social force able to provide an effective basis for genuine democracy.[77] A year earlier he had endorsed Neumann's account of the systematic oppression of German labour under national socialism and stressed the need for 'deeper levels of analysis and strategy'.[78] Yet during the following decade, Mills produced a series of analyses and 'collective portraits' which progressively denied to the working class a significant political role in the struggle to resist the trend towards bureaucratisation and, ultimately, totalitarianism.

As the title of his study *The New Men of Power: America's Labour Leaders* suggests, Mills was concerned with the increasingly important role played by the labour bureaucracy in political decision-making.[79] He pointed to the ambiguous structural position of the labour leader, a question familiar to Marxists, particularly at the level of national policies. As the labour leader's security of position rests primarily on his ability to 'deliver the goods', he is dependent upon the loyalty of other trade unionists; but at the same time, his activities lead him into the sphere of the national power élite. In this dual role, the labour leadership exercises a powerful influence towards the structural incorporation of the trade unions as a whole.[80]

To some extent, Mills' account of the co-opting of the labour bureaucracy is expressive of a more general pessimistic mood among American left intellectuals during the early post-war years. While the working class internationally had achieved substantial social reforms in the field of welfare, and consolidated the strength of its economistic organisations, the notable absence of mass revolutionary movements throughout the capitalist world seemed to many to rule out the likelihood of a decisive shift towards socialism. But Mills went further and spoke of the 'collapse' of labour as an agency of radical change. The working class, while still a structural fact, becomes a class-for-itself only in the early stages of industrialisation or within the political context of autocracy. Mills thus rejects the revolutionary potential of the working class as 'a labour metaphysic . . . a legacy from Victorial Marxism that is now quite unrealistic'.[81]

While Mills had from his earliest writings recognised Marx as a seminal social theorist, it was not until relatively late that he attempted a systematic coming to terms with Marxist theory. A more detailed study of Marxist thought did not, however, decisively change Mills' attitude towards labour as an agency of social change: labour unions and parties 'function politically and economically in a reformist manner only, and within the capitalist system'.[82]

Behind Mills' social behaviouristic approach to the incorporation of the working class is his synthesising conception of the 'classical tradition' of sociology. His 1954 essay, *IBM Plus Reality Plus Humanism=Sociology*, distinguishes the 'classical sociological endeavour' from the over-abstract grand theorists on the one hand, and the obsessively statistical scientists on the other.[83] While this classification in its essentials anticipates the critical themes of *The Sociological Imagination* five years later, the 1954 formulation is significant in that Marx is excluded from the mainstream of positive humanist thought which Mills sees to be alone 'worthy of the name sociology'.

Mills' *Two Styles of Social Science Research*, written a year earlier, suggests an alternative classification of 'macroscopic' and 'molecular' forms of sociological procedure. He includes Marx within the macroscopic style of enquiry, but his principal concern is the social significance and institutional context of the microscopic model. The practitioners of this form of enquiry typically work in applied organisation bureaux and agencies, aiming to clarify alternatives of practical, mainly pecuniary and administrative, action for specific clients with particular interests.

Mills raises the question of a possible synthesis between the two styles of research. He views microscopic enquiry as the most 'objective' type on the grounds that, working at a lower level of abstraction and more easily codified, it is repeatable, relatively open to cumulative development and essentially verifiable. This largely Popperian conception of scientific procedure was modified when Mills suggested that the macroscopic approach allows for a more adequate connecting overview of observations and explanations to develop. The optimal goal is to be able to 'shuttle between levels of abstraction' in the course of research, to effect a meaningful interpenetration of the two orientations: 'We must build up molecular terms: we must break down macroscopic conceptions.'[84]

It was only from the late 1950s that Mills began to elaborate on the specific status of Marxian theory. *The Sociological Imagination* remains notably ambivalent: Marx is listed with Comte, Spencer and Weber as a practitioner of the 'theory of history', which 'can all too readily become distorted into a trans-historical straitjacket into which the materials of human history are forced and out of which issue prophetic views (usually gloomy ones) of the future';[85] at the same time, the sociological imagination is the source of 'all that is intellectually excellent in Karl Marx'.[86] Mills' main concern here is to debunk the dominant contemporary mystifications of academic sociology and to specify an alternative type of intellectual craftsmanship. His definitive coming to terms with the theories of Marx is to be found in *The Marxists*. To a large extent Mills, consistent with his own advice, returned to his academic file, that 'continually growing store of facts and ideas', and re-oriented some of his prior formulations on the general theme of Marx.[87] The range of the assessment which results is unparalleled in Mills' work and offers a unique opportunity to identify the continuity between his early and later studies.

Mills reformulates his view that Marxism is part of the classical tradition of sociology, emphasising the absence of a 'Marxist social science' as such. There is, rather, one social science which would be notably deficient without the insights of Marxist theorists. As against the 'vulgar' and 'sophisticated' types, Mills is concerned with the 'Plain Marxists' who understand Marx to be firmly grounded in the classical tradition. He adopts an independent stance, taking the view that Marx 'is a spectator of audacity about virtually every realm of man and society in history. He is also full of genuine murk.' This approach allows a selective and eclectic use of Marx: 'We are able to use whatever of his we feel the need of, and to reject what we do not.'[88]

In fact, little of Mills' conception of social structure, as expressed in *The Marxists* or elsewhere, derives from Marxist theory. On the question of class, for example, Mills contrasts his own essentially Weberian view of status and occupation as components of social stratification to Marx's supposed one-factor model centred on production relations:

> Property as an objective criterion of class is indispensable to the understanding of the stratification of capitalist society. Alone it is inadequate and misleading, even for understanding economic stratification.[89]

Now while the Marxist theory of class does focus on the relations of various social groups to the means of production, a definition formulated in these terms alone implies a static conception of socio-economic structure. Class, by this criterion, constitutes a category to depict the positions of various social aggregates as a snap-shot of hierarchically-connected variables within a system of stratification. Marx saw classes to be necessary aspects or expressions of a particular society's productive system as developed in definite historical conditions. Thus, in order to understand their concrete significance, it was necessary to theoretically reconstruct the basic features of capitalist society – the dual nature of the commodity, the money form of value, the production of surplus value, the growth of the division of labour, the process of capital accumulation: in short, the forms of reproduction and circulation of social capital as a law-like process – before formulating what would otherwise have been a necessarily simplified and misleading descriptive 'model'.[90]

Mills errs in conceiving of the Marxian categories as tools for sociological description rather than theoretical abstractions expressing historically specific and necessary laws of motion. He does this by skirting the underlying issues of political economy, in particular the labour theory of value, without which Marx's analysis of commodity society, including capitalism, is quite incomprehensible. Mills, in fact, is quite explicit that the Marxist conception of exploitation is an ethical proposition, 'a moral judgement disguised as an economic statement'.[91]

Now for Marx, profit consists of surplus value, or that part of the total value of a commodity in which the surplus or unpaid labour of the worker is realised. The worker sells his labouring power to the capitalist, creating surplus value when his expended labour exceeds that amount socially necessary for his own material reproduction.[92] Mills' only recognition of this view of the basic production relations of capitalist society is a dismissive reference to 'arguments about "theories of value" quite apart'.[93] Marx's analysis is interpreted as a polemical denunciation of a perceived immoral social order.

Mills, in fact, held an essentially technicist conception of economic structure; his analyses of particular power structures are unquestionably sensitive to the influence of the corporate élite on the process of political decision-making. The Power Elite, in particular, documents its relations and increasing convergence with the military and political élites in the United States. Nevertheless, Mills' formal typology of possible forms of industrial development is constructed in terms of technicist criteria. He distinguishes the 'underdeveloped' from the 'overdeveloped' society: whereas in the former, the means of production are insufficiently developed to permit a standard of life above that dominated by the struggle for simple existence, the latter's productive forces sustain a social order centred on conspicuous production, waste, the 'fashion principle' and built-in obsolescence. Here

> the means of livelihood are so great that life is dominated by the struggle for status, based on the acquisition and maintenance of commodities.[94]

The third type of industrial arrangement, that of a 'properly developing society', allows men a choice among different styles of life, free from the struggle for basic survival. Although he does distinguish between the capitalist and communist models of industrialisation, nowhere in this general typology does Mills differentiate industrial systems in terms of their relationships of ownership and control. The structure of industry is seen from the viewpoint of technological development, broadly interpreted to include the productive powers of labour itself, as is apparent from Mills' characterisation of communism as a form of 'substitute capitalism'. Its success is conditional upon the failure of capitalism to provide a level of industrialisation adequate to allow a post-poverty social existence.[95] In spite of his seemingly Marxist emphasis on the importance of the development of the productive forces, Mills' model of production relations is built on an essentially technocratic conception of economic organisation.

One consequence of this technology-centred perspective is Mills' impressionistic and descriptive view of post-war capitalism. While he saw its long-term stabilisation to be an open question, Marx's theory of crisis is decisively rejected as inadequate to the conditions of twentieth-century imperialism. Crises, for Mills, are now essentially military and political rather than economic problems. The post-war U.S.-centred revival of capitalism provides an international scenario in which slumps are episodic rather than secular, while new forms of 'organized' private economy replace the earlier anarchy of production by bureaucratic, rationalised economic structures:

> Capitalism and bureaucracy, in brief, are not polar opposites. They have been integrated. The anarchy of production has not

been genralized; to a considerable extent it has been rationalized.[96]

Underlying this interpretation is a narrowly materialistic view of productive development. Echoing Paul Baran's conception of a 'potential' economic surplus,[97] Mills sees a gap between capitalism's actual and potential productivity, but denies that any fundamental economic contradictions underlie it. Rather, he stresses 'the fabulous capacities (technical, economic, political) of fully developed capitalism as we know it today'.[98]

Viewed from a technocratic standpoint, this reluctant celebration of advanced capitalism's productive potential appeared plausible during the heyday of the post-war boom. During this period, several interpretations of the apparent new stability of the capitalist world were developed by commentators either directly affiliated to currents in the labour movement or claiming to write from the viewpoint of Marxism, among the most prominent being the writings of Baran and Sweezy, Michael Kidron, and Herbert Marcuse.[99] In terms of a consistently Marxist analysis, however, a number of developments were taking place which suggested that the period of economic expansion following the Pax Americana would not last indefinitely. The growing role of credit in international transactions, the increasing build-up of constant capital in the growth centres of industrial activity and, above all, the progressive weakening of the American dollar, the chief currency for foreign trade, all revealed a potential achilles heel at the heart of the new economic order.[100]

Mills saw none of this. He formally recognises the Marxist distinction between the forces and relations of production, but holds these categories at a high level of abstraction, not attempting to apply them directly to the concrete conditions of the post-war world. The perspective he offers is a strongly Weberian-influenced model of organised, bureaucratic capitalism, securely founded on a stable technical and administrative basis and reinforced by a systematic and effective political order. Mills' claim to be working in the tradition of the 'Plain Marxists' must be seriously questioned in the light of his actual theories. Always assuming a single if heterogeneous sociological tradition, he seeks to incorporate the most valid contributions of Marxism into it by isolating and assessing each apparently discreet element, and accepting or rejecting it accordingly. Mills' understanding of Marxism, however, leaves much to be desired. He criticises Marx for assuming that the functional indispensability of a class in the economic system leads to its political supremacy in society as a whole; according to this interpretation, the working class is seen as progressively the most indispensable and in consequence the ascendant class within capitalism.[101]

Consistent with his discussion of productive forces, Mills confuses a historical socio-economic trend with an aggregative view of strata and their respective technical roles in narrowly economic activity. The theoretical foundation of Marx's view of the proletariat as an agent of revolutionary change is the fundamental contradiction between the socialisation of the productive forces and the private ownership of the means of production.[102] This underlying contradiction finds expression in a series of crises, centred on the tendency of the rate of profit to fall. Far from being concerned with the purely technical roles of different social strata, Marx's programme for proletarian revolution is based on a structural and historical theory of capitalist development.

Mills further presents a mechanical and inadequate interpretation of the Marxist theory of revolutionary consciousness when he writes:

> The workers will become increasingly class conscious and increasingly international in their outlook. These economic and psychological developments occur as a result of the institutional and technical development of capitalism itself.[103]

Marxists have always denied the evolutionary, 'automatic' development of socialist consciousness that Mills' caricature implies. From the foundation of the First International in 1864, it has been a fundamental assumption of Marxist politics that successful revolutionary preparation requires the presence of appropriate organisational forms. The classical expression of the Marxist theory of revolutionary organisation, Lenin's *What is to be Done?*, was not written primarily as a theory of ideology as such, and Lenin does not explicitly account for the dominance of bourgeois ideology in trade-union consciousness in terms of the political economy of capitalist society. Nevertheless, his conception of a trained 'organization of revolutionaries capable of maintaining the energy, stability and continuity of the revolutionary struggle'[104] derives its rationale from the 'fetishism of commodities' in capitalist society.

By commodity fetishism, Marx meant the objective appearance of the social characteristics of labour. The proportions of labour time expended on commodities appear to their producers only in the external form of the magnitude of their exchange value, determined by the average socially-necessary labour time required to produce them.[105] The consciousness required to orientate the working class towards the abolition of capitalism's specific forms of alienation and domination, corresponds to a theoretical understanding totally distinct from this immediate sphere of fetishistic appearances, of which the everyday trade-union practices of economism are a direct, if militant, expression. The theoretically-trained vanguard organisation is, for Lenin, the necessary bearer of this consciousness and its corresponding practices.

Mills, by contrast, identifies the subjective factor of a Marxian 'class-for-itself' strictly in terms of psychological states and spontaneously-emerging 'revolutionary urges' within the proletariat.[106] His interpretation entirely misconceives the underlying purpose of Marxist theory: the freeing of social reality from the grip of fetishistic appearances for the purpose of conscious revolutionary preparation:

> The philosophers have only intepreted the world in various ways; the point is to change it.[107]

Mills' crucial misinterpretation of Marx concerns his pragmatist rewriting of the Marxist conception of human essence. According to Mills, Marx

> emphasized that very little about society and history can be explained by reference to the innate limits or capacities of 'human nature' as such. . . . The principle of historical specificity includes the nature of human nature. . . . Man has an almost infinite potential.[108]

Certainly, Marx insisted against Feuerbach's abstracted conception of 'humanity' that the human essence is not a quality or property of individuals, but comprises 'the ensemble of the social

relations', themselves having a determinate historical existence.[109] But Mills' remarks on human essence imply a thoroughly relativistic notion which is not to be found in Marx, and
more closely resembles Dewey's socio-psychological view that 'it
is only within the situation that the identification of the needs
with a self occurs'.[110] Mills, in fact, compares Marx's anthropology with G. H. Mead's social behaviourism.

Marx's ontological conception of man actually contrasts
sharply with Mead's idealistic account of cultural existence in
general.[111] In the *Economic and Philosophic Manuscripts*, Marx
develops his basic image of how man exteriorises himself *through*
labour *within* class systems. The more the worker produces in such
a context, the more impoverished he becomes: 'With the
increasing value of the world of things proceeds in direct
proportion the devaluation of the world of men.'[112] How does
such a paradox come about? Man's life activity, the clue to his
'species character', is 'free conscious activity', but in conditions of
estranged labour, this activity, man's essential form of being,
becomes a mere means to his existence. The product of his labour
is 'alien, a coerced activity', and the secret of alienation lies in
social formations, rather than, as Marx sarcastically suggests,
with 'The Gods':

> If his own activity is to him related as an unfree activity, then
> he is related to it as an activity performed in the service, under
> the dominion, the coercion, and the yoke of another man.[113]

Labour is the key category in Marx's philosophical anthropology: while the free, unalienated development of human
potential is, of necessity, suggested in non-reductionist terms, the
objective circumstances which constrain man's existence are
specified as precisely the social relations which have been
historically created. These relationships constitute, first and
foremost, those undertaken in the course of labour, productive
life, which is 'the life of the species'. Some of the consequences of
Mills' ambivalence of the question of labour and culture are
taken up in the following, concluding section.

TWO VIEWS OF HISTORY-MAKING

Divorcing Marx's philosophical anthropology from productive life, skirting the implications of the labour theory of value, interpreting Marx's conception of class as a variant of sociological stratification theory, and effectively de-politicising his analysis of ideology. Mills is able to conflate his personal reworking of Marxist theory into the tradition of classical liberalism. Together, Marxism and Liberalism 'practically exhaust the political heritage of Western civilization'. Liberalism sanctifies the value of the personality, affirms the ideal of the rational acquisition and use of knowledge, and asserts the status of the individual's conscience. Marx assimilates the ideals of the enlightenment, giving them a specific critical content:

> . . . from the ascendant bourgeoisie of his day, he takes over the rationalist, optimistic idea of progress itself, and reseats it in the lower depths of liberal society.[114]

Authentic Marxism, for Mills, is liberalism made concrete and applied to those societies which adopt a hollow liberal rhetoric in their own self-estimation. This interpretation buttresses Mills' perennial concern to articulate a coherent and effective link between theory and political action. At the same time as history assumes, in men's experience, an irreversible and juggernaut-like character, so too the sources of intelligible biography become exhausted. 'Nowadays men often feel that their private lives are a series of everyday traps', *The Sociological Imagination* begins.[115] This, the juncture of biography and history, is the tragic leitmotif of Mills' writings. He implicitly characterises life in contemporary society as chronically alienated: the 'cheerful robot', the 'crackpot realist', 'rationality without reason', all testify to a social world in which 'human development will continue to be trivialized, human sensibilities blunted, and the quality of life impoverished and distorted'.[116]

Seeking a potentially creative agent of social change, Mills abandons the industrial working class to incorporation and ineffectivity at the hands of a co-opted labour bureaucracy, and appeals instead to the intellectuals to repossess their appropriated cultural apparatus and constructively explore the historical possibilities now open. For Mills, such a collective endeavour would embody 'the politics of truth':

> It is an affirmation of one's self as a moral and intellectual
> centre of responsible decision: the act of a free man who rejects
> fate; for it reveals his resolution to take his *own* fate, at least,
> into his own hands.[117]

Mills did not underestimate the difficulties of developing a
political strategy from the critical intellectual milieu: in 1944, he
wrote of the decreasing impact of intellectuals' thinking on the
centres of political initiative. His tough-minded conclusion was
that to think in a realistic political way the intellectual must
cultivate an awareness of the actual sphere of strategy open to
him,[118] although fifteen years later he could still affirm that the
intellectual was faced with 'a unique opportunity to make a new
beginning'.[119]

In another context, Mills raised the possibility of ameliorative
social change initiated by a liberally-reformed state bureaucracy,
by 'men selected and formed by a civil service that is linked with
the world of knowledge and sensibility'.[120] The question is not, as
for Marx, to destroy and replace the State power of the ruling
class, but to rework the forms of relations between the power élite
and its subjects in such a way as to recreate a society of publics, to
whom the national leadership would be constructively responsive. Mills adopts Weber's definition of the State as the
territorial monopoly of legitimate coercion, and specifies the
primary political need to be a corresponding, that is non-class,
movement of social renewal against the prevailing trend of
bureaucratisation and, in terms of the chances for creative
history-making, social petrification. The intellectuals, above all,
would comprise a public in the classical liberal sense, a critical
strata located between the power élite and the emerging mass
society. But the resulting liberal forms of sociation would draw on
the critical reserves of Marxism as a liberating creed.

Now Mills' linking of liberalism and Marxism has a limited
historical validity in terms of their respective defence of the
interests of historically ascendant and progressive classes. The
liberal conceptions of socio-economic order in the writings of
Smith and Quesnay assumed that the rights to private property
and freedom were inseparable, and that the 'natural order' of
social economy corresponds to the free competitive market

economy, guaranteeing liberty, economic democracy, equilibrium, dynamic growth and the justice of equivalent exchange;[121]
supporting the progressive demand for formal freedom before the
law, they sought to liberate the social economy from the
constraints of the mercantilist *ancien régime*. J. S. Mill's criteria for
the validity of State regulation were the practices of the
expanding commodity economy itself:

> . . . as a general rule, the business of life is better performed
> when those who have an immediate interest in it are left to take
> their own course, uncontrolled either by the mandate of the
> law or by the meddling of any public functionary.[122]

The conscience and good sense of practical men in the market
would, under conditions of political equality, maximise the
values associated with the private economy.

Marx revealed that formal freedom and equality before the
law had, under the conditions of capitalist development, forced
the working class into the position of a systematically and
structurally oppressed class. His political concern was the
realisation of substantive freedom in social and economic life, an
accomplishment which assumed the negation of private
property. In communism, the alienated objective dependence of
capitalist society would be superseded by

> Free individuality, based on the universal development of
> individuals and on their subordination of their communal,
> social productivity as their social wealth.[123]

An illusory freedom of property rights would be replaced by a
substantive one based on the common social ownership and
control of the production process, the antithesis of the classical
liberals' political programme.

Mills' interpretation of the historical and structural aspects of
Marx's thought is, as we have seen, inadequate and incomplete.
Furthermore, he is inconsistent in his verycelebration of Marx,
distinguishing Marx's 'method', his most valid theoretical contribution, from his 'model'.[124] Yet Mills nowhere actually indicates
what he saw to be the character of Marx's method. Certainly, he
rejects the 'laws of dialectics', the 'dialectical method', as 'either
a mess of platitudes, a way of doubletalk, a pretentious obscuran-
tism, or all three . . . the know-it-all confusion of logic with

metaphysics'.[125] Equally, Mills dismisses most of what he sees to be Marx's substantive sociological theories, the labour theory of value, and even the possibility of a strictly 'Marxist social science'. Formally, Marx is incorporated into the sociological tradition, yet it is difficult to see exactly which aspects of his thought Mills does accept as valid.

In place of Marx's view of class conflict as the driving force of historical progress, Mills' work is permeated by a powerful pessimistic ethos:

> If this – the politics of truth – is merely a holding action, so be it. If it is also a politics of desperation, so be it. But in this time and in America, it is the only realistic politics of possible consequence open to intellectuals.[126]

The source of this pessimism is that Mills wants a political programme for the making of meaningful history, but at the decisive moments abandons the humanistic image of man as history-maker that underlies both his pragmatist conception of the individual's role in social action and the ideal of unalienated craftsmanship as an alternative to intellectual subordination to the power élite. In *White Collar*, labour is portrayed as the substance of alienation, the appropriation of human abilities through social institutions whose continuance is inconceivable without those activities:

> Being alienated from any product of his labor, and going year after year through the same paper routine, he [the white-collar employee – D.B.] turns his leisure all the more frenziedly to the *ersatz* diversion that is sold him . . . such traits as courtesy, helpfulness, and kindness, once intimate, are now part of the impersonal means of livelihood. Self-alienation is thus an accompaniment of his alienated labor.[127]

Yet in terms of his search for agencies to make history, Mills reduces this fundamental role of labour in social life to a 'dependent variable', while institutions have an autonomous, strictly external form of existence. They are objective complexes which function to maintain the 'organization of roles'.[128]

A reified conception of social institutions recurs in Mills' writings. White-collar man 'has no culture to lean upon except the contents of a mass society that has shaped him and seeks to manipulate him to its alien ends'.[129] Finding no communities or organisations which are truly his own, he is vulnerable to the systematic and insidious influence of manufactured loyalties and cultural preoccupations.

Concluding *Character and Social Structure*, Mills proposes that man

> creates his own destiny as he responds to his experienced situation, and both his situation and his experiences of it are the complicated products of the historical epoch which he enacts. . . . Only within the limits of his place in an historical epoch can man as individual shape himself, but we do not yet know, we can never know, the limits to which men collectively might remake themselves.[130]

An ambivalence in his view of history means that this implicit glimpse of praxis as the potential collective remaker of history is only mooted in Mills' writings directly concerned with a programme for the future. Divorcing a potentially revolutionary conception of labour from his political programme and general sociology, Mills denies an agency of historical change whose potential he had at other times implied. His struggle to make history is, in this sense, a struggle against his own pessimistic paradigm of rulers and ruled, of self-sustaining social institutions. The consequence of this is a desperate search for what must, given his reified account of social structure, be a *deus ex machina* to re-vitalise the decaying forms of cultural existence.

The appeals for publics, for constructive intellectual and political programmes, for the renewal of a critical sense of social life as recreation, even Mills' support for the Cuban revolution, assume an increasingly formal and pragmatic nature. We see in Mills an attempt to develop a radical and committed sociology on the basis of a convergence of currents drawn from Weberian, Marxist and pragmatist thought. That such an eclectic programme should fail to produce the politically-credible synthesis that Mills desired should not surprise us, despite the impact of his writings on contemporary and subsequent social scientists.[131] His work, both sociologically and politically, represents liberalism extended to a critical extreme at which point it assumes a powerful and radical content. Its deeper theoretical implications of an infinitely flexible problematic of rulers and ruled impose a conceptual barrier to social and political practice; and it is within this internal contradiction that Mills' personal, political and sociological radicalism flourished and floundered.[132]

7

Parsons and the
Functionalist Utopia

Parsons' sociology represents an attempt to develop a unified theoretical approach to the social sciences. It embodies a perspective which has been influential for several decades in academic sociology, although its unquestioned dominance has been challenged from a number of directions in recent years.[1] Parsons' seminal work, *The Structure of Social Action*, indicates some of the theoretical questions that were to influence his work as a whole. While not accepting all Weber and Sombart's major propositions, especially in so far as they were pessimistic concerning the future of Western-type societies, Parsons drew attention to Sombart's notion of a historically-unfolding, capitalist 'Geist', and to Weber's analysis of the protestant ethic. He discovered in both a recognition of the autonomy of 'value elements' in society and, more generally, saw this 'same system of generalized social theory' to be a distinctive focus of nineteenth-century sociological thought.[2]

Parsons sought to lay the foundations for a general theory of social action by locating the springs and orientations of human action within the normative sphere of social life. This concern with social order and the moral dimension of social existence, together with Parsons' later development of system analysis, evidence his continuity with the functionalist tradition of social theory. In Parsons' earlier writings, the individual is seen to play an active and dynamic role in social life, and especially in social change. Functionalist thought, in fact, has rarely if ever conceived of society as a purely static system: 'statics' and 'dynamics' have been universally viewed as different aspects of sociological analysis, rather than two discreet subject matters. Comte insisted that the two aspects must be combined by a truly scientific sociology:

> The very fact that Progress, however viewed, is nothing but the development of Order, shows that Order cannot be fully manifested without Progress.[3]

Comte's emphasis on progressive change in time is not without historical significance. His famous Law of the Three States[4] reflects the social conditions of Europe in the early nineteenth century, when the relatively fixed categories of feudal society had dissolved beyond the point at which reality could be convincingly accounted for in non-dynamic terms. Even before the French Revolution, political movements throughout the Continent, including areas as far east as Poland, were challenging the accepted traditions and institutions of the despotic *ancien régime*, and the series of essentially bourgeois revolutions of 1848, while also witnessing the emergence of more radical demands, essentially served to consolidate the hold of the developing bourgeois classes on European political life. Comte diagnosed a generalised social crisis in Western societies, deriving from the advance and application of science during the late medieval period and the limited development of an organic successor to the old catholico-feudal regime. Scientific sociology alone could provide the basis for a new form of social integration by formulating 'a plan fitted to the existing state of knowledge'.[5] Human intervention in the historical process can operate only within the limits established by the immanent development of society itself. Consequently, Comte demanded as a precondition of social reconstruction 'an exact and complete representation of the relations naturally existing'.[6] Social reconstruction, to be effective, must operate in accordance with the natural laws that the scientific or positive method reveals to be at work in history.

As Comte's positivist system implies, many of sociology's founding fathers envisaged social change as an evolutionary process, developing in terms of increasing structural complexity and differentiation. Comte himself spoke of cooperation of effort as the basis of 'the consensus of the social organism' in 'all settled states of society'. The need for consensus is especially pronounced in the modern world of large industrial undertakings, 'for which the combination of efforts required is so vast'.[7] Before Darwin's *Origin of Species* was published in 1859, Herbert Spencer had written a series of synthesising studies on the theory of natural and social evolution as a process involving change to increasingly coherent and multiform states, consequent on the dissipation of motion and the integration of matter.[8] Nevertheless, the major evolutionary sociological theories of the nineteenth century developed largely under the influence of contemporary ideas in natural history, and often sought to explain social change in terms of wider accounts of natural evolution viewed as a whole. Spencer, among others, analysed the changing yet resilient nature of societies in relation to the organic qualities of biological life:

> Not only has a society as a whole a power of growth and development, but each institution set up in it has the like – draws to itself units of the society and nutriment for them, tends ever to multiply and ramify. Indeed, its instinct of self-preservation soon predominates over everything else.[9]

Until the 1830s, the embryological theory of preformation, assuming the 'givenness' of species and races, had been the dominant perspective in natural history. Doubts had been expressed by individuals, including Erasmus Darwin, but prior to the work of Lamarck, leading naturalists such as Linnaeus had, noting the apparent constancy of types, assumed the fixity of species.[10] Lamarck's account of the transmission of new organs corresponding to new needs was effectively attacked by Cuvier and his supporters, and it was only with Charles Darwin's explanation of change through natural selection that evolution became an accepted doctrine.

The cornerstone of Darwin's theory is the proposition that the struggle for existence has positive consequences for the evolution of species. Pressure on resources ensures that those variations within a species which are more fitted to adapt in changed environmental conditions will survive and reproduce. Advantageous variations will be passed on to the animal's offspring and, over a long period of time, cumulative changes will become so pronounced as to constitute a new species.[11] Chains of dependence in nature assure, moreover, that such changes affect wider ecological processes beyond the area of individual species. Darwin's theory assumes above all the unity and inter-dependence of nature as a material process.

Although the analogy of the social organism had been used by political philosophers since Plato and Aristotle, organismic social theory derived a new and immediate impetus from nineteenth-century developments in natural history. Plato had used the analogy in order to express the interdependence of social strata and functions, but gave it a static meaning, despite the critical implications of *The Republic* for Greek society.[12] The nineteenth-century evolutionary social theorists, by contrast, grounded the analogy in history and considered social structures in terms of medium- or long-term processes of change. Timasheff's identification of the conception of integration and inter-dependence of parts as the connecting thread between the earlier organicists and sociological functionalism[13] is supported by Durkheim's adoption of an essentially Darwinian view of evolution. Durkheim suggested that the most widespread forms of social organisation must, at least in their aggregate, be the most advantageous and offer the greatest chance of survival and progressive development. As in biology, a species' normality can only be assessed in relation to its place in the evolutionary scale.[14] Durkheim's early works of the 1880s were largely concerned with the German tradition of organicist social theory. While approving of Shäffle's metaphorical use of the organic analogy, Durkheim, like Spencer, insisted that it did not imply a literal identity between social and biological forms. He contrasted, for example, the relative constancy of species within the biological realm to the potential for a rapid development of new forms of organisation in social life.[15]

Durkheim explains his use of the organic analogy as an analytical and expository device in terms of sociology's early stage of development as an independent science. The existent sciences, and in particular biology, 'contain a treasure of experiences which it would be foolish to ignore'.[16] *The Division of Labour in Society* is concerned to document and examine the historical movement from mechanical to organic solidarity. In the former, solidarity is based upon the 'likeness of consciences': there is a relatively undifferentiated division of labour within which individuals socially resemble one another, engage in more or less uniform beliefs and practices, and are consequently mutually replaceable.[17] Organic solidarity, by contrast, involves a progressive differentiation of individuals and functions. Each individual has a sphere of action peculiar to himself, and there is correspondingly greater scope for the free play of initiative. The division of labour increasingly becomes the dominant integrative principle, displacing the 'collective conscience', and constitutes 'the principal bond of social aggregates of the higher type'. Durkheim postulates a 'historical law' of the sequential relation between the two types of solidarity:

> Mechanical solidarity which first stands alone, or nearly so, progressively loses ground, and organic solidarity becomes, little by little, preponderant.[18]

The interdependence of differentiated social functions is the basis of organic solidarity in Durkheim's theory:

> The members are united by ties which extend deeper and far beyond the short moments during which the exchange is made. Each of the functions that they exercise is, in a fixed way, dependent upon others, and with them forms a solidary system.[19]

Parsons similarly notes a number of 'striking analogies' between his own sociological theory and dominant concepts in biology.[20] Comparing the processes of personality and biological development, he suggests that, as both fields of science advance, a common conceptual scheme may be seen to underlie their theoretical systems. Society and personality exist 'in nature' rather than 'set over against' it. Moreover:

> Biology is our nearest neighbour in the community of sciences and . . . substantive relationships should be expected. We are both part of the same larger 'community' of knowledge.[21]

Parsons elsewhere evidences his intellectual debt to classical physics as well as the biological sciences. During the seventeenth century, when rapid advances were being made in physical science, a number of philosophers, in particular Hobbes, developed models of society viewing man as part of the material world and subject to the universal principles of mechanics.[22]

While the organic analogy appeared to be the dominant model adopted by the founders of modern sociology, more mechanical analogies were also influential in the functionalist explanation of the division of labour and social order. Spencer, in particular, drew on the discoveries of the physical sciences in elaborating his heavily biologised model of social structure and function:

> . . . all actions going on in society are measured by certain antecedent energies, which disappear in effecting them, while they themselves become actual or potential energies from which subsequent actions arise.[23]

The functionalist view that the general principle of mutual dependence of parts is the basis of the scientific analysis of society[24] is, in fact, as much the basis for adopting a mechanical as a biological metaphor. The former has figured significantly in twentieth-century systems theory, most notably in Pareto's use of concepts such as 'fields of force'.[25] Parsons similarly posits four fundamental laws of social equilibrium corresponding to the principles of Newtonian natural philosophy: the principles of inertia, action and reaction, effort, and system-integration are, he proposes, applicable to the working of social systems.[26] Concerning the principle of system-integration, a 'pattern element' will tend to be confirmed in its place within the system, or eliminated as a function of its contribution to the integrative balance of the system as a whole.[27] Mechanistic analogy, the functionalist counterpart of the Hobbesian model of civil society, thus also serves to express Parsons' conception of the social system.

SOCIAL SYSTEM AND SOCIAL ACTION

It is in *The Social System* that Parsons' general theory is most systematically elaborated: the energy for social action derives ultimately from the individual organism, but the actions themselves are organised through social interaction into 'a system in the scientific sense'.[28] Selective ordering among the possibilities of orientation implies that 'a component of "system integration"' is operative, and the actual integration of the system as a whole constitutes a 'compromise' between the 'strains to consistency' of its personality, cultural and social components.[29] While integration is rarely, if ever, complete, Parsons defines a society as a system which meets all the essential functional prerequisites of long-term survival from within its own resources: a society contains 'all the structural and functional fundamentals of an independently subsisting system'.[30] The criteria for significance of any social process are to be found in its functional contribution to the maintenance and survival of the system as a whole.

Following Durkheim, Parsons emphasises the determining priority of values in social life, but his voluntaristic conception of social action, by introducing purposive elements into the historical process, modifies the naturalistic perspective that systems analysis is otherwise liable to generate. To this extent, Parsons' theory has a limited affinity with the work of a variety of sociologists who have, with different emphases, been concerned with the interactive aspect of social life. Not least, George Simmel's formal sociology, while ostensibly concerned with the formal conceptualisation of types of human phenomena, examines social interaction as a process undertaken by social actors. Rejecting both organicism and the ideographic method of German Geisteswissenschaft, his field of study, as Coser observes, is *association* rather than *society* in the abstract.[31] Despite his fears of cultural alienation and creative atrophy in modern society,[32] Simmel adopted a dialectical view of the relationship between the individual and society: man is 'both product of society, and life from an autonomous centre'.[33] He examined social actions not as discreet phenomena, but in relation to those of other individuals and to particular social structures and processes. Competition in social life, for example, may be at least partly reduced by either a voluntary agreement to renounce certain practices, or an outside, imposed restriction in the form of law or morality.[34] Again, conflict generally is a form of sociation functioning positively to resolve contrasts and achieve some kind of resolution to tensions in social relations, even though at one extreme this may involve the annihilation of one party to the dispute.[35]

Simmel's writings were a seminal influence for a number of trends in twentieth-century sociology, including his adherent Leopold von Wiese and the members of the Cologne school in the inter-war years. Perhaps more widely read today are the writings of the Chicago school, an important current in American sociology during the 1920s. Albion W. Small, a leading figure in this school, emphasised the fluid, associational nature of human experience as the basis of all structural relationships, social forms and institutions.[36] R. E. Park similarly broke macro- and medium-scale sociological concepts relating to structures down into the processual, interpersonal relations that construct, sustain and modify them: 'collective behaviour' is thus 'the behaviour of individuals under the influence of an impulse that is common and collective, an impulse, in other words, that is the result of social interaction'.[37]

Around the same time in Britain, L. T. Hobhouse was attempting to establish the role of ideas in history while avoiding the excesses of neo-Hegelian objective idealism. He saw mind, 'not a unitary mind, but mind acting in millions of distinct centres, as many centres as there are individuals', as the moving force of history. Ideas and institutions are developed in a single process, 'the living tradition', in which institutions mould and are themselves remoulded by men.[38] History in this way represents the growth and unfolding of the power of the human mind as a social process, operating through tradition, selection and cooperation. Mutuality is the most crucial quality of progress in social life, since social development, seen by Hobhouse as a multifactorial process, rests on mutual need and cooperation rather than on coercion and constraint.[39]

Finally, Dewey and Mead's symbolic interactionism, focusing on the experiential context of reflective processes, anticipated the more recent interest of ethnomethodologists in, to borrow Garfinkel's expression, 'the rational accountability of practical actions as an ongoing, practical accomplishment'.[40] The significance of some of these theories for contemporary Weberian sociology is taken up elsewhere in this book. All of them represent attempts to avoid the 'oversocialized conception of man' that Dennis Wrong has identified as a central feature of much recent social theory.[41]

As against these and many other non-holistic accounts of social life, Parsons' conception of social action is distinguished by its direct line of descent from Max Weber's sociology. Parsons defines values as symbolic elements which serve as criteria for actors' selection among alternative orientations in social situations.[42] He emphasises the largely self-maintaining character of social integration. Thus, in the social system

> . . . the complementarity of role-expectations, once established, is not problematical. . . . No special mechanisms are required for the explanation of the maintenance of complementary interaction-orientation.[43]

Alongside this holistic and homeostatic model co-exists a Weberian view of social action. While drawing a distinction, only partially explicit in Weber, between meaning systems which express a coherent and scientific relation to the objective world and those which do not, Parsons adopts the essential elements of Weber's interpretive or Verstehen sociology.[44] For Weber, action is behaviour to which the individual attaches subjective meaning; social action is that action in which the actor takes into account and is oriented by the behaviour of others.[45] Parsons reformulates Weber's proposition in the following terms:

> Concrete motivation involves an intrinsic relation between the meaningful elements and the others in the action complex.[46]

The conception of a common value system is the theoretical bridge between the systematic and voluntaristic aspects of Parsons' work, and is central to his analysis of social stratification and power. The assumption of shared moral beliefs and values does not for Parsons merely relate to the orientations of individual actions, but is central to and constitutes the crucial determining variable of his model of the social system. He suggests that, as yet, social science is unable to attribute primacy to any variable in the determination of social change. Formally, he adopts an agnostic view of the 'plurality of possible origins of change'.[47] Nevertheless, Parsons generally attributes particular importance to the part played by value elements in social processes. In his discussion of deviance, the context of social behaviour is identified as the sphere of value elements: 'All social action is normatively oriented.' Parsons sees this value system to be essentially shared or homogeneous:

> The value orientations embodied in these norms must to a degree be common to the actors in an institutionally integrated

interactive system. It is this circumstance which makes the problem of conformity and deviance a major axis of the analysis of social systems.[48]

At the same time, Parsons points to the ubiquitous absence of complete integration as the social basis of 'romantic—utopian' cultural elements. Utopian ideas, values and movements arise because

> every complex social system is in fact shot through with conflicts and adaptive patterns with respect to whatever value-system it may have.[49]

Actual societies are thus characterised by conflict, but specifically at the level of values. The structural and historical primacy that Parsons attributes to value elements is apparent in his account of the influence of Christianity on Western society, which has, he suggests, 'produced a great society and culture'. Especially in its Protestant form, it has been responsible for the growth of free enterprise, the nineteenth-century educational revolution, and a historically unparalleled development of individual character and autonomy.[50] 'The millennium,' Parsons concedes, 'definitely has not arrived.' Nevertheless, he proclaims a profound enrichment of social life: Christian ideals, for him, have been a major source of both order and progress in Western society, not least in relation to the growth of the humane welfare state.[51]

Elsewhere, Parsons suggests that differences between societies often 'reside in' differences in the context and range of the general moral consensus. Moral standards, furthermore, have a generalised and central significance for particular action systems, 'they draw on all the elements of cognitive, cathectic and evaluative selection from the alternatives of action'.[52] Now, if the notion of causality is not implied in this formulation, Parsons' contention has little explanatory value. He clearly does not mean that different societies have different systems of moral consensus and are otherwise the same: his differentiation of forms of kinship organisation, for example, precludes this interpretation.[53] He can only be saying that structural differences are generated by variations and changes in the moral consensus of particular societies, a proposition which implies a monocausal idealist theory of social causation, despite his agnostic reservations in *The Social System*.

ON POWER AND CLASS: PARSONS' VALUE-ADDED TAXONOMY

Parsons' assumption that deviant values are to be explained in terms of their relation to an otherwise common symbolic system has immediate implications for the analysis of power. The economic and political content of large-scale social confrontations such as those in Russia in 1917, Britain in 1926 and Portugal in 1974 suggests that the concepts used in analysing them should reflect material social processes and relations; but Parsons' analysis systematically overlooks the material basis of social power and inequality.

In his early work, *The Structure of Social Action*, Parsons suggests that force is a marginal or residual aspect of social life. While the role of force and fraud has been typically underestimated by liberal theorists of progress, Parsons proposes that they often perform an integrative social function.[54] They are, moreover, used primarily by the State in order to enforce commonly accepted rules. Coercion and, by implication, the divergence of material interests that typically accompanies its exercise, are thus theoretically transformed by Parsons into the corporeal agency and effect of a more or less universally-accepted value system. Both the scale of coercion and its significance as a determining factor in social structure and change are assumed to be minimal.

A similar assumption underlies Parsons' analysis of social control in *The Social System*. His thesis is that when special strains develop, corresponding control mechanisms such as those of the North American youth culture are required to reinforce the more conventional forms of social interaction, the normal means of social control lying in 'a complex system of unplanned and largely unconscious mechanisms'.[55] Social control in its overtly coercive form is schematically isolated from the typical patterns of everyday social interaction, which Parsons sees to be largely automatic and self-sustaining. In effect, he generalises Adam Smith's conception of the spontaneously harmonising 'hidden hand' from a theory of economic equilibrium into one of social relations in general.

Consistent with this quasi-cybernetic model of the social system, Parsons characteristically minimises the importance of power and coercion in the determination and maintenance of social ranking. In his seminal 1940 essay, Parsons defines social stratification in terms of the differential evaluation of system units and their resultant hierarchical placing. Central to this process is the normative ranking of social actors in terms of the familiar context of a shared value system or 'generalized pattern'.[56] Illustrating what Nagel has aptly termed his 'architectonic system of distinctions', Parsons identifies six principal bases of differential evaluation. They are, in order of presentation, membership of a particular kinship unit, possession of esteemed personal qualities, accomplishment of valued achievements, ownership of material and symbolic possessions, possession of authority and, finally, possession of power. Authority is defined as the institutionally recognised right to influence other social actors. Power, appendaged to Parsons' list as a 'residual category', entails the social ability to influence others and secure possessions in situations which lack the sanction of legitimacy. Operant only outside the framework of legitimate social actions and relations, it occasionally augments, rather than permeates and plays a persistent part in structuring, social stratification.

Thirteen years later, Parsons extensively revised his 1940 study, developing its central themes and applying them to contemporary North America. Whereas the original essay was concerned primarily with the ranking of the individual social actor, in the revised version the unit of analysis is the status-role complex, which may refer to an individual or a collectivity.[57] Stratification is again viewed as an essentially consensualist process, ranking individuals according to a socially-shared value system, and the difference between this and the earlier study is basically one of increased sophistication rather than of fundamental revision or qualitative theoretical development.

As against Parsons' emphasis on the process of normative evaluation and ranking, much functionalist analysis of stratification has been concerned to demonstrate the inevitability of inequality as a consequence of social differentiation as such. Davis and Moore's influential version of this thesis, first published in 1945, may be retrospectively regarded as a definitive theoretical justification of the meritocratic case for social inequality, developed through the last century in response to egalitarian political programmes and given a new impetus in the 'business as usual' conditions of the restored, highly-socialised capitalist societies after the Second World War. The authors propose that in any differentiated society only a limited number of persons have talents which are 'trainable' for the most functionally important positions. The conversion of these talents into actual skills requires training, involving sacrifice, and consequently their bearers must be induced to forgo immediate gratification by the promise of privileged access to scarce and desired rewards. Material and symbolic inequality is thus both inevitable and functionally advantageous for the system as a whole.[58] Similarly, B. Barber, defining stratification in terms of the unequal flow of desired scarce resources on the one hand, and of punitive measures on the other, sees the differential functional importance of activities and roles to be its primary criterion. Echoing Davis and Moore, Barber concludes that 'Some system of stratification is a functional requirement of societies'.[59]

While indicating a more adequate empirical recognition of the complex effects of stratification, Tumin's attempt to correct the theoretical simplicity of the Davis and Moore thesis is similarly written from the functionalist perspective and shares its most basic theoretical assumptions. Tumin's main objection is that the conception of 'functional importance' is imprecise and may provide the basis for a legitimisation of existing patterns of inequality. Differential esteem need not be reflected in unequal rewards, social duty being a possible alternative basis for individual motivation. The only items that society must distribute unevenly are the power and property demonstrably necessary for the performance of particular tasks, and these constitute resources rather than rewards. Stratification, moreover, has dysfunctional consequences in so far as it serves to repress as well as to foster the emergence of talent, limits the expansion of productive resources, and encourages inter-class hostility. The consequence is a negative influence on social integration.[60]

The essential criterion of Tumin's critique of Davis and Moore is the dysfunctionality of prevailing patterns of social stratification. While lacking the theoretical rigour of Durkheim's identification of meritocratic principles and the 'normal' form of the division of labour, Tumin's thesis is based on a critical but nevertheless functionalist interpretation of social inequality.[61] Tumin, like Schwarz,[62] raises the possibility of other than inegalitarian cultural means to 'help get important positions conscientiously filled by able personnel', but in both cases the alternatives to inequality are perceived primarily in terms of their advantages for the technical-integrative potential of the system as a whole. The question 'functional for what?' remains, as in the Davis and Moore thesis, posed at the indeterminate conceptual level of 'the social system'. For Tumin, inequality is one of a number of alternative means for determining the positional structure of social actors, their activities and efforts within an enduring pattern of social interaction. As such, it is not a phenomenon systematically examined in terms of the objective interests that benefit differentially in particular stratified societies. This failure to examine the structured relations of conflicting interests, the most general weakness of the Davis and Moore analysis, is not fundamentally corrected by their critics within the functionalist perspective.[63]

Parsons is not concerned with the inevitability of stratification in terms of purely technical criteria of efficiency and social differentiation. His initial assumption is the primacy of normative evaluation in the hierarchical structuring of system units, and his substantive studies are developed accordingly. The imperatives of economic and political power are minimised in favour of perceived legitimate structures of social obligations, often leading Parsons to virtually transcribe the idealised portrayals of legal and constitutional documents as adequate accounts of social reality. On democratic electoral procedure, for example, he offers little more than a description of the legal framework of voting practices, quite abstracted from the economic interests which they both sustain and are sustained by. Thus, he asserts that in the advanced Western countries 'the power element has been systematically equalised through the device of the franchise'.[64]

Again, in the dynamic departments of modern industry, especially in the United States, functions are fulfilled primarily in occupational roles separated from the family, a development which for Parsons constitutes 'the most crucial change in the economy since the Marxian diagnosis was made'.[65] Parsons makes much of this fairly commonplace observation, concluding that large-scale productive enterprises are now run 'as if' they were no longer first and foremost profit-making organisations:

> . . . it is of dubious value to continue to speak of the 'free enterprise' sector of the economy as 'capitalistic' at all.[66]

Characteristically, the question of sectional power is avoided, but in this instance the source of that avoidance concerns Parsons' perception of the structure of the capitalist enterprise itself. Anticipating Galbraith's technocratic conception of the industrial firm,[67] Parsons suggests that its control focus lies within its own organisational interest, the manager occupying an essentially administrative position comparable to that of the university professor.

That the administrative and managerial groups in the private sector coordinate economic activities subject to the imperative to attain at least a minimal level of profitability is overlooked in Parsons' formulation. As H. I. Ansoff's recent manual of corporate strategy puts it, 'the primary [managerial – D.B.] economic objective is to optimize the long-term rate of return on the equity employed in the firm'.[68] A century ago, Marx distinguished between the owning and the functioning or working capitalist, and noted their increasing empirical differentiation within the capitalist division of labour.[69] This process speeded up rapidly during the merger boom which took place in Britain, America and elsewhere around the turn of the present century.[70] Viewed historically, the rise of the salaried capitalist manager – elevated by Burnham into a new global ruling class embracing such disparate political developments as Stalinism in the Soviet Union, Fascism in Germany and the New Deal period in Roosevelt's America[71] – has taken place broadly as a function of the increasing centralisation and concentration of capital both within and between nations.

Concentration of capital refers to the tendency of capital units to increase in size; centralisation to their tendency to lose their individual identity and autonomy, coming under the control of their, usually larger, rivals. Measuring the latter in terms of the 'concentration ratio', or the percentage of an industry's sales, employment or output accounted for by its five largest firms,

Aaronovitch and Sawyer reported the trend shown in Table 3 for the 1935–68 period in Britain.[72]

TABLE 3

Year	1935	1951	1958	1963	1968
Per cent	52·0	55·8	58·7	63·5	69·0

The ratio persistently rose over the three decades up to 1968, from 52·0 per cent in 1935 to 58·7 per cent in 1958 and 69·0 per cent by 1968. The rise is particularly striking for 1963–8, when the ratio rose by 5·5 per cent over five years. This rise of over 1 per cent per year is indicative of an especially rapid phase of centralisation during a period of social democratic rule.

One way of representing the concentration of capital is to compare the rate of growth of firms with that of productivity. Over the half decade covering 1962–7, Rowthorn documents the average growth rate of firms as in Table 4. While the rate of concentration was slower in Britain than in most other advanced capitalist countries, the average annual rate of growth of firms of 8·1 per cent was considerably more than twice as rapid as that of productivity, which increased at approximately 3 per cent.[74] The scale of both the concentration and centralisation of capital was clearly substantial during the peak years of the post-war boom.

TABLE 4

Average growth rate of firms, 1962–7 (per cent per annum)[73]

U.K.	8·1
All (sample of 10 leading capitalist countries and blocs, including U.K.)	9·4

It is further the case that in Heath and Wilson's Britain, just as much as in Bismarck's Germany, the trend towards increasingly large and monopolistic units was to a large extent associated with deliberate State policies. M. Burrage points out that an important similarity between the public and private sectors in the British economy is the long-term tendency for the State to encourage concentration in both. Thus, corresponding to the monopolistic tendencies within the nationalised sector, 'the governments of both parties have often tried to increase the concentration of private enterprise'.[75] The conceptual distinction between the public and private sectors conceals, of course, the reality of a single national economy, itself hardly discreet from the point of view of the actual world division of labour, within which the State substantially and systematically intervenes, albeit characteristically in an *ad hoc* and reflexive form. While viewing the capitalist economy as a unitary entity, it remains the case that the overall unprofitability of State expenditure as a whole implies a burden on the material sources of capital accumulation. In Britain, the eleven years following 1963 registered an average annual public-sector deficit amounting to 9·43 per cent of G.N.P., rising to over 10 per cent in 1972−3.[76] Government spending may promote capital formation, but cannot *of itself* enlarge total social capital, which can only accumulate through and for profitability. The costs of capital accumulation are to a large extent directly socialised through State intervention. Nevertheless, this policy on the one hand generates inflationary pressure through the practice of deficit spending, and on the other is sustained by surplus value which can only come from the sectors of profitable production. When used on a regular basis, the alternative use of overseas lending agencies as a source for funds for State expenditure raises the serious danger of increasingly large deficits culminating in *de facto* state bankruptcy, as the experience of Britain, Italy and a number of other countries during the mid-1970s has dramatically demonstrated.

In attempting to resolve this Hobson's choice, both the State and private industrial interests stand to benefit from the competitive advantages associated with the development and utilisation of economies of scale, and it is with the growth of increasingly large and complex economic units that the technical, as against the control-oriented need for the skilled administrator, has arisen on the scale it exists today. Parsons, however, fails to discriminate between the day-to-day empirical administration of the enterprise on the one hand, and the ultimate responsibility of the managerial strata to profit criteria on the other. Despite the important structural changes, including the relative decline of the family firm, which have taken place, profitability remains the yardstick of both success and failure in the capitalist enterprise. The widespread academic, editorial and political concern at the rapid fall in profit rates in Britain, the United States and other countries since the mid-1960s[77] is based on a realistic recognition, more or less sophisticated, that the system of private property is faced with a crisis at the most basic level when profits – crudely, the difference between the value produced by labour power and that required to maintain it for further rounds of production – become problematic.

But while Parsons conceptually democratises the socio-economic structure of contemporary Western societies, his important essay *Evolutionary Universals in Society* makes explicit the assumptions which lead him to generalise their distinctive features into the properties of social systems in general. Culture, Parsons observes, is shared through the basic evolutionary universals of language, religion, kinship organisation and technology. Power is excluded from the list of recurrent cultural phenomena, which centres upon the 'solidarity and integrity of the system as a whole, with both common loyalties and common normative definitions of the situation'.[78] In this paper, Parsons universalises the most basic social relations of commodity society by positing the necessity of money and markets for the stable functioning of developed societies. Market exchange, he suggests, is the most general means of mobilising economic resources, although other means, such as the use of political power, are also empirical possibilities. Constituting a generalised resource, money is able to effect a potentially unlimited range of economic transactions.[79]

Superficially, Parsons' characterisation of money as 'the great mediator of the instrumental use of goods and services' resembles Marx's rather less prosaic observation concerning the power of universal purchase and sale inherent in the money form of capital: 'Money is the pimp between man's need and the object, between his life and his means of life.'[80] Parsons, however, goes on to assert that the market system rests upon universalistic norms, which are defined in *The Social System* in terms of their 'generality' or universal applicability.[81] As such, they are the sociological counterpart of the Kantian categorical imperative to the rational being: 'Act by a maxim which involves its own universal validity for every rational being.[82]

Leaving his analysis at this point, Parsons avoids the corollary of his thesis, a corollary crucial for a deeper understanding of the relation between money and the structure of social relations which it mediates. Immediately following the sentence quoted above, Marx continues:

> But that which mediates my life for me, also mediates the existence of other people for me. For me it *is* the other person. [my emphasis – D. B.][83]

Money mediates not only, or even primarily, between person and thing, but first and foremost between person and person: it is an essentially social relation. While formally equalising the exchange relations between individuals, the transactions which money effects will reflect and be structured by wider patterns of more or less unequal relations between social classes. E. Preiser observes that in capitalist society, property-less labour is structurally placed in a disadvantageous position within the total complex of economic relations: 'Behind the elasticity of supply lies the power embodied in property.'[84] As Preiser's objection to the unaugmented supply and demand paradigm implies, economic exchanges are inseparable from the power structure which they both sustain and express.

The conflict of interest between wage labour and capital constitutes the major challenge to Parsons' notion of a common value system by posing exploitation as the relational foundation of the capitalist social structure. Prevailing forms of stratification are intrinsically unfavourable to the emergence of value consensus, systematic social inequality fostering competing forms of typical consciousness. Parkin distinguishes the dominant, subordinate and radical value systems, each deriving from a distinct structural source, and promoting deferential or aspirational, accommodative and oppositional orientations respectively.[85] While it should not be confused with revolutionary consciousness,[86] the solidaristic ethos of traditional working-class communities derives directly from the occupancy of a shared class position, the crucial feature of which is the common sale of labour power.[87] Parsons can speak of 'the solidarity and integrity of the system as a whole' only because he assumes the existence of underlying universalistic norms. This, however, is a utopian assumption in that it involves the superimposition over social reality of a set of idealised hypothetical social conditions.

Parsons' covert recognition of the social relations specific to commodity-producing societies is especially apparent in his discussion of scarcity, the social context of which is a Hobbesian struggle of *individual* wills and purposes;[88] the social aspect of scarcity is identified as its fundamental feature. Parsons thus defines possessions as rights, or bundles of rights, 'a set of expectations relative to social behaviour and attitudes'. Explaining the source of their perennial scarcity, he distinguishes 'relational' from 'non-relational' factors. The latter are 'extrinsic to the social system as such' and include physical limitations to the availability of objects as well as those objects which can only be produced 'at a cost in the economic sense of the term'. Through this inclusion, Parsons generalises the cost–profit criteria of capitalist society as the basic mechanism for the allocation of goods 'in every social system'.[89] Historically, specific production and distribution relations are again built into Parsons' model of the social system, although he also includes in the category of non-relational factors the natural constraints of time and space.

The most fundamental limitations on human action comprise of those mechanisms which systematically structure otherwise incompatible social actions and practices into a patterned system.[90] Following Hobbes, Parsons terms this the 'relational problem of order', or 'the problem of power'. He adopts Hobbes' usage of power as 'a man's present means to any future goal', in situations where those means are dependent upon his relation to other actors. Its significance in society is determined primarily by the degree of differentiation in the societal role system, the incidence and influence of universalistic orientations, and the extent of operant effectiveness or 'drasticness of means'. These factors, together or singly, constitute the basis of the 'struggle for power' and necessitate a legitimate framework for the orderly attainment of what are often mutually cross-cutting social goals:

> Only by some sort of control operating on both parties to a conflict can the vicious circle be broken.[91]

Whereas economic power lies in the possession of means to maximise advantages in exchange transactions, political power entails the control of the interactive system as a system, the 'mobilization of the total relational context as a facility relative to the goal in context'.[92] Parsons' holistic orientation thus intrudes into and structures the voluntaristic ('mobilization') dimension of his analysis of political power. Its goals are characteristically indeterminate, and his analysis assumes the form of an ideal–typical description of a *mode of exercise* of power. Explanation in this way becomes mere accounting, and theory is replaced by narrative.

These assumptions are developed by Parsons in a number of more recent studies of power, although they constitute elaborations of rather than departures from the model presented in *The Social System*. Implying a revision of the earlier analysis, his *On the Concept of Political Power* challenges the theoretical diffuseness of the Hobbesian view of power as a generalised capacity to attain social goals irrespective of the medium employed and the status of the authorisation in question. Parsons defines power as an analytically distinct phenomenon functioning to effect changes in the actions of other system units.[93] Conceptually parallel to the economy and empirically controlling its output for the goals of the social system, the actual political process is nevertheless irreducible to its, at least partly, economic components:

> Power is . . . the means of acquiring control of the factors in effectiveness; it is not itself one of these factors, any more than in the economic case money is a factor of production.[94]

In this paper, Parsons suggests a direction of analysis which, if consistently pursued, would lead to a qualitative theoretical advance from the position developed in his critique of C. Wright Mills, whose 'zero sum' conception of power is criticised for interpreting its sectional aspect, in fact a secondary factor, as the crucial feature of the relational complex as a whole.[95]

In his *On the Concept of Political Power*, it is no longer immediately clear that the 'collective' as against the 're-distributive' or sectional aspect of power has unambiguous primacy in Parsons' model. But in spite of Parsons' more conspicuous recognition of 'conflict elements' and ' "interest" problems in the system',[96] he continues to conceive of conflicting interests as subordinate to and constituted within a wider environment of shared purposes, a position which recalls Simmel's model of 'opposition between associates'.[97] Parsons' idiosyncratic usage thus defines power in terms of its legitimacy as perceived by social actors, or its 'bindingness'. A generalised circulating medium, it operates on a decentralised basis through such social institutions as the family to mobilise resources for shared goals. As against force, which is monopolised by the government and is reserved for exclusive use in 'a special set of conditions',[98] power is incorporated into Parsons' general model as an extension of consensus and a mode of reconciliation, rather than a particularistic defence of social and economic interests.

Parsons accounts for the concentration of political power in the State by, on the one hand, tautologically noting the empirical monopolisation of coercive capacity on a territorial basis and, on the other, by asserting the functional need for such a focus of power.[99] For Parsons, the State has a functional *raison d'être* independent of the class interests which it represents. He is unconcerned with the nature of the conflicting interests that he sees to be integrated through the political process. His analysis of the social sources of aggression in Western societies is confined either to the feelings of injustice and insecurity engendered by the competitive emphasis on achievement, or to a passing look at the structural relations of private property which condemn the majority to be at best, in Parsons' own words, 'good losers'.[100] He draws a sharp conceptual division between the kinship system, where the individual personality is crystallised, and the occupational order in which the individual achieves social status.[101] This sequence of biographical development is then transposed into a model of social causality, the environment of which is a systematic and essentially shared moral order.

Working with this model, Parsons pays little serious attention to the wealthy and their persistent disproportionate influence over the development of society as a whole. Stratification in contemporary America is accounted for in terms of the universalistic-achievement dichotomy. He identifies occupational achievement and kinship-group membership as the two principal determining elements of the stratification system. The former is governed by the universalistic criterion of equality of opportunity, but kinship relations provide differential advantages for opportunity which guarantee some stability to the system.[102] Kinship mediates the universalistic principles of the occupational order, but not in such a way as to undermine its basic operation.[103] Through the inheritance of property, wealth to some extent becomes a source of status independent of the norms of achievement and universalism; but in general, wealth is, for Parsons, not a primary determinant of status: 'Like office; its primary significance is as a symbol of achievement.'[104]

The overwhelming majority of empirical and historical studies of the U.S. power structure demonstrate that this is not the case. Commentators as otherwise distant as C. Wright Mills and J. K. Galbraith concur on the view that the top few hundred American corporations exercise a decisive power in the economy as a whole.[105] Domhoff's synthesising study of the corporate rich confirms the large overlap between the industrial chiefs and wider American élite strata, concluding that the 'interacting and intermarrying' social élite is very much a 'psychosocial reality'.[106]

The roots of Parsons' achievement-oriented model lie in his idealisation of a particular stage of the United States of America's history. The wide distribution of the means of subsistence in expanding colonial America probably did allow for a relatively high level of social mobility and status to exist. Traditional aristocracies of the European type were notably absent, and as late as the 1830s de Tocqueville was impressed both by the broad equality of social conditions and the general fluidity of what class lines did exist. He wrote: 'Wealth circulates with inconceivable rapidity, and experience shows that it is rare to find two succeeding generations in the full enjoyment of it.'[107] Nevertheless, even for this early period the evidence is far from conclusive. Richard B. Morris cautiously warns that: 'We lack the basic data needed to make valid generalizations on whether there was in fact a rigid caste system or a considerable degree of mobility within the social structure.'[108] Even de Tocqueville was alarmed by the generally downward pressure exerted on wages by small groups of industrialists in otherwise democratic countries.[109] Certainly, by the 1850s the period of corporate ascendancy was already well advanced in the United States.[110] The rise of privileged corporations with rights guaranteed by law and the rapid growth of privately-owned factories during the latter half of the nineteenth century both competed favourably with the rival industrial centres in Britain and Europe and established the concentration of wealth which was to remain relatively stable during the present century.[111]

Parsons is wilfully naïve as regards the roots of power in social and economic life. Far from simply empirically misreading the class nature of his own society, his schematic analytical separation of the economic and political orders precludes a structural account of their forms of interrelation in terms of political economy. The question of class power and its source is systematically conceptualised out of court.

PARSONS AND WEBER: THE TRADITION OF PATHOS

Yet while he theoretically obscures the class character of contemporary capitalism, Parsons, as we have seen, implicitly structures his analysis of 'the social system' in accordance with the production and market relations of specifically capitalist commodity society. This thoroughgoing ethnocentricity is reflected in Parsons' ambivalent fascination for the Hobbesian model of man, which C. B. Macpherson has convincingly related to the development of the 'possessive market society' where labour power becomes a commodity. Macpherson draws attention to the classlessness of Hobbes' atomised model of social relations and the erroneous conception of the State that it sustains.[112] This criticism is also applicable to Parsons' analysis: while elaborating a theory of the social system which is formally agnostic towards the class nature of the State, he at the same time incorporates economic relations specific to capitalist society. In this sense, there are elements in Parsons' work which, when their implications are realised, challenge the theoretical adequacy of the model itself. His universalisation of capitalist social relations serves, however, to reinforce an underlying theme which denies the possibility of a non-stratified social order.

In this approach, Parsons is adopting a central assumption of Weber, who formally excludes non-domination oriented forms of social life from his theory. While the three ideal types of traditional, charismatic and legal rational authority are distinguished, domination in one form or another is an invariant feature of social life; other than domination-oriented, social forms are quite simply not envisaged.[113] Socialism would merely complete the process, prepared by capitalism, of expropriating the private owners alongside the workers.[114] The only historical alternative to total bureaucratic petrification is some form of charismatic renewal, a revitalisation of social systems which are otherwise tending towards an atrophied and petrified state. In either case, relations of domination are unavoidable.

Weber emphasised that he saw the functionalist frame of reference to have a strictly heuristic value in sociological analysis.[115] In fact, he approached the study of domination in a functionalist manner which in important ways anticipates Parsons' model of structured legitimate social relations. Parsons' claim that Weber held norms to be at all times central to social action is misconceived:[116] for Weber, social action may and often does rest on other than normative principles. Values are unambiguously paramount only in the area of 'value rational' action, while with 'instrumentally rational' action the choice of ends may be made according to utilitarian criteria, that is without reference to norms or values. 'Affective action' is oriented to no clear ideal, but rather is motivated by an emotive state and as such is located on the border between meaningful and non-meaningful action. Finally, 'traditional action', performed under the influence of custom and habit, is equally distinct from the commitment to an overriding ideal involved in the value rational type.[117]

Even in the context of a legitimate order, actual belief in its legitimacy in the form of a conscious normative orientation may not be the principal factor maintaining order. Accountability rather than normative orientation is, for Weber, the *essential* hallmark of social action, incalculability being 'the privilege of the insane'.[118]

Nevertheless, it remains the case that Weber wrote little about the possibility of 'illegitimate' forms of domination. He explained legitimate domination in terms of the motivations which induce subjects to obey the commands of their rulers: domination 'can only mean the probability that a *command* will be obeyed'.[119] Legitimate domination implies that in a given setting, actors' motivations are consistent with and reinforce, or at least do not directly serve to undermine, the stability of existing patterns of political rule. Parsons' definition of power in terms of its bindingness on social actors thus has its antecedent in Weber's sociology of domination, despite the over-normative implications of Parsons' own reading of Weber.

Nevertheless, Parsons' shared value system has no direct counterpart in Weber's theory, a distinction which reflects the fundamental difference between their respective conceptions of the social system. Although Weber made little formal reference to Durkheim in his writings, his objections to the illegitimate reification of collective concepts are primarily applicable to Durkheim's notion of *sui generis* social facts, and by the same count imply a critical attitude towards Parsons' holistic sociology. Despite his recent interest in social evolution[120] Parsons draws heavily on the tradition of ahistorical or synchronic analysis, which interprets society in terms of concepts relating to structure and function. Weber, by contrast, believed that all human reality can be understood only in the dimension of time and by the methods of the historian.[121] His individualising approach to social and historical study is associated with an anti-holistic distrust of super-individual social categories,[122] and it is in accordance with this methodological postulate that Weber examines classes at the level of market encounter and interaction.

Unlike Parsons, Weber sees class conflict to be ubiquitous in capitalist society. At the same time, he saw contemporary class divisions to be essentially reconcilable through the sphere of politics. Whereas classes and status groups are located in the economic and social orders respectively, political parties reside and function in the sphere of power. Their activity lies in the acquisition of social power and in influencing social action, whatever its content may be. The actions of classes and status groups may comprise of the strategies of individuals or loose clusters of individuals, but party-oriented social action, always coordinated and directed towards a particular goal, necessarily has an associational character, even when its aims do not directly coincide with economic or status interests.[123]

While his own political life was in the main one of anticipation and frustration, Weber conceived of the political sphere as an arena in which an appropriate leadership would be able to unify, or at least balance, the various contending interest groups which persistently undermined the realisation of German national unity around the turn of the century. His diagnosis of Germany's political malaise centred on the absence of classes capable of providing the State with genuine leaders and the failure of German political institutions to engender such a leadership. The immediate balance of political forces meant that the idea of the nation as a symbol of common interest and membership must above all embrace the working class.

Weber's 1918 Vienna speech to Austrian officers stresses the urgency of subordinating socialist tendencies within the labour movement to the principle of national unity, especially as it concerns military interests.[124] Class compromise could not be achieved on the basis of economic policy alone, since the essence of capitalism is the free organisation of economic interests, which by themselves assume a sectional character. Rather, national unity must and can only be a specifically political accomplishment. Towards the end of the First World War, Weber looked to the German parliament for a democratically-elected plebiscitary leader who would rule with authority and be personally responsible to the people. In the following years, he advocated the direct election of a president with separate powers, who would both represent a check to parliamentary power and be directly accountable to the electors. Until at least 1908, Weber assumed that a vigorous capitalist economy depended upon geographical expansion, and accordingly he supported a great power overseas policy. His later view, that imperialism would guarantee not only economic benefits but also the survival of German culture, deepened, but did not fundamentally alter his commitment to the ideal of a unified Germany with a decisive but responsible role in world political affairs.[125]

In his essay on 'ethical neutrality', Weber challenges the view that economic science can provide other than strictly technical solutions for 'given' problems with an example which explicitly assumes the increasing internationalisation of capitalist economic activity. The problem he considers is that of whether or not the profitable destruction of goods in order to raise producers' prices may be viewed as 'economically correct'. An affirmative answer ignores the possibility of irreconcilable conflicts of interest between political groups and takes an *a priori* stand in favour of the free-trade position. But an economic system which is not based on the competitive market would not reflect its particular interest blocs and consequently would not necessitate the deliberate withdrawal and destruction of consumable goods. If 'the political unity of the world economic system' is assumed, which Weber observes is 'theoretically allowable', the focus of criticism shifts towards the capitalistic forms of market provision and exchange.[126]

The nationalistic values that permeate Weber's political writings lead him to endorse a conscious partisan commitment to Germany's political interests in the existing, territorially-divided world order. In the 1894 Freiburg Address he wrote: 'Economics, as an explanatory and analytical science, is international, but as soon as economics expresses values, it becomes bound up with the substance of our life as a nation.'[127] Three years later, Weber offered a more explicit rationale for the development of such a nationally-oriented economic science on the basis of his view of global economic trends. The inexorable drive of bourgeois nations to 'expand economically' is again

> approaching a point where it will be *power only* which decides the size of the share of the individual nations concerned with the economic control of the globe, this being identical with the margin of facilities for the livelihood of their population, in particular their working classes.[128]

The national idea is, for Weber, an ultimate value which has primacy in both political and economic activity; it is, in terms of his own conception of social science, associated with a clear value orientation. To this extent it is, as Mommsen points out, inseparable from Weber's conviction that society ought to be kept as dynamic as possible in the face of the increasing rationalisation of political as well as social needs.[129] Weber assumes that authentic political leadership within the nation state is unlikely to be spontaneously forthcoming, and that would-be aspirants must accordingly adopt a systematic and active overall strategy in order to win a broadly-based support:

> It is not a question of the politically passive 'mass' throwing up a leader of itself, but rather of the political leader recruiting a following and winning the mass by demagogic appeal. This is true even in the most democratic constitutions.[130]

Weber's methodological nationalism remained, in Raymond Aron's words, 'ruthlessly lucid,'[131] allowing him, with the war lost in autumn 1918, to advocate the Kaiser's immediate abdication 'in the interest of the reich and the dynasty'.[132] The opening paragraphs of *Politics as a Vocation* specify the sociological focus of political activity to be the struggle for power within or among states.[133] Weber's analysis of the relationship between State and nationality in *Economy and Society* dismisses all mono-factor attempts to equate the two concepts, in particular the linguistic and racial variants. National identity appears as a complex empirical combination of social, political and cultural allegiancies and identifications which may or may not cor-respond with the geographical boundaries of a formal polity. It is thus defined in general cultural (values) rather than state-oriented (territorial) terms.[134]

Propagation of the idea of the State is closely associated with 'prestige interests' and the notion of a 'culture mission', and is anchored in the uniqueness of 'the culture values that are to be preserved or developed only through the cultivation of the peculiarity of the group'.[135] There is unquestionably a manipu-lative element in Weber's view of intellectuals as the conscious bearers of the national idea:[136] but he could conceive of their project attaining success only to the extent that it corresponds to the reality of socio-cultural existence. In modern capitalist society the functions of the State include law enactment and the protection of personal safety and public order and, as such, the State does not objectively represent a 'community of interests'.

Weber is clear that the State's activities benefit the bourgeoisie in particular.[137] Nevertheless, he saw the nation State to rest on sentiments and emotional elements which are irreducible to the purely economic effects of imperialism on workers' incomes.[138] Through the propagation of shared 'culture goods', intellectuals are able to synthesise a national unity which has its preconditions in the forms of existing *cultural* life and which expresses the common *economic* interest of the various classes in the per-petuation of capitalism. Weber saw the possibility of a divergence between formal and substantive rationality on the basis of the pursuit of profit and class conflict.[139] Despite this, he consistently advocated the rallying of the working class behind an imperialist policy for Germany, the changes in direction of which were determined by the purely pragmatic needs of the day. While his opposition to socialism in Germany adduced the 'hard' expedient reason that post-war industrial reconstruction required foreign credit which only the bourgeoisie would be able to secure,[140] his defence of nationalist power politics had deeper roots in his analysis of the development of capitalism.

Basically, Weber saw the economic expertise of businessmen to be superior to that of the State bureaucracy in terms of substantive rationality.[141] By proposing a programme for national unity against the background of incipient class conflict that capitalism implies, he wrote from what may be termed a non-dogmatic functionalist viewpoint. Whereas for Parsons integration is inherent or intrinsic in the social system, Weber pursued it as a practical accomplishment, derived from underlying values and achieved on the problematic ground of shared cultural life in spite of ubiquitous crosscutting economic and symbolic pressures. Behind this scenario stands Weber's pessimism concerning the possibility of self-government in social life. Domination is defined as a universal quality of social existence, while the particular instance of workers' control of the productive process is rejected as technically not feasible.[142] In 1918, Weber dismissed the practical possibility of a socialist reorganisation of industry in Germany:

> I cannot see the manpower for the running of production in peacetime either in the trade union members themselves or among the syndicalist intellectuals.[143]

Bureaucratic domination represents, for Weber, the characteristic mode of domination in mass democracies. Viewed technically, all the people cannot govern themselves and, as a consequence, their political parties assume bureaucratic tendencies in accordance with the prevailing trend of modern life. The pessimism that pervades this view of man's historical potential is a major influence on the Parsonian system, where power is equally, though by different mechanisms, defined into the essence of social existence. Parsons' fatalism derives from the tacit and often ironically cheerful generalisation of capitalist production relations into properties of 'the social system' as such. Weber, by contrast, soberly examines domination as a variable but inevitable feature of social organisation. For both, no real alternative to the pathos of timeless domination is envisaged. Some of the assumptions and implications of this deep sociological pessimism, especially as they concern developments in economic science during the last quarter of the nineteenth century, are examined in our final chapter.

8

From Natural Law
to Sociology

GREECE: THE BEGINNINGS

The development of systematic social thought is inseparable from the changes in social organisation consequent upon the genesis, growth and periodic disruption of commodity production. With the emergence of an enduring international economy during the Iron Age came the universalistic ethical creeds of Lao-tse, the Buddha and the Hebrew prophets. Medieval feudalism was intellectually dominated by doctrines as hierarchical and predictable as the social relations which they justified. While ascendant capitalism, to take a number of polar cases, saw Adam Smith and Marx, J. S. Mill and Machiavelli, Weber and Lenin. The historical growth of the productive forces has, in an irregular and anything but linear fashion, transformed the social relations of mankind, and it is in relation to the principal points of transformation that the major developments in social theory have mainly taken place.

Schematically, social philosophy and political economy may be distinguished as two characteristic modes of theorising on these developments. The distinction, of course, is essentially one of abstraction: while rarely abandoning its ethical origins, political economy has been more concerned with the 'substantial' study of social and economic physiology. Classical social philosophy, especially that of Plato and Aristotle, formed the point of departure for the subsequent discussion of exchange and value. Periodically, doctrines of natural law surfaced openly, for example in the form of the physiocrats' 'ordre naturel'; but against its origins, political economy, since around the seventeenth century, has persistently sought to rid itself of directly ethical considerations.

The practice of social philosophy, especially since the classical Greeks, has mainly been concerned with the underlying theme of social integration. Its overall orientation is towards the total nexus of social relations and centres on the question of political obligation. How may relations between persons and classes be harmonised? How do we reconcile the idea of the social good to the realities of State and political power? Despite the abstract form of these questions, their changing content reflects, as we have implied, revolutionary historical developments in economic life. By the seventh century B.C., Greece had a flourishing industry in pottery, and was building a mass export market of cheap products based on Athens, Corinth and the other major urban centres. The ties of economic exchange were further sealed by an increasing dependence upon imported food, and large-scale production for the market provided a stimulus to the developing division of labour.[1] The production of goods for exchange had already undermined much of the local, small-scale social organisation of the earlier Aegean settlements by the sixth century B.C.

By this time the Milesian philosophers had effected an intellectual revolution by seeking to explain the natural world in terms of its underlying material constitution. Indicative of their interests and success is the attribution to Thales, the founder of the Milesian school, of the prediction of an eclipse and the introduction of geometry into Greece from Egypt.[2] Thales' concern with the constitution of natural phenomena (he conceived water to be the basic constituent of matter) was developed by his followers Anaximander and Anaximenes, the latter taking a particular interest in meteorology.

Now, although the Pythagorean school departed from the Milesian emphasis on the natural world and the laws that govern it, their preoccupation with number as the key to the universe posited an abstract quantity as the measure of phenomena. Thus, while shifting attention from the actual material composition of the cosmos, the rationalist Pythagoreans both affirmed a correspondence between the analysis of mathematical properties and the structure of the world and, through their preoccupation with the properties of numbers, anticipated a more precise form of investigation than the Milesians had been able to develop.

The initiative in the development of the theory of change, however, was taken by the materialist atomists in response to Parmenides' proposition of a static world. Around 500 B.C., Heraclitus propounded the doctrine that change is the essence of reality, and that as such reality is unattainable. Parmenides countered with the assertion that change and motion are illusory, the world of 'Being' having an eternal, unchanging character.[3] The materialist atomists replied that Parmenides' static schema overlooked the phenomenal world of motion by ignoring the atomic constitution of matter. Democritus, and later Epicurus and Lucretius, argued for a world comprising of space and atoms, the latter engaged in ceaseless and unavoidable movement.

By the later years of the fifth century B.C., a differentiation between natural philosophy and the philosophy of social and political conduct was becoming more pronounced in Greek thought. Socrates, in particular, examined the conditions required to allow the development of an intelligently organised society: popular crowds, he believed, are prone to manipulation at the hands of orators and demagogues, and the management of the State is accordingly best conducted by its wisest men. Socrates' aristocratic answer to the problem of political stability was formulated consciously as a reply to what he saw to be the irresponsible and debunking influence of the sceptical and relativistic Sophists.

Socrates' interests were overwhelmingly concerned with questions of human conduct and social order rather than the natural world. But in terms of the overall movement of Greek philosophy, his profound influence on Plato was tempered by the latter's preoccupation with the earlier problems of mathematics and natural philosophy. Plato deduced the necessity of society from the human condition of mutual need and the difference of aptitudes between individuals. The division of labour in production, he observed, allows the development of individual talents, and in doing so benefits society as a whole.[4] Wider society comprises the three main classes of rulers, auxiliaries and, for want of a more concise term, the third class. Whereas the first two groups are required to live austere and simple lives, removed from all possible influence of personal interests, the third class of

Plato's ideal republic effectively represent civil society as it is usually understood. They are allowed to own property, but are prevented by the guardians from the extremes of both wealth and poverty, for 'One produces luxury and idleness and a passion for novelty, the other meanness and bad workmanship and revolution into the bargain'.[5]

While substantively a reiteration of Socrates' objections to the instability of popular rule, Plato's opposition to democracy and its tendency to degenerate into class war and eventually tyranny[6] rests on a particular conception of the role of the philosopher in society and of the relation between the real and the ideal. The philosopher-ruler's appropriate intellectual object, as depicted in *The Republic*, is the unchanging world of 'Forms', the sphere of ultimate reality which stands behind the sensual realm of appearances.[7] This doctrine is developed further in Plato's *Timaeus*, where he opposes the world of becoming to that of being: becoming is the visible world of flux and change, the object of empirical knowledge which, while modelled by the Creator on the pure realm of being, lacks its eternal quality as 'uncreated and indestructible' form.[8]

Plato rejects the ultra-rationalist proposition that the world is a product of reason alone, suggesting instead that it is only in combination with necessity that reason could operate.[9] The very anthropomorphism of Plato's account of creation invites a comparison of his conception of the modus operandi of divine intelligence and philosophical rule. Just as the Creator brought the world into being by moulding, yet at the same time obeying the physical laws of 'indeterminate cause', so the philosopher-ruler governs and seeks to engender rationality within the necessary relations of civil society. 'Indeterminate cause' and the necessary division of social labour are the objects which divine and philosophical reason respectively must harmonise. In the former, 'a constant disequilibrium is maintained which ensures that the perpetual motion of the constituents shall continue unceasingly':[10] whereas the philosopher guardians overlook the general state of social order and justice in which each of the three classes 'does its own job and minds its own business'.[11]

Now Plato ascribes to the guardians the function of supervising social mobility in the case of individuals whose character is not in keeping with their class position.[12] Nevertheless, his account of the social division of labour has a tone of finality, which has been correctly charged with assuming the 'hypostatized limitation of human capacities'.[13] Indeed, Plato writes: 'No two of us are born exactly alike. We have different aptitudes, which fit us for different jobs.'[14] The historically-specific rigidity that this formulation reflects is the slave economy of classical Greece. Thus, when Plato enumerates the various economic functions that society must fulfil, he neglects to mention the slave category; the slaves are, implicitly, subsumed within the categories of their owners.[15] Aristotle similarly, if more forcefully, defined the slave as the 'mere chattel', the 'instrument for use' of his owner.[16] The social order that Plato and Aristotle so painstakingly sought was well adjusted to the conditions of their own society, both in its general ideal of class reconciliation and in its taking for granted of the underlying slave economy.

Plato's philosophy is illustrative of both the stimulus which was given to social thought by the development of Greek civilisation, and the obstacles faced by philosophy in the context of the limits to Greece's productive development. In the later stages of Greek civilisation, as in the subsequent Roman Empire, the reciprocal influence of slavery and a highly concentrated form of power and wealth undermined the incentive to develop science, and with it the inclination to explore the nature of the world.[17] Within the sphere of social thought Plato, as we have seen, saw the basis of social differentiation and the possibility of social order to derive from the division of labour, firstly between productive occupational categories, and secondly in the form of the relations between the three great social classes, each with its proper or natural place and function.

This conception of the operation of natural law in society was developed further by Aristotle, whose *Treatise on Government* contains the ethical rationale of inequality in property, the seminal critique of communism on the basis of its inability to provide a stimulus to proper industry and care.[18] Not only in his discussion of property, but in his wider account of social life, Aristotle blends his observations on economic relations with normative prescriptions for how people ought to behave. Thus, alongside his analysis of money as the necessary medium of exchange in trade, he condemns usury as 'censurable' and 'detestable', a form of economic activity which is 'most against nature'.[19] Aristotle's philosophy is imbued with teleology, based on an often implicit conception of natural law: all phenomena in the world are impelled by an inner impulse arising from their form and function, and move towards their distinctive and inherent mode of being. Just as 'it is the intention of nature to make the bodies of slaves and freemen different from each other',[20] so a 'natural' economy geared to the production of food eschews luxury and 'has its bounds'.[21] Teleology is the means by which Aristotle translates accounts of social and economic relations into normative statements about the good life in society. Man, for Aristotle, is naturally social, finding his conditions of existence and possibilities of fulfilment in a common life with others. But the imperfections of human nature allow the possibility that the State will be used for private purposes, and the three regular types of government (kingdom, aristocracy and state) are prone to degenerate into tyranny, oligopoly and democracy respectively.[22]

Constitutional government, with the decisive influence of the middle ranks, provides, Aristotle believed, the desired combination of aristocracy and democracy.[23] The existing class divisions of Greek society are taken for granted, and the good life rests upon the correct balance between their proportions and forms of relations. Aristotle's strictures against imperfect forms of government derive not from the alienated forms of labour appropriation by which they are sustained, but from their failure to correspond to the 'ideal' mode of political organisation, the optimal state.

Aristotle defines craft as the exercise of productive disposition accompanied by reason. The 'bringing into being' that craft and skill effect has its origin in the maker, the producer of artefacts, whose creations constitute a category distinct from those things which 'exist by nature' and 'have their starting point in themselves'.[24] But the forms of sociality are precisely such a product of nature, ontologically distinct from and superior to the productive practices of their particular human constituents. Already the glorification of 'natural' alienated institutions and the reification of crystallised social effort has gained ascendancy over the seeds of a political economy of commodity production and exchange.[25]

BACON, DESCARTES AND THE NEW SCIENCE

The social philosophy of Plato and Aristotle suffered as a consequence of the low productive development of classical Greece and the static conception of human activity and social structure that it fostered. The development of more modern social thought can be likened to the changes in the forces and relations of production which accompanied the rise of the bourgeois class. Alongside the growth of natural science stands the revolutionary break-up of the static categories of feudal society, and its philosophical reflection in the enlightenment emphasis on 'natural reason' and the social contract. The medieval period is too easily relegated to a residual and homogeneous stage of stagnation in social thought. Despite the overriding hegemony of Christian doctrine, controversies such as those between the nominalists and the realists, or between the theological mystics and the more worldly classifiers of natural phenomena, punctuated the transmission of speculative thought between the final collapse of the Roman Empire and the emergence of systematic scepticism from around the fourteenth century.[26]

A qualitative change took place with the critique of scholasticism at the hands of Bacon who, confronted by what he saw to be the petrifying edifice of Aristotelian thought, offered both a diagnosis and a remedy for the obstacles thus posed to social and intellectual progress. Positive advance, he argued, could only be gained by making a thorough and decisive break with the 'idols' of current learning in favour of the inductive method of scientific enquiry.[27] The movement from particulars towards the general, the compilation of observations and facts, and the use of experimental reason to draw conclusions from them were at the heart of Bacon's teaching. In advocating this procedure he appealed to the material benefits and increased human comforts, the 'many things of excellent use stored up in the lap of Nature', that would derive from the development and application of science.[28] The innovations – and horrors – of the industrial revolution were as yet but distant possibilities, but Bacon's advocacy of scientific experiment anticipated the upsurge of empiricism and materialist thought that was to figure so prominently in subsequent British philosophy.

Bacon was ambiguous in this context. A deep understanding of philosophy, he believed, leads us to a belief in God;[29] but when the scientific procedure he advocated became effectively harnessed to the powers released with the break-up of feudalism, it was to provide a powerful weapon in the reconstruction of both philosophy and the world. The cult of the experiment, while anticipated by Bacon's premature propaganda work in the opening decades of the seventeenth century, became a powerful philosophical movement only as this crucial century proceeded. Deistic and other theological doctrines co-existed with a materialist approach to natural phenomena for many proponents of the new scientific method, not least Bacon and Hobbes. Systems builders of the Leibniz variety also attempted at this time to construct completed models of the workings of the universe, in form if not in substance following the style of the medieval scholastics.

Yet the new science found an ally in the rationalist philosophers, in particular Descartes. Like Bacon, Descartes' starting point was the conscious break with classical speculative philosophy of the Aristotelian type. In the *Discourse on Method*, Descartes describes how he 'quit the authority of my preceptors' to seek only that knowledge which could be found in himself and in 'the great book of the world'.[30] While his philosophical dualism allowed the postulate of both objective and subjective spiritual autonomy to find a place in his metaphysics, Descartes affirmed the lawlike nature of material being and hence its accessibility to scientific investigation. The mind is spiritual and may function independently of bodily existence but matter, in all its forms, has a spatial nature and is subject to mechanical laws. Furthermore, while Descartes suggests that it is easier to 'know' the contents of one's own mind than those of the external world,[31] his account of the relationship between body and mind allows for the attainment of objectively valid cognition.[32]

The radical empiricism of Bacon is subdued, Descartes' primary concern being the understanding of the laws of the physical universe through the use of reason, especially in its development and application of the principles of geometry. Nevertheless, he reiterates Bacon's plea for the pragmatic effect of science in human life, and his precepts for the correct exercise of reason are in the main a rationalist version of the Baconian inductive scientific method. The rejection of authority, the movement from simple to complex problems, and the exhaustive enumeration of phenomena so as to 'be sure of omitting nothing', together constitute the pursuit of observation and experiment within the sphere of pure reason.[33] Above all, Descartes discerns an essential unity in the relations of nature, a common basis in cognisable reality which will ensure their access to the enquiring mind. 'All things which fall under the knowledge of man,' he wrote, 'succeed each other in the same way.'[34] Even if the extension of mechanistic materialism to society was beyond the scope of Descartes' project, and although his own enquiries produced such unscientific offspring as the theory of vortices, his programme for rational enquiry comprised an aspect of the scientisation of social philosophy which reached a turning point with Hobbes and established the terms of the ensuing debate.

HOBBES AND THE EMBOURGEOISEMENT OF NATURE

The post-medieval revolution in philosophy was epitomised by the emphasis on physical law and motion in the writings of Galileo and Hobbes. The bringing of Galileo to trial for claiming that the earth is a moving object well expresses the political import of his dictum: 'There is one rule of physics (or set of rules) for heaven and for earth.' 'The Bible,' he asserted, 'is not chained in every expression to conditions as strict as those which govern all physical effects.'[35] Such opinions were understandably viewed as heretical and dangerous. Even Roger Bacon, who had written of the benefits to be derived from scientific knowledge, saw the investigation of the natural world primarily in terms of a support for religion.[36] Considerable advances were made in the field of medicine in the later years of the thirteenth century, and the medieval period as a whole saw technical improvements in such specialised areas as lens-making, printing and the technology of firearms. Despite this limited progress, the propagation of empiricism in science by Francis Bacon, the discoveries of Galileo and, later, Newton's theory of gravitation, symbolised a shift away from the mysticism that was much of medieval science towards a view of the universe as rational, intelligible, and potentially amenable to human purpose.

The importance of Hobbes derives from his rigorous application of materialism to the study of man in society. Whereas Descartes had introduced, or rather reformulated, a dualism in the investigation of man by affirming the 'specially created' nature of the soul,[37] Hobbes asserted the material character of thought itself. He saw the act of mental deliberation to be the consequence of a variety of sensory impulses, the final link in a far-reaching causal chain of internal events.[38] Strict paths of causation determine the development of all phenomena in nature, man not excluded.

Hobbes' method of exposition was to proceed from an account of the most fundamental qualities of matter, to the laws of human cognition and behaviour and, finally, to the level of social, that is political, organisation.[39] He begins his account of social life with the assumption that in the natural state, men approximate to a condition of mental and physical equality. But from this equality of ability there develops an antagonism over access to 'Ends', or scarce resources.[40] Whether or not actual conflict occurs, the uncontrolled struggle over resources constitutes a generalised state of social war, in which individuals are impelled by 'a perpetuall and restlesse desire of Power, that ceaseth only in Death'.[41] Man's natural existence, Hobbes believed, is that of an egoistic and acquisitive struggle, ended only by the attainment of a social covenant. 'Articles of peace' were drawn up in order to remove the sources of insecurity and create a power, Leviathan, armed with sanctions to ensure the observance of the agreed laws.[42] Hobbes does not claim an actual historical basis for the social covenant; his thesis is analytical rather than historical in a literal sense. The anarchy of 'natural' egoism is intended to indicate how men *would* behave if the power of authorised government were removed, and Hobbes drew on his own experience of the English Civil War to reinforce the point.[43]

In proposing this pre-covenant struggle of all against all, Hobbes was not merely reproducing the billiard-ball universe of the Greek atomic materialists. The 'desire of Power after Power' is explicitly a social phenomenon, a power over men, defined in terms of political 'eminence'. Hobbes distinguishes between the ambitions of those who seek 'vain glory' and the reactive egoism of the others who are compelled to defend themselves against this original threat. Nevertheless, the clash of antagonistic individuals has a homogeneous character, deriving its regularity from the competitive, lawlike determination of the market:

> For every man looketh that his companion should value him, at the same rate he sets upon himself: And upon alle signes of contempt, or undervaluing, naturally endeavours, as far as he dares . . . to extort a greater value from his contemners, by dommage; and from others, by the example.[44]

The abstract, amoral decisions of buyers on the market establish the value or worth of all men, and Hobbes accepts this as natural. Furthermore, the covenant which establishes the State is itself a social product, a compact freely and rationally arrived at in order to humanise the egoism of this very market. Whereas Plato implied a direct parallel between divine and social order, Hobbes saw the essence of natural law in society to lie in the triumph of reason over the original state of war. For Hobbes, there are 'no other precepts of *natural law*, than those which declare unto us the ways of peace'.[45] Reason is no less a part of the nature of man than passion, since the will of all men is directed towards their own good, which lies in the reasonable, ordered state of civil peace. The state, Leviathan, is the embodiment of the triumph of reason and the guarantor of peaceful social continuity.

By using the analytical fiction of the social covenant, Hobbes removed human relations from the sphere of nature (Aristotle) and the framework of theology (St Augustine and the scholastics) for a strictly social interpretation. His portrayal of capitalistic economic relations is partly implicit, being transposed into a hypothetical natural state. Nevertheless, the substantive idea of society as a human creation, as the product of men and their reciprocal practices, is present beneath the symbolism of the state of nature and its subsequent pacification. With Hobbes, the problem of order in capitalist society is posed in all its historical specificity, and his solution exercised a decisive influence, both positive and negative, over later controversies.

AFTER HOBBES: THE PACIFICATION OF NATURE

Hobbes' uncompromising portrayal of egoistic man did not, of course, go unchallenged. Some thirty years before the appearance of *Leviathan*, Lord Herbert of Charbury, writing from the rationalist camp, attempted to pre-empt the strife of market competition in the nascent bourgeois society with the doctrine of consensus as the criterion of truth:

> Whatever is believed by universal consent must be true and must have been brought into conformity in virtue of some internal faculty.[46]

But whereas Charbury's view that to doubt the authority of the moral laws would 'upset the whole natural order'[47] recalled the inflexibility and hierarchical absolutism of the old feudal régime, a subsequent generation of social philosophers, while still endorsing the basic image of market man, interpreted natural law in such a way as to present man as inherently good, just and sociable. The dominant influence here was John Locke, for whom the state of nature was a Golden Age, where far from existing in a state of war, all men naturally observed the laws of nature and reason. But even in this idyll, there were some whose behaviour contravened the natural laws and by doing so rendered the property of others insecure. In order to remedy this situation, men entered into the social contract as a guarantee that the happiness and freedom given by nature would be confirmed and strengthened.[48]

The wider social context of Locke's theory was the development of private property. He distinguishes the original common property of land, the earth which is 'common to all men', from man's property in his own person. By applying his bodily labour to the material of nature, man establishes his products as his own property, appropriates them.[49]

Locke's account of property centres on its character as the product of individual labour, but the use of money is introduced in order to explain the obvious actual inequalities, especially in the ownership of land. In the absence of money, an individual's property is restricted by the limitations imposed by the amount of perishable goods that he can use. In society, however, the individual enters into contractual relations which involve the alienation of his capacity to labour, thus permitting inequalities of property to be established beyond the bounds of what particular men can actually use. In this way, an individual may acquire a surplus of goods beyond his needs in the form of gold and silver 'without injury to anyone'.[50] In order to guarantee the right to such inequalities of wealth and property, 'the community comes to be umpire, by settled standing rules, indifferent, and the same to all parties'.[51] The particularism of feudal right is thus negated by the formal legal and civil equality of the bourgeois market.

Even in the face of the ascendant rule of market relations, Locke tries to preserve the notion of a natural basis for moral law. He believed that 'moral good' lies in conformity to some law to which sanctions are attached by the law-giver, either divine, civil, or in the form of public opinion. Divine law, 'the only true standard of moral rectitude', is given either by the light of nature or the voice of revelation. While moral law survives in this religious form, Locke discerned a meaningful regularity in the strictly social estimation of moral actions: 'Everywhere,' he observed, 'virtue and praise, vice and blame, go together.'[52] In the determination of the will, the mind is immediately impelled 'by the most pressing uneasiness a man is at present under'. Nevertheless, human liberty lies in man's constitution as a responsible moral agent, and this liberty is most perfect when he is determined by 'the greater good'.

Consequently, education plays an especially important role in Locke's theory. Rejecting the Cartesian notion of innate ideas, he developed a sensationalist theory of cognition with the mind as the recipient of the raw data of experience. His celebrated 'white paper' theory of knowledge, the denial of mental impressions derived from other than sensory data and the active reflection of reason upon it,[53] underpins the radical doctrine of the perfectibility of man that was to become such a powerful intellectual and political force in the course of the eighteenth century. 'I imagine the minds of children as easily turned, this way or that, as water itself,' Locke wrote.[54] The human character, according to this revolutionary view, is socially malleable and may be trained to appreciate and value that which is morally good, even though it is often a distant goal and contrary to the impulses of immediate desire. Education, in other words, is an intermediary factor between the actual and the possible in social life.

TOWARDS ENLIGHTENMENT

The writings of Locke had a decisive influence on the ideas of the French enlightenment, and with it the subsequent development of European history. D'Alembert cites his critical approach to the metaphysical concerns of traditional speculative philosophy as, together with the scientific discoveries which followed Galileo's work in astronomy, having 'lifted, so to speak, a corner of the veil that concealed truth from us'.[55]

The philosophes did not only inherit a sensationalist psychology from Locke. Just as his account of the growth of inequality had as its referent the growth of the bourgeois class and the industrial revolution that it bequeathed to the world, so the philosophes expressed a recurrent interest in the useful effects of technology in social life. D'Alembert expressed a common sentiment when he observed: 'Too much has been written on the sciences; not enough has been written well on the mechanical arts.'[56] Economic development was inseparable from the fight against all political and religious tyranny, a struggle that the philosophes waged with an unprecedented collective energy. Locke's political theory had introduced a note of accountability that was conspicuously absent from Hobbes's monolithic Leviathan. Government power, for Locke, was essentially fiduciary, held in trust on behalf of the people who can replace it in times of abuse. Behind his theory is the idea, crystallised under the impact of the glorious revolution, of a society as little molested by government as possible and ruled by a minimum of simple, preferably non-coercive, laws of reason and good sense.[57]

A pervasive theme throughout the writings of the French enlightenment was the polemical concern to reform social institutions in accordance with precisely these principles of reason and natural order. In Becker's words, they were prompted by 'a didactic impulse to set things right'.[58] Voltaire's influential *Philosophical Letters*, written in Britain, was to a large extent an appreciation of British social pluralism at the expense of the absolutist French monarchy. Of special interest is his plea for commercial liberty and toleration: commerce, Voltaire wrote, is an important source of freedom, bringing the possibility of both wealth and liberty to the people at large. He contrasted the 'well-powdered lord who knows precisely what time the king gets up in the morning' to the 'great merchant who enriches his country . . . and contributes to the well-being of the world' with great effect.[59] Montesquieu similarly praised the English support for international commerce, even though it often involved considerable restrictions on the permitted activities of individual merchants.[60]

Basing themselves upon Locke's epistemological doctrine of perfectibility, the prophets of progress, whose numbers included Saint-Pierre, Mercier and Volney, were concerned, though with different emphases, with the historical transformation of social institutions in the interest of the greater freedom of humanity as a whole. Voltaire, Fontenelle, Mably and Montesquieu, together with Hume and Gibbon in Britain, studied history from the point of view of the unity of social life and politics.[61] The attacks of the barbarians and Christians, political disruptions within Rome itself, the plunder and abuse of Rome's material culture, and not least the inexorable process whereby the products of man perish 'in the boundless annals of time', all contributed, in Gibbon's monumental account, to the ruin of Rome.[62] *The History of the Decline and Fall of the Roman Empire* may indeed be read as a testimony to historical decay, as a powerful vindication of Rousseau's warning that 'The body politic, as well as the human body, begins to die as soon as it is born, and carries in itself the causes of its destruction'.[63] Gibbon even cites the prophecy of the venerable Bede: 'When the Coliseum falls, Rome will fall; when Rome falls, the world will fall.'[64]

Yet Gibbon knew well that the world had not fallen with the ruins of the Capitol. The monuments of the Empire, he wrote, are now visited by 'a new race of pilgrims from the remote, and once savage, countries of the north'.[65] Gibbon's history ends at this point, but it was from the inroads made into the territories of the old empire by the Germanic and Scandinavian peoples that the social relations of feudal Europe, and later those of capitalism, were to emerge. History as conceived by the philosophes involved the search for the principles governing the behaviour of people in society, the forms and mechanisms by which institutions develop and change over time. The British moral philosophers had affirmed that morality, far from being an entirely external constraint on the behaviour of individuals, is an essential component of the structure of the world. Cudworth, Hutcheson,

Shaftesbury, Cumberland, Locke and Hume all in their different ways pointed to the natural benevolence and sociability of man.[66] An individualistic utilitarian theme appears in many of these writers, as in Locke's proposition that things are good or evil 'only in reference to pleasure or pain'.[67] Again, Cumberland observed that the divinely-ordained natural law 'has reward annexed to its observance and punishment to its transgression'.[68]

The notion of a specifically *social* utility is present in the most developed expositions of British moral philosophy at this time, Hume's discussion of benevolence being a case in point. He denied the proposition that man has faculties for self-love alone, appealing to 'common feeling' and 'our most unprejudiced notions' for confirmation that sympathy and benevolence are components of 'the original frame of our temper'.[69] The great majority of enjoyments are extracted from nature by labour and industry. Consequently, the institution of property is of fundamental importance in society, and it is from property that Hume saw justice to derive its social utility.

Hume supported the establishment of laws that are useful and beneficial for society as a whole. The four principles which he suggests will meet this criterion are: that the individual ought to be allowed to keep whatever he produces or improves by his own labour; that property should be inheritable; that property may be alienated by consent, in order to promote beneficial commerce; and that all contracts and promises should be fulfilled, so as to secure the mutual trust and confidence which advances 'the general interest of mankind'.[70] The ultimate good of all such laws, which together constitute the rules of social equity and justice, derives from 'that utility which results to the public from their strict and regular observance'.[71]

The transition from individual to social utility produced some remarkable works in social philosophy, not least that of Mandeville. His largely doggerel *Fable of the Bees* documents the fortunes of a beehive whose initial state of well-being derives primarily from the prevalence of vice and egoism:

> Vast numbers thronged the fruitful Hive;
> Yet those vast numbers made 'em thrive;
> Millions endeavouring to supply
> Each other's Lust and Vanity.[72]

But an irate Jove reacts by overthrowing the established order and replacing it with a virtuous ruler who propagates the doctrine of altruism. The consequence of the well-intentioned coup, however, is the progressive growth of poverty until the community collapses and a few remaining survivors leave the ruins to live in a tree.

Mandeville's pointed tale did not seriously dent the enlightenment derivation of a spontaneous social harmony from the pursuit of proper self-interest. The doctrine of natural law that underlay these speculations had a long and varied ancestry. It had figured prominently in the social theories of Plato and Aristotle, and was developed during the later medieval period by both Jesuit theologians and the secular tradition of legal thought represented by Grotius.[73] Hobbes, as we have seen, identified it with the conditions of the social covenant. The innovation of the enlightenment philosophes was their association of the postulate of an intrinsic or potential harmony of social interests with the historically unprecedented rise of acquisitive activity augured by the birth of the industrial bourgeoisie. By philosophically endorsing the individualism which lay at the heart of the emerging property relations, they gave voice in the sphere of thought to the needs of what was arguably to become the most powerful ruling class in world history. Natural law was no longer a synonym for social duties, but rather a rationale for the assertion of rights, not least the economic rights of the bourgeoisie.

Morelly was virtually unique among the enlightenment thinkers in combining the doctrine of human perfectibility with a radical critique of all forms of private property. In the primitive state, he believed, little or no property existed and natural affection was the basis of a benign paternal authority. But with the gradual growth of communities and the emergence of property, this natural equilibrium was broken up, bringing about the perversion of man's social character and the possibility of class conflict. Morelly was radically optimistic in his belief that the eradication of private property would allow the reassertion of benevolent human impulses:

> Destroy property, the blind and pitiless self interest which
> accompanies it, wipe out all the prejudices and errors which

support them, and there are no more furious passions, ferocious actions, notions or ideals of moral badness.[74]

Morelly's communistic leanings were the exception and, in general, the philosophes were no advocates of an egalitarian social order. Holbach, for example, appealed to the 'code of nature' as the only source of a valid morality which could correspond to the true interests of both the individual and the community. The laws of nature, for Holbach, are obvious and immutable: 'Listen to nature, she never contradicts her own eternal laws.'[75] The content of these laws, however, centres on an imperative of mutual benevolence within class society. Nature, Holbach continues, proclaims the right of men to happiness and the duty to submit to legitimate authority: 'In short, be a man, be a sensible rational being, be a faithful husband, a tender father, an equitable master, a zealous citizen.'[76] The class nature of Holbach's natural morality was one of compromise and reconciliation within the institutions of private property.

The philosophes rarely conceived of enlightenment as a universal phenomenon, let alone a weapon in the struggle against property. Their reformism was no more a preview to Babeuf's conspiracy of equals than had Locke's *Treatises on Civil Government* been the political programme of the landless diggers. In eighteenth-century France, the general low esteem of the non-noble bourgeoisie and their limited access to channels of social mobility, bred among them a widespread resentment towards the political institutions of the old régime.[77] The philosophes' view of the world, which in many ways reflected the demands of the frustrated bourgeoisie, was often at best ambiguous on the relationship between enlightenment and the working classes. In *The Age of Louis XIV*, Voltaire wrote that the philosophical spirit had 'penetrated practically every class of society save the lowest'.[78] Diderot, and even Rousseau, expressed similar doubts about the ability or even desirability of extending enlightenment to *le peuple* in the wider sense.[79] This paradoxical partisanship on the part of the self-proclaimed citizens of the world had its intellectual seeds in the moral theories of Hume and Smith. Here, sympathy and human benevolence are the ethical counterparts of a society based on commodity production and exchange, the two being mediated by natural reason for the benefit of both man in general and men in particular. The distance between the doctrine of moral sentiments and the free accumulation of the *Philosophical Letters*, in its economic content a propagandist anticipation of *The Wealth of Nations*, was not as great as may appear.

The typical philosophe view of history emphasised the role of ideas rather than class struggle as the agency of progressive change. D'Alembert, with more than a little of the Pangloss, wrote about the improvement in learning and general culture since the Renaissance, making the remarkable suggestion that 'The invention of printing and the patronage of the Medici and of Francis I revitalized minds, and enlightenment was everywhere.'[80] Fontenelle and Turgot also at times tended to equate progress with the increasing scope and influence of knowledge in society. Voltaire wrote of Descartes: 'He was the greatest geometrician of his age; but geometry leaves the mind where it finds it.'[81]

Bacon, Galileo, Huygens and the other practitioners of natural science were, for Voltaire, the bearers of the 'spirit of reason' who had 'contributed to extend the enlightenment of the human spirit'.[82] The pedagogic stance of the philosophes is apparent in Diderot's suggestion that 'To instruct a nation is to civilize it',[83] and found an even stronger expression in Helvétius' uncompromising materialist doctrine of human modifiability.

Such views were an inevitable consequence of the common philosophe self-conception as the very embodiment of the forces of rationality in history. As Plekhanov's excellent critique of eighteenth-century French materialism makes clear,[84] even the most consistently materialist philosophers of this period were unable to systematically overcome the idealist belief that opinion is the primary force governing social development. Holbach begins his *Nature and Her Laws* with a radically materialist statement of the relationship between human existence, including consciousness, and the natural world: 'Man . . . is the work of nature. – He exists in nature. – He is submitted to her laws. – He cannot deliver himself from them. He cannot step beyond them even in thought.'[85] The 'moral' dimension of man, for Holbach, is no more than his physical being considered from the point of view of certain aspects of his behaviour, which are themselves the work of nature. Yet in the same work, he attributes human misfortune to a mere cognitive failing: 'For want of clearly understanding his own peculiar nature, his proper tendency, his wants, and his rights, man has fallen in society, from freedom into slavery.'[86] Oppressive social and political conditions are thus reducible to a pedagogic problematic of ideas.

Social being alone was exempted from the systems of the eighteenth-century French materialists. Implicitly, as we have seen, their conception of what would constitute a progressive development in social organisation linked up closely with the ambitions of the rising bourgeoisie. But although the philosophes as a tendency harnessed much of their collective polemic to the progressive entrepreneurial forces that were transforming the social and intellectual world, above all in Britain, an anticipatory shadow across the prospect of unlimited progress and perfectibility emerged from within their own ranks in the person of Rousseau. As early as 1749, Rousseau had thrown down the gauntlet in his *Discourse on the Arts and Sciences*, a work which reads very much like a point by point refutation of all that the philosophe movement stood for. Far from representing the fruits of enlightened reason, he argued, the arts and sciences are born of human vices and thus tainted in their very origins. While Voltaire, Diderot and Turgot had welcomed an increasingly effective rational orientation in recent history, Rousseau associated the development of the arts and sciences with the growth of moral decadence: 'Being the effect of idleness, they generate idleness in their turn.'[87] Even philosophers of the stature of Newton and Descartes, Rousseau claimed, have brought little or no positive benefit to their fellow-men.

'Is virtue inconsistent with learning?' Rousseau polemically asked. His answer takes the form of an antithesis of nature and artifice. True morality, although little more than an abstraction at this stage of Rousseau's career, is associated with the natural life rather than the sophisticated society of the philosophes: 'Let men learn for once that nature would have preserved them from science, as a mother snatches a dangerous weapon from the hands of her child.'[88] The source of civil society, Rousseau insists, must be sought in the origin of property, in the original impulse to enclose a piece of land and assert 'This is mine'.[89] Primary differentiation among styles of living arose from environmental variations, but the second decisive and irreversible step in the development of human society derived from the pursuit of metallurgy and agriculture. The ensuing enslavement of mankind by the usurpation of 'a few ambitious individuals' assured the parallel growth of poverty and inequality, irretrievably destroying natural liberty and securing the new powers of the rich minority. The moral retrogression of humanity in this way derived directly from the combined assault of property and industry.

Yet while Rousseau's paradox of the irreconcilability of virtue and knowledge struck at the heart of many fundamental enlightenment assumptions, his doctrine of the general will was in one sense perhaps the most precise expression of its approach to social order. The problem Rousseau considers is that of finding a form of association which will protect the goods of each associate without at the same time restricting his original freedom. He elaborates a deductive argument to suggest that it is a common element between different particular interests which forms the basic social tie, and that sovereignty lies in the exercise of the general will thus created. Distinguished from the 'will of all', which is the mere arithmetic sum of all particular interests, the general will is concerned only with the 'common interest', the essence of sociality itself. While deceit or ignorance may empirically obscure the common interest, the general will which it represents is infallible and always 'tends to the public advantage'.[90]

Rousseau expresses the unitary nature of the general will in terms of the familiar organic analogy.[91] The will of the community has a *sui generis* and authoritative existence, with regard to which sectoral interests must be judged as correct or incorrect. The social contract represents a collective act of alienation on the part of all those constituent interests: 'The total alienation of each associate, together with his rights, to the whole community.'[92] But at the same time, the moral and civil equality that the contract creates assures, through the representation and harmonisation of all particular interests, the realisation of a form of liberty appropriate to man's true sociality. This liberty, Rousseau believed, constitutes a collective obedience to a self-prescribed law.

By accounting for the unity of the general will in terms of the harmony of legitimate particular interests, Rousseau was drawing on the essential postulate of natural law that inspired the more orthodox enlightenment thinkers to campaign for social and political reform. Even in Montesquieu's *Spirit of the Laws*, for example, we find the assertion of a natural law of equity in social relations, a proposition which stood in sharp contrast to the monarchical and aristocratic domination of his own society. While viewing 'extreme equality' as incompatible with true democracy, Montesquieu opposed slavery as 'in its own nature bad', since it denies both master and slave of the power to act through a motive of virtue.[93] The philosophes applied the principles of natural law and right to the institutions that they found around them, and their inevitable primary target was the weakening edifice of feudal power. As Engels appraised their project:

> Religion, conceptions of nature, society, political systems, everything was subjected to the most merciless criticism: everything had to justify its existence at the bar of reason or renounce all claim to existence.[94]

This attack on the *ancien régime* was as diverse in content as it was significant in the history of European society. The materialism of Diderot and Holbach, Bayle's scepticism, Voltaire's satire and the educational theories of Rousseau, converged in the common assault on the many aspects of feudal reaction. That Rousseau should have viewed the attainment of a rational social order as a contradictory historical process indicates the advances he made over the unilinear evolutionism of some of his co-thinkers. But in the last analysis, he shared their near-unanimous concern to affirm the property rights of the revolutionary entrepreneurial class and with them, so they thought, the well-being of mankind.

THE SOCIOLOGICAL SYNTHESIS: I, CAPITALISM SANCTIFIED

By the nineteenth century, when the founding fathers of modern sociology were writing, the classificatory style pioneered by Montesquieu[95] had developed in a number of directions. Centrally, the historical dimension of social structure, often ideationally conceived by the enlightenment thinkers, was systematised by Comte and others into a theory of the stages of social development. Comte's theological, metaphysical and scientific or industrial stages, like the historical trinity of social systems developed earlier by Saint Simon,[96] is significant both for its diachronic form and for the primacy that economic life is given in the most recent historical form of social organisation.

The social organisation of industry was forced to the attention of these theorists not only by the remarkable growth in world economic activity since at least the seventeenth century, but perhaps more crucially by its wider effects on social relations and its very irregularity. Voltaire had endorsed the benefits in terms of welfare and liberty which accompanied the growth of commercial freedom in Britain. The sociological problem for Comte was the opposite, that of overcoming the disorder and apparent social fragmentation that had followed in the wake of this same industrial revolution. The major European economic crisis of the seventeenth century had been followed by a sequence of industrial depressions which, looked at retrospectively, raised serious doubts as to the validity of the earlier, more optimistic belief in a potentially linear path of economic growth and opulence. Partly in response to the effects of these economic crises, the European capitalist countries had witnessed a series of peasant revolts and, more significant for the future, the beginnings of organised resistance on the part of the new industrial working class.

Faced by these developments, Comte diagnosed the need for social planning on an unprecedented scale. The rational plan on which the new order was to be founded would guarantee a maximum of freedom and social welfare on the basis of cooperative productive work.[97] Society is increasingly organised with production as its aim, and it is the task of positive social science to bring the emerging system to a state of organic maturity. In the consummate positive social order, industry will no longer merely satisfy material wants, but will be brought into closer accord with the affective aspects of human life. Then, 'our only science would be the "Gay Science", so artlessly preferred to any other in the knightly times of old'.[98] Science and industry will take their place in the moral celebration of humanity, under the inspiration of an enlightened sociocracy.

Whereas the philosophes had appealed for a dynamic transformation of the sources of inertia, oppression and ignorance in society, Comte's scheme for social reconstruction has the character of a conscious culmination of the trends discovered by positive science to be already at work.[99] The glorification of the facts of history that this form of interventionism implies finds expression in the social functions that he designates in the reconstituted social order for the actual social forces of the nineteenth century. The continued existence of private property is, for Comte, essential. History has demonstrated that the means to accomplish the production of wealth tend to accumulate in the hands of those best able and most willing to use them, which in the modern period means the bourgeois class:

> Capitalists then will be the temporal chiefs of modern society. Their office is consecrated in Positive religion as that of the nutritive organs of Humanity.[100]

But left alone the capitalists are liable to develop a sense of false pride in their activities and to abuse their power through compulsion and coercion.[101] Consequently, it is necessary in the interests of society as a whole to moderate their authority with the exercise of a wider morality, a spiritual authority which acts in the benevolent interests of all classes. The presence of a spiritual power behind the temporal authority of the economic sphere is a guarantee that the benefits of industrial society will be regulated in accordance with the principles of social order and well-being. Their socially responsible use will be facilitated by the relatively highly-developed 'social feelings' of the working class, in whom are present (this written in 1848!) 'sincere and simple respect for superiors, untainted by servility'.[102] Comte's religion of humanity, the apex of his work, was in fact little more than a heavily theologised capitalism directed towards the narcissistic glorification of man and his works.

THE SOCIOLOGICAL SYNTHESIS: 2, DURKHEIM AND WEBER: THE REJECTION OF NATURAL LAW

Comte denounced the division of labour, or 'the system of dispersive speciality now so much in vogue', on the grounds of its 'brutalizing' social consequences. In particular, it condemns the intellect of the workman to 'the most paltry mode of culture', denying him the ability to engage in abstract and general thought.[103] By restricting the workman's thoughts, the division of labour undermines the universal sentiments upon which positive social order rests. For Comte, the development of intelligence is the moving force of historical development, in the course of which the growth of industry and production provide, when regulated by the insights of positive social science, a scenario for the truly human fulfilment of mankind. But the incorrect application of specialisation in economic life is an obstacle to this realisation, obstructing the emergence of the appropriate mental state for social unity.

Gouldner is undoubtedly correct when he suggests that an important element in Durkheim's critique of the Comtian outlook was his view, first systematically elaborated in *The Division of Labour in Society*, that science cannot of itself be expected to provide the new morality adequate to bind the emerging industry-centred society into a unified system. Gouldner goes on to suggest that in opposition to Comte's belief in the primacy of ideas in the determination of social order, Durkheim generalised Marx's philosophical anthropology into a wider view of the influence of social relations in general on the development of morality.[104]

In order to understand fully the significance of Durkheim's reaction against Comte's idealism, it is necessary to locate it within the former's overall conception of historical change. Comte's rather cavalier dismissal of economics was another aspect of his belief in the primacy of ideas in history. Since the theories of the political economists reflected the growth of the division of labour in capitalist society, and since this division of labour was incompatible with the kind of moral solidarity for which he appealed, it was obvious to Comte that their theories were incorrect. He even went so far as to attribute the development of the division of labour to 'the irrational endeavours of our Anglo-maniac economists', among whom Adam Smith and Ricardo must presumably be numbered.[105] Contemporary economics, he believed, erred in abstracting the phenomena of economic life from their function within the wider social entity. Only the enlightened high priests of sociology could provide a satisfactory means of resolving the crisis into which the previously undirected advance of science and technology had led society.

By the 1880s, when Durkheim was formulating the outlines of his own approach to sociology, the view that the division of labour could be reversed by a purely moral force was far less plausible. This was the period that saw the consolidation of imperialism, an unprecedented rise in the concentration of capital, the beginnings of systematic mass production within capitalist industry, and the emergence of the working-class parties of the second international as an effective political force. Throughout Europe as a whole, including tsarist Russia, industrial capitalism was developing at a revolutionary pace, and with it the transformations in the labour process that everywhere accompanied the rise of the modern factory. In the face of such developments, either the division of labour had to be accepted as an aspect of whatever new form of solidarity might be developed, or the possibility of social harmony in any other than a non-revolutionary state would have to be rejected as a hopeless utopia.

Durkheim, of course, followed the former assumption. Perhaps the most immediately striking aspect of his sociology is the dual proposition that while the integration of society is above all a moral problem, the conditions for the realisation of moral solidarity are at the same time amenable to a naturalistic mode of scientific enquiry. At the heart of this perspective is Durkheim's conception of the sphere of social facts as a *sui generis* reality, conceivable only in the context of the interaction of individuals, yet irreducible to it. In this, Durkheim was challenging the influential view of Spencer that the path of causation in social life proceeds from the individual to the collectivity, from the part to the whole. Spencer, too, affirmed the need to ground the scientific study of society in the analysis of lawlike processes comparable to those operant in the sphere of nature, but assumed that the qualities of system units are reproduced in the distinctive traits of the social aggregate. 'Given men,' he wrote, 'have certain properties, and an aggregate of such men must have certain derivative properties which form the subject matter of a science.'[106] Society, for Spencer, has organic properties of growth and development, and his objections to the 'great man' theory of history reveal an underlying recognition of the social constitution of man. Nevertheless, his observations on the power of 'social arrangements' in promoting or retarding the attainments of individuals[107] are overshadowed by the primacy he attributes to psychological factors, conceived in utilitarian terms, in the determination of social phenomena. In the last analysis, the needs and aspirations of individuals colour the outlines of the social state rather than vice versa.

Durkheim attacked this individualistic approach to society on the grounds that 'it is only applying the old principles of materialist metaphysics to social life. It claims, that is, to explain the complex by the simple, the superior by the inferior, and the whole by the part, which is a contradiction in terms.'[108] In order to distinguish the subject matter of sociology from that of the other sciences, he posits the existence of phenomena which are exclusively sociological. Laws, currencies, languages and customs are not only external to the individual, but are endowed with a coercive power in relation to him. The proper domain of sociology, they above all have the positive properties of 'facts':

> It is not realized that there can be no sociology unless societies exist, and that societies cannot exist if there are only individuals.[109]

The second part of this proposition in particular, it appears to us, affirms an ontological dualism between society and the individual, rather than being, as Giddens has suggested, a strictly methodological postulate.[110] Durkheim's intention was to develop a 'sociological naturalism', a science which explains social facts in terms of natural causes.[111] But while the autonomy of social life must be the fundamental assumption of sociology, the existent sciences offer valuable analytical precedents for the study of society. Biology, in particular, has accumulated 'a treasure of experiences which it would be foolish to ignore'.[112] Durkheim adopts the biological metaphor, already used by Shäffle and a common analogy in nineteenth-century social thought. His conception of the organic nature of a society integrated through the division of labour is quite explicit, as the following passage indicates:

> The members are united by ties which extend deeper and far beyond the short moments during which the exchange is

made. Each of the functions that they exercise is, in a fixed way, dependent upon others, and with them forms a solidary system.[113]

The simplest type of society, which Durkheim concedes to be a hypothetical entity, is the 'horde', defined as 'the veritable social protoplasm, the germ whence would arise all social types'.[114] The horde is characterised by mechanical solidarity based upon the absolute resemblance and non-differentiation of individuals. A clan is a horde which, while solidarity is still based upon the likeness of consciences, has lost its independence by becoming an element within a more extensive complex of social groups. The association of clans, in turn, produces what Durkheim terms 'segmented societies with a clan-base'. Such societies, again dominated by the mechanical solidarity of likeness, embody Durkheim's conception, antithetical to that of Marx, of communism. Their purely aggregative form of cohesion 'absorbs the individual in the group, the part in the whole'.[115]

As against Marx, Durkheim locates communism proper at the dawn of social evolution, its hallmark being the poverty rather than the enrichment of individual development. The organic solidarity characteristic of developed societies, by contrast, is bound up with and inseparable from the division of labour:

> In effect, individuals are here grouped, no longer according to their relations of lineage, but according to the particular nature of the social activity to which they consecrate themselves.[116]

Since the Middle Ages, the earlier form of segmental organisation has been in decline. Integral to this process is the development of an inter-regional division of labour and the growth of city specialisation. At the same time, occupational specialisation becomes dominant within the social structure. The division of labour increasingly becomes the major integrative principle, displacing the 'collective conscience' from this position, and constitutes 'the principal bond of social aggregates of the higher type'.[117] On the basis of this distinction, Durkheim formulates a 'historical law' of the sequential relation between the two types of solidarity.[118] Organic solidarity is a historical phenomenon, emerging with the development of the division of labour and the growth of functional specialisation in society.

Durkheim does not confine the concept of the division of labour to the forms of economic differentation. Rather, it is a general tendency developing in all spheres of social life, not least in that of politics.[119] But whereas Comte saw only a negative threat to social cohesion in the division of labour, Durkheim suggests that in so far as it assumes the 'normal' form, it spontaneously generates the type of solidarity appropriate to the differentiation of social functions. The State is the overall directive organ standing above the web of social, especially economic, functions, but their mutual dependence and coordination is grounded directly in the mode of operation, in 'the very practices', of each special function: 'What gives unity to organized societies . . . as to all organisms, is the spontaneous consensus of parts.'[120] Patterns of reciprocal reaction are repeated and become habitual; the resultant social habits, in turn, are transformed into rules of proper social conduct.

Durkheim's concern is to establish the immanent solidarity of society as against the relative sovereignty of the State and juridical law. But in order for the division of labour to produce an organic solidarity, certain substantive conditions must be present. Essentially, these are what Durkheim termed 'the principles of 1789'. Liberty, equality and fraternity, he believed, were not merely the political demands of the French Revolution, but pervasive social facts reflecting the state of mind of an entire age and society, 'some general change which occurred in the structure of European societies'.[121] The task of the 'higher' societies is to realise these principles, the potential for which is unique to social life. Organic solidarity entails 'doing away with external inequalities as far as possible'.[122] While the 'perfect spontaneity' that would distinguish a pure meritocracy is conceded by Durkheim to be 'never met with anywhere as a realized fact', a close approximation to it is an essential aspect of the normal form of the division of labour.[123]

Organic solidarity reconciles the apparently opposing forces of individualism and social interdependence. Durkheim's conception of individualism is antithetical to the utilitarian egoism of Herbert Spencer and the classical economists. Rather, he draws on the theories of Kant and Rousseau, 'the basis of our moral catechism',[124] to affirm a form of social individualism which recognises the rights of the collectivity as well as those of the individual. There are, Durkheim proposes, moral ways of acting which are applicable to all men, and which derive from the common condition of humanity. Individuals receive dignity from a higher source, their society, in relation to which the 'cult of man', the autonomy of reason, and the right of free enquiry are fundamental.

In reply to the conservative objection that such an individualistic creed is subversive of social unity, Durkheim subjects the authority of existing powers to the very criteria of reason that the historical growth of individualism gives to mankind:

> Respect for authority is in no way incompatible with rationalism so long as the authority is rationally grounded.[125]

For authority to be rational in the context of the developed division of labour, it is essential that the greatly expanded area of economic transactions is organised in accordance with the principle of equity. Whereas primitive societies are impelled to maintain as intense a collective life as is possible, equitable social relations alone can assure the free development of all the socially useful forces in the higher types. Indeed, not only the harmony of functions, but also the very survival of modern society depends upon this condition.[126]

In his inaugural lecture of 1887 at Bordeaux, Durkheim expressed the view that sociology differs from economics in that the former considers economic phenomena within their wider social context rather than in isolation.[127] This contextualisation of the subject matter of economics is a central concern of all the major figures in the foundation period of modern sociology. Pareto's *Treatise on General Sociology* begins with the assumption that the task of sociology is to analyse and classify those elements of human behaviour that do not constitute economic activity of a logical kind.[128] The 'residues' which figure so prominently in his writings are the recurrent elements of non-scientific thought which evidence the presence of 'sentiments', the source of non-rational, though not necessarily non-useful, social behaviour.

Pareto believed it necessary to augment economics by a complementary social science of the non-logical, whereas Weber and Durkheim in their different ways undertook the actual reconstitution of economic science within the totalising study of society itself. This was the hallmark of classical sociology, the reconstitution of the subject matter of the different social disciplines within the area of a science of the 'social as such'. We saw in Chapter 2 how Weber took over the essential assumptions of neo-classical economics and reformulated them in terms of his theory of class structure and class conflict. Durkheim undertook a parallel project in his study *The Division of Labour*, where he praises the classical economists for recognising the spontaneous character of social interdependence.[129] His own account of the division of labour reflects the contemporary rise of marginalist doctrines, and adapts them in such a way as to construct the theoretical basis of a solidary organic system. Every object of exchange has a social value which is determined by the amount of useful labour which it contains. By this, Durkheim refers not to the material costs of production of the commodity, the object of the classical theory of value, but to that expenditure of energy which is capable of producing 'useful social effects', which 'reply to normal social needs'.[130] Economic transactions multiply along with the growth of the division of labour. As they increase in social importance, so the conflicts associated with market exchange become potentially more serious, and can only be avoided by the placing of the parties to a contract in conditions of external equality.

What Durkheim has in mind is by no means the formal equality of juridical law. True equivalence in exchange requires the radical removal of all coercive and unjust advantages in the conditions of the contract, above all those deriving from the inheritance of wealth: 'There cannot be rich and poor at birth without there being unjust contracts.'[131] To function in its normal form, the division of labour must reflect the spontaneous qualities of its members, the voluntary character of which requires that the services exchanged have an equivalent social value. This condition is necessary to ensure both that individuals are legitimately bound to their social function, and that the different functions are harmoniously integrated.

Far from being mere ideological abstractions, the ideals of justice, equality and fraternity are thus all grounded in the normal development of the division of labour. The identity of interest between the individual and society as a whole is neither spontaneously derived from the enlightened pursuit of self-interest as Smith and the eighteenth-century moral philosophers had believed, nor, as Comte imagined, the creation of an elect body of Platonic social scientists. Moral solidarity is a function of the division of labour, a natural consequence of the process of social evolution. Abnormal forms of the division of labour develop with the growth of a world market and the resulting anarchy in economic activity. Anomie, or normlessness, expresses precisely this absence of operative regulations in economic life. With the appearance of dislocations between the process of production and the distribution and consumption of industrial output, production becomes unbridled and arbitrary.[132] The worker is reduced to a mechanical component of the industrial system, unable to relate his activity to an identifiable end, and no longer a living cell of the social organism. The ensuing class conflict, characteristic of the anomic state, represents a partial break in organic solidarity, the failure of society to morally regulate 'the free unfolding of the social force that each carries in himself.'[133]

Durkheim's well-known programme to reconstruct the conditions of moral solidarity centres on the establishment of occupational corporations as an intermediary institution between the individual and the State. As well as assuming a directly technical function in the restoration of economic order, the corporations reinforce and foster moral cohesion through undertaking educational and other cultural activities. Durkheim places the revolution in social life that accompanied the rise of capitalism at the heart of his analysis of the crisis of modern society. His very conception of sociology and its subject matter, however, directs attention away from a systematic examination of the core relations of capitalist society, as is especially apparent in his discussion of the 'forced' division of labour. Dissatisfaction among the lower classes with their customary social position is the basis of class conflict, which expresses a widespread desire to perform traditionally closed functions. With external constraint as the sole link between individuals and their functions, only an imperfect and troubled form of solidarity is possible. Each individual must have a task which is fitting to his potential if the division of labour is to produce an enduring solidarity.[134]

It is at this point that a paradoxical convergence between the sociologies of Durkheim and Weber becomes apparent, the basis of which is the view of both that social harmony is attainable within the framework of the production relations of private property. Weber, as we have seen, bracketed away the substantive irrationalities associated with capitalism into a residual sphere of contingent quasi-phenomena, and portrayed the rational core of the capitalist system as an intrinsically equilibrating entity. Certainly, he saw class conflict to be unavoidable. The potential of the rational capitalist economy to match production to needs, and the common interest of all classes in the technical and managerial abilities of the bourgeoisie serve, nevertheless, to neutralise its socially disruptive effects. Weber's capitalism may not be a peaceful world, but at least it possesses an intrinsic rationality which can guarantee its own survival.

Now in his account of occupational corporations, Durkheim also assumes the survival of capitalist property relations. He suggests that in the present state of industry, where the interests of employers and employees are 'often rival and antagonistic', the two groups must be represented in independent representative organisations, meeting only in the overall directing councils of the corporation.[135] The corporations which are to provide the stimulus to moral solidarity are thus themselves the embodiment of the antagonistic interests of a class-divided society.

In his attempt to establish the immanence of organic solidarity, Durkheim obscured the divisive nature of property as a social relation: 'Property,' he observes, 'is definitive only of the extension of the person over things.'[136] His conception of organic solidarity rests substantially on a metaphorical comparison with the structure and functioning of living organisms in the natural world.[137] When he considers the actual relations between society and the natural world, his account is structured by a one-sided, dichotomous conception of their mode of interaction. 'Liberty', Durkheim contends, 'is the product of regulation.' Unique to social life, it constitutes 'a conquest of society over nature'.[138] The essence of this proposition is that it is only through the subordination of nature to social control that liberty can be realised. Liberty in this sense is a supra-natural quality of human existence, attainable

only in so far as man raises himself above things and makes law for them, thus depriving them of their fortuitous, absurd, amoral character; that is, in so far as he becomes a social being. For he can escape nature only by creating another world where he dominates nature. That world is society.[139]

As in his proposition that there is an exclusively sociological sphere of reality, Durkheim effectively drives a wedge between society and nature, substituting a formal evolutionary account of their mode of relation *as qualitatively discreet sectors of the world* for an analysis of the way in which man transforms his material environment through the medium of specific, structured production relations. Thus set off from the social relations entered into in order to transform nature for their own requirements, Durkheim's humans are available for integration with only 'sociological' phenomena as their referents. In particular, the realisation of the solidarity of interests latent in the division of labour requires the substantive condition of a meritocratic social order. With this condition met, the social organism attains a rationality in relation to which the rights of the individual and the moral solidarity of the system are mutually reinforcing.

The 'natural rights' of liberty, equality and justice are no longer the revolutionary demands of a rising class, but instead the necessary conditions as well as the product of a determinate evolutionary process. In their eighteenth-century form, they had implied the break-up of an entire structure of class rule, the abolition of feudal right. By the late nineteenth century, they were adopted by Durkheim as the substance of a new form of moral solidarity whose realisation is latent in the division of labour and is conceivable without the agency of class struggle. With Durkheim, the legitimising sanction of natural law need no longer underpin the doctrine of social unity, for unity itself is the essence of the gradual development of social evolution. Weber developed this aspect of Durkheim's sociology even further by defining natural law as a primarily legitimising doctrine 'with definite class obligations'.[140] The study of capitalism that both writers differently undertook no longer assumes even the secular conception of natural law that had been developed by Hume and directed against the institutions of the *ancien régime* by the eighteenth-century philosophes.[141] 'Social' evolution and the 'rationality' of formal capitalist activity are,

Durkheim and Weber believed, adequate to the task of elaborating the conditions of social continuity.

Some twenty-five years ago, Gunnar Myrdal suggested that the most promising areas for advance in the social sciences were the 'borderlands' between the formal disciplines.[142] Such, the reconstitution of social knowledge within the framework of a wider totalising perspective, had also been the vision of the founding fathers of sociology. Exchange theory is, not without good reason, often associated with economics rather than sociology. Adam Smith took the propensity to barter and exchange as the starting point in his discussion of the division of labour, and the concept has, in one form or another, been central to the theories of virtually every major economist since. Yet the non-appropriating contract of Weber's formally free labour relation and Durkheim's vision of a meritocratic social order based on the equivalent exchange of social services are also core elements in what, as is well known, was largely a response to the intellectual and political challenge of Marxism.

H. Stuart Hughes has spoken of Marx as 'the midwife of twentieth century social thought'. Durkheim, Pareto, Sorel and Croce, he observes, were all in their distinctive ways concerned with Marxism's claim to scientific validity and, through this, to a consideration of what is meant by the very project of a science of society.[143] Their shift of attention from economics to the wider moral and cultural aspects of life in society allowed a 'decontaminated' Marxism, Hughes writes, to be absorbed into the mainstream of European thought.[144] There is much in this account of the intellectual roots of sociology that is still valid. Pareto, for example, both affirmed the 'Marxist' idea of class struggle, but denied its socialistic implications by generalising his conception of class conflict to encompass 'an infinite number of groups with different interests'.[145] With the nature of social interests thus conceived, Pareto could pay lip-service to the 'essential truth' of historical materialism, but at the same time deny any special significance for the relationship between labour and capital.

Yet Hughes minimises the importance of marginalism in the formation of the new synthesis represented by the efforts of Weber and Durkheim. Their approach to class conflict is meaningful only against the changing climate of economic thought. A century earlier, the historians of the French Reformation had located class conflict at the centre of the historical movement. By promoting the social forces of 'civil equality and unfettered industry', Thierry wrote, the bourgeoisie had emerged as a revolutionary agent of change between the medieval strata of nobility and serfdom.[146] Mignet similarly described the division of pre-revolutionary France into hostile provinces and rival classes that inevitably accompanied the survival of feudal distinctions:[147]

> France was in an utter confusion of arbitrary administration, of class legislation and special privileges to special bodies. For these abuses the revolution substituted a system more conformable with justice, and better suited to our times.[148]

But the development of bourgeois society in post-revolutionary France soon belied the expectations of Mignet and Thierry alike in the formal equality of capitalist social relations. It was of course Marx who, on the theoretical basis of the appropriation of surplus value, sought to interpret the laws which seemed to inexorably determine the social reproduction of structured class antagonisms. It was Marx who affirmed that the very existence of these classes is 'only bound up with *particular historic phases in the development of production*'.[149] Both Durkheim and Weber were aware of the inequalities in actual exchange relations within capitalist society, yet both found the conceptual means to depict a non-exploitative nexus of exchange without conceiving of a necessary intermediate historical rupture. At the apparent poles of functionalist and social action thought we thus find a glimpse of social unity, or at least a dynamic equilibrium, behind the sociology of conflict. Lying behind this dual-faceted synthesis we find the unavoidable stimulus of Marxism and the invaluable aid of neo-classical economics.

It is not misleading to view the Durkheimian and Weberian approaches to class conflict from their very inception as replies to the Marxian synthesis, debates with the celebrated ghost. Perhaps we can best conclude by noting the failure of Western capitalist society to either approximate the meritocratic ideal, or attain an enduring substantive rationality of economic activity in the Weberian sense in the long years that stand between the original diagnoses and our own experience. World war, international depression and the resilience of gross material inequality even in the 'happy' phases of economic expansion, have overshadowed the diversification of the sociology of conflict throughout the twentieth century. Finally, of course, Marxism itself has not stood still, but continues to develop as a living and active movement.

Notes and References

Publication details of works cited are given in the Bibliography.

CHAPTER I

1. M. Weber, 'Capitalism and Rural Society in Germany', in H. Gerth and C. W. Mills (eds), (1970), p. 382.
2. M. Weber, *General Economic History* (not dated), p. 227.
3. A. Giddens (1971), p. 164.
4. D. Beetham (1974), p. 242.
5. M. Weber (1968), p. 302. See also parallel definition in ibid., p. 927.
6. Ibid., p. 304.
7. Weber's 'property classes' are structured by the acquisition of expensive consumers' goods, the presence of sales monopoly, the monopolisation of 'wealth accumulation' out of unconsumed surpluses, the monopolisation of capital formation from savings, and the monopolisation of status privileges (ibid., p. 303). The positively privileged incumbents are typically rentiers, and Weber locates their sources of income in the spheres of men (in the case of slave-owners), land, mines, installations and securities. By focusing on income source rather than role in the production process, Weber particularises his conception of class as an aggregative distributive category.

   Again, 'social' classes exist in so far as individuals are able to move freely within a common cluster of class situations. On this criterion, Weber identifies the 'working class as a whole', the property-less intelligentsia and specialists, the petty bourgeoisie and, finally, 'the classes privileged through property and education' as the social-class composition of capitalist society (ibid., p. 305). This four-category schema of social classes is, in essence, a compressed or condensed summary of the principal divisions within his classification of commercial classes. As such, it simply adds the dimension of mobility to his conception of commercial classes, with 'the marketability of goods and services' as its primary determinant.

   Finally, Weber's class typology is augmented by the notion of 'status groups'. He defines status as 'an effective claim to social esteem in terms of positive or negative privileges' (ibid., p. 305). It may or may not correspond to, or 'rest on', class position, and as such is concerned with subjective evaluation in a way that class, in its various forms, is not. But while contending to account for objective structures, Weber's conception of class focuses analytical attention on the surface forms assumed by economic activity within the market system, forms which are immediately accessible to his Verstehen methodology. Thus, the procuring of goods, the gaining of a position in life, and the essentially subjective pursuit of 'inner' satisfaction are central to Weber's general definition of class situation. Class and status, in brief, are essentially complementary and interrelated rather than discrete phenomena in Weber's formal schema, and cannot be said to represent poles along a continuum of objectivity and subjectivity.

8.   Ibid., pp. 13–14.
9.   See R. Bendix and G. Roth (1971), p. 253.
10. 'A Critique of Eduard Meyer's Methodological Views', in Weber (1949), p. 128.
11. Ibid., pp. 128–9.
12. See E. Whittaker (1960), pp. 206–7.
13. 'The Meaning of Ethical Neutrality', in Weber (1949), p. 38.
14. W. Windelband (1958), p. 648–60.
15. W. Dilthey (1961), p. 79. See also P . Hamilton (1974), pp. 90–1 and J. Freund (1972), pp. 37–9.
16. Quoted in W. M. Urban (1949), p. 199.
17. ' "Objectivity" in Social Science and Social Policy', in Weber (1949), p. 74.
18. Ibid., p. 77.
19. Ibid., p. 73.
20. The two stages of analysis implied by this procedure broadly correspond to an academic division of labour envisaged by Weber among the social sciences. Sociology, Weber proposes, is concerned with the formulation and presentation of general principles and generic or ideal concepts in relation to social action. History, by contrast, 'is directed towards the causal analysis and explanation of particular, culturally significant, actions, structures, and personalities' (Weber, (1968), p. 19). The formulation of general principles, while an important and valid general activity in its own right, at least in part takes the form of a means towards the end of reconstructing actual, causal historical sequences. Thus, Weber observes that the task he set himself in *Economy and Society* constitutes 'a very modest preparation' for the study of particular historical phenomena: 'It is then the concern of history to give a causal explanation of these particular characteristics' ('Letter to Georg von Below', 1914), quoted in A. Giddens (1971), p. 146.
21. W. G. Runciman (1972), p. 16.
22. ' "Objectivity" in Social Science and Social Policy', in Weber (1949), p. 93.
23. Ibid., p. 68.
24. Ibid., p. 90.
25. 'Objective Possibility and Adequate Causation in Historical Explanation', in Weber (1949), p. 173.
26. 'The Meaning of Ethical Neutrality', in ibid., pp. 18–19.
27. 'Objective Possibility', in ibid., pp. 169–70.
28. ' "Objectivity" in Social Science', in ibid., p. 84.

29. 'Science as a Vocation', in H. Gerth and C. W. Mills (1970), p. 139.
30. '"Objectivity" in Social Science', in Weber (1949), p. 110.
31. 'Science as a Vocation', in H. Gerth and C. W. Mills (1970), p. 142.
32. Ibid., p. 155.
33. M. Weber (1968), p. 4.
34. Ibid., p. 18.
35. Economic action is defined by Weber as that action which seeks, through peaceful means, to acquire the control of desired utilities (Weber (1968), p. 63). Defined thus, economic action is primarily a market and distributive concept: its objects are goods and services rather than the production relations which define their social character as the products of determinate forms of joint production.
36. H. Gerth and C. W. Mills (1970), p. 133.
37. M. Weber (1957), p. 123.
38. Ibid., p. 123.
39. M. Weber (1970), p. 78.
40. M. Weber (1968), p. 137–8.
41. M. Weber (1970), p. 17.
42. J. E. T. Eldridge (1971*b*), p. 33.
43. Ibid., p. 24.
44. Weber, *General Economic History* (not dated), p. 361.
45. Some of the major criticisms are summarised in P. Honigsheim (1968), pp. 139–41.
46. R. H. Tawney (1938), pp. 283–5.
47. M. Weber (1970), p. 163.
48. M. Weber, *General Economic History* (not dated), pp. 275–6.
49. M. Weber (1968), p. 334.
50. M. Weber (1957), p. 185.
51. Ibid., p. 186.
52. M. Weber (1968), p. 946.
53. Ibid., p. 1111.
54. Ibid., p. 1008.
55. Ibid., p. 975.
56. Ibid., pp. 956–63.
57. H. Marcuse (1968), p. 215.
58. M. Weber (1968), p. 941.
59. C. J. Friedrich, 'Some Observations on Weber's Analysis of Bureaucracy', in R. K. Merton *et al.* (eds), (1964), p. 31.
60. A. W. Gouldner, 'On Weber's Analysis of Bureaucratic Rules', in ibid., p. 48.
61. M. Weber (1968), p. 975.
62. Ibid., p. 998.
63. M. Weber (1957), p. 337.
64. Ibid., p. 333.
65. T. Parsons (1951), p. 67.
66. M. Weber (1968), p. 984.
67. M. Weber *General Economic History* (not dated), p. 338.
68. Ibid., p. 342.

69. Ibid., pp. 347–9.
70. Ibid., pp. 350–2.
71. M. Weber (1968), p. 291. See also ibid., p. 314.
72. Ibid., p. 333.
73. Ibid., p. 334.
74. Ibid., p. 905.
75. Ibid., p. 908.
76. M. Weber (1957), p. 214.
77. We discuss the Marxist conception of class, in particular its supposed 'monofactorial' character, in our critique of C. Wright Mills' analysis of social structure. See Chapter 5, *C. Wright Mills: the Struggle to Make History*.
78. M. Weber (1968), p. 259.
79. Ibid., pp. 107–9.
80. We have paid particular attention to Weber's account of class conflict and the prominence it attains in contemporary society. In our chapter on Talcott Parsons we return to Weber and examine his doctrine of the State and the national interest, both in his general sociology and in his political writings on Germany. Our reason for discussing these themes separately is not a belief that they can be adequately considered independently of one another, but rather a concern to confine our introductory chapter to the formal aspects of Weber's analysis of class structuration as a general guide to the basic Weberian model. Additional substantive issues are examined as our exposition requires.

CHAPTER 2

1. A. Smith (1970), pp. 109–17.
2. Ibid., p. 169.
3. Ibid., p. 184.
4. D. Ricardo (1911), pp. 21 and 80.
5. Ibid., p. 34.
6. Ibid., p. 45.
7. Ibid., p. 75.
8. D. Yaffe (1973), p. 49.
9. Ibid., p. 49.
10. D. Ricardo (1911), pp. 54–5.
11. Appendix D, 'Development of the doctrine of wages', in A. Marshall (1946), pp. 430–1.
12. D. Ricardo (1911), p. 75.
13. A. Smith (1970), pp. 429–33.
14. Ibid., p. 433.
15. Ibid., p. 434.
16. The basic tension in Smith's theory is between the notion of productive labour as that which, when exchanged against capital, produces value, and the ahistorical conception of mere embodiment in a vendible commodity (A. Smith, (1970), pp. 429–30). Marx's analysis of these two

meanings and his rejection of the latter may be found in K. Marx (1969), pp. 69—77.

17. R. L. Meek (1956), pp. 18—44. Pre-Adam Smith labour-value doctrines are discussed in H. R. Sewall (1968), esp. chaps 2 and 3.
18. E. Roll (1938), pp. 128—37.
19. K. Marx (1973*b*), p. 128.
20. A. Smith (1970), p. 133.
21. K. Marx (1972*c*), p. 181.
22. G. Pilling (1972).
23. Quoted in G. Routh (1975), p. 33.
24. D. Ricardo (1951), p. 361.
25. Ibid., pp. 402—4.
26. D. Ricardo (1911), p. 267.
27. Ibid., p. 13.
28. See K. Marx (1972*c*), p. 179.
29. *McCulloch, quoted in ibid., p. 185.*
30. D. Ricardo (1951), pp. 381—2.
31. See J. Foster (1974), p. 107.
32. K. Marx (1972*c*), p. 453.
33. The minutiae of the various nuances in economic theory at this time are discussed in B. B. Seligman (1963), R. L. Meek (1956) and M. Berg (1975). But above all, see Marx's three-volume study *Theories of Surplus Value*, especially Volume 3 (1972*c*) where he traces the outlines of the fragmentation of post-Ricardian political economy.
34. 'On Liberty', in J. S. Mill (1925), pp. 114—21.
35. 'Utilitarianism', in ibid., pp. 5—6.
36. Ibid., pp. 7—9.
37. Ibid., pp. 10—11.
38. Ibid., p. 16.
39. J. S. Mill (1875), p. 220.
40. Ibid., p. 147.
41. Ibid., p. 123.
42. See M. Berg (1975) for some of the theoretical antecedents.
43. J. A. Schumpeter (1959), pp. 493—6.
44. M. Dobb (1937), p. 51.
45. J. A. Schumpeter (1959), p. 740.
46. D. Ricardo (1911), pp. 228—9.
47. V. Gordon Childe (1965), pp. 260—9.
48. Most notable are the works of J. M. Gillman (1965) and P. A. Baran and P. M. Sweezy (1968).
49. In developing his critique of the Narodniks' economic theory and political programme, Lenin attacked Sismondi's analysis of crises on the grounds that he saw their basic cause to lie outside of production, in particular in the limited scope for working-class consumption. The basis of Lenin's critique is the proposition, derived from Marx's reproduction schema in *Capital*, that developing capitalist production 'creates its own market mainly for means of production and not for articles of consumption' (V. I. Lenin, *A Note on the Question of the Market Theory*,

p. 55). Even Sismondi's consumption-dominated analysis did not, however, fundamentally go outside the costs of production-value orientation of the classical school: consumption determines the course of accumulation, but only in so far as the surplus value created in production cannot be effectively realised in the limited sphere of consumption (personal, as opposed to productive consumption) that Sismondi considers (Lenin, *A Characterisation of Economic Romanticism*, 21). Thus conceived, consumption has a quite different role in the total economic process than that envisaged by marginal utility theory.

50. E. H. Chamberlin (1950).
51. D. H. Heathfield (1971).
52. Some of the major positions adopted are discussed in F. Machlup (1950).
53. O. Lange (1950), pp. 181–5.
54. J. M. Cassels (1950). pp. 106–8.
55. C. Menger (1950), pp. 121–3.
56. B. Rowthorn (1974), p. 64.
57. S. Jevons (1970), p. 254.
58. Ibid., pp. 226 and 258.
59. Ibid., p. 104.
60. A. Marshall (1946), pp. 252–3.
61. E. H. Chamberlin (1950), p. 150.
62. Ibid., pp. 149–50.
63. J. Robinson and J. Eatwell (1973). See also M. Dobb, 'The Sraffa System and the Critique of the Neo-Classical Theory of Distribution', in E. K. Hunt and J. G. Schwartz (1972). Still a fine introduction into the general area is N. Bukharin (1972), although his identification of marginal utility theory with the interests of the rentier class fraction is notoriously reductionistic.
64. D. G. Champernowne (1973), pp. 188–9.
65. G. Therborn (1974), pp. 134–5.
66. J. S. Mill (1875), pp. 465–76.
67. A. Bhaduri (1969), p. 534.
68. G. Myrdal (1953), p. 12.
69. M. Weber (1957), p. 159.
70. Ibid., pp. 244–5.
71. Ibid., p. 158.
72. Ibid., p. 163.
73. Ibid., p. 164.
74. Ibid., p. 165.
75. Ibid., p. 193.
76. Ibid., p. 193.
77. Ibid., pp. 101–2.
78. Ibid., p. 191.
79. Ibid., p. 235.
80. Ibid., p. 275.
81. Ibid., p. 169.
82. Ibid., p. 238.
83. Ibid., pp. 246–7.

84. Ibid., p. 192.
85. Ibid., pp. 164–5.
86. Ibid., p. 216.
87. Ibid., p. 278.
88. See previous chapter.
89. M. Weber (1957), pp. 320–1.
90. Ibid., p. 193.
91. Ibid., p. 169.
92. Ibid., p. 221.
93. M. Weber (1949), pp. 43–5.
94. P. Honigsheim (1968), p. 63.
95. Quoted in T. B. Bottomore (1966), p. 48.
96. J. Burnham (1945). See also T. Veblen (1954), very much a precursor of Burnham's ideas.
97. T. H. Marshall (1950), p. 77.
98. B. M. Gross (1966), p. 61.
99. S. M. Lipset and R. Bendix (1959), p. 266.
100. See R. Dahrendorf (1959), pp. 97–100.
101 Lipset and Bendix (1959), p. 73.
102. F. Parkin (1972), p. 14.
103. Ibid., pp. 23 and 123.
104. In particular, he nowhere attempts to theoretically account for the relationship between the two sources of inequality in property and occupation. Their mutual causal significance is left unexplained, is not even recognised as a problem to be theoretically resolved.
105. F. Parkin (1972), p. 18.
106. H. H. Ticktin (1973) describes the growth and increasing differentiation of the technical strata in the Soviet Union. Our concern here, however, is the experience of the capitalist societies.
107. See, for example, D. V. Glass (ed.) (1954), C. W. Mills (1951).
108. E. J. Hobsbawm (1972), p. 286.
109. K. D. George (1971), p. 16.
110. Ibid., p. 17.
111. The definitive scholastic idealisation of this phenomenon is still probably that of W. H. Whyte (1957). By way of complete contrast, Wilensky's study of 108 relatively highly-skilled blue-collar workers and thirty-nine lower white-collar workers in a large parts-supplying factory found that only 45 per cent of the total sample gave any evidence of an ordered progression in status or function over time (H. L. Wilensky, 'Work, Careers and Social Integration, in T. Burns (ed.) (1969).
112. K. Marx (1972a), pp. 369–80.
113. M. Weber (1957), pp. 225–8.
114. Ibid., pp. 228–38.
115. Ibid., p. 247.
116. Weber, *General Economic History* (not dated), pp. 276–8.
117. J. Ure (1973), p. 178.
118. See R. Dahrendorf, 'The Service Class', in T. Burns (ed.) (1969), pp. 141–2.

119. Ibid., pp. 146–7.
120. This skill-based differential market capacity has been elevated into the theoretical model of a 'dual labour market'. See C. Palloix (1976).
121. G. Routh (1965), p. 147.
122. Ibid., p. 148.
123. A. Rees (1961), p. 70.
124. *Politics and Money*, 4, No. 1 (Jan.–March 1973), 30.
125. W. Baldamus (1961), p. 114.
126. Ibid., p. 114.

CHAPTER 3

1. A. Giddens (1973), pp. 105–6.
2. Ibid., p. 19.
3. Ibid., p. 48. See also Giddens (1974).
4. A. Giddens (1973), p. 107.
5. Ibid., p. 221.
6. Ibid., p. 107.
7. Ibid., p. 103.
8. K. Marx (1973c), p. 99.
9. Ibid., p. 99.
10. K. Marx (1967), p. 57.
11. K. Marx (1973c), p. 99.
12. See the selection of passages on this theme, especially from Marx's 'Theories of Surplus Value', in M. Nicolaus (1967).
13. A. Giddens (1971), p. 48.
14. K. Marx (1959), p. 187.
15. K. Marx (1973a), p. 27.
16. A. Giddens (1971), pp. 228–9.
17. K. Marx (1972a), pp. 369–80.
18. K. Marx (1973b), pp. 106–19.
19. Ibid., p. 115.
20. A. Giddens (1973), p. 262.
21. Ibid., p. 141.
22. Ibid., p. 142.
23. Ibid., p. 19.
24. Ibid., p. 280.
25. Ibid., p. 292.
26. Ibid., pp. 156–64.
27. Ibid., p. 292.
28. Ibid., p. 142.
29. The metaphor used by Marx to describe the isolated and socially atomised condition of the nineteenth-century French peasantry (K. Marx, (1954), p. 106).
30. A. Giddens (1971), p. 41.

CHAPTER 4

1. M. Weber (1970), p. 55.
2. Ibid., p. 54.
3. 'Gesammelte Politische Schriften', in G. Roth (1976), p. 314.
4. See Chapter 1.
5. 'The Logic of the Cultural Sciences', in M. Weber (1949), p. 124.
6. M. Weber (1968), p. 8.
7. Ibid., p. 11.
8. Ibid., p. 21.
9. Ibid., p. 4.
10. Cited in G. Roth (1976).
11. M. Weber (1968), p. 18.
12. P. Lassman, 'Phenomenological Perspectives in Sociology', in J. Rex (1974a).
13. A. Schutz (1962), p. 43.
14. Ibid., pp. 5–6.
15. Ibid., pp. 76–7.
16. Ibid., p. 10.
17. A. Schutz and T. Luckmann (1973), pp. 59–61.
18. A. Schutz (1962), pp. 11–12.
19. Ibid., pp. 74–5.
20. See P. Lassman (1974), p. 130.
21. A. Schutz (1962), pp. 38–9.
22. Ibid., p. 36.
23. Ibid., p. 43.
24. Ibid., p. 40.
25. Z. Bauman (1976), p. 44.
26. A. Schutz and T. Luckmann (1973), p. 18.
27. Ibid., pp. 62–4.
28. Ibid., pp. 66–7.
29. Ibid., pp. 69–70.
30. Ibid., p. 80.
31. Ibid., pp. 88–90.
32. Ibid., pp. 91–2.
33. Ibid., pp. 83–4.
34. A. Schutz (1962), pp. 34–5.
35. A. Schutz and T. Luckmann (1973), pp. 66–7.
36. Ibid., p. 68.
37. See, for example, P. Lassman (1974), J. Coulter (1971), A. W. Gouldner (1971).
38. R. Turner, 'Introduction' to R. Turner (ed.) (1974), p. 7.
39. S. Freud (1966), p. 239.
40. Ibid., p. 279.
41. 'The Question of Lay Analysis', in S. Freud (1962), p. 105.
42. H. Garfinkel (1967), p. 1.
43. Ibid., p. 76.
44. Ibid., pp. 41–2.

45. Ibid., p. 3.
46. Ibid., p. 283.
47. Ibid., p. 265.
48. Ibid., pp. 277–9.
49. Ibid., p. 4.
50. Ibid., p. 282.
51. Ibid., p. 31.
52. The story of Agnes is recounted in ibid., pp. 128–84. In a well-known Appendix to *Studies in Ethnomethodology*, Garfinkel reveals that Agnes' account of her biography had in fact been fictitious. Garfinkel adapts to this discovery by terming his own original account a situated report, demonstrating the very qualities of indexicality that ethnomethodology is concerned to explore. In our opinion, this unexpected irony, although widely cited by subsequent commentators, neither adds to nor substracts from Garfinkel's case. If, as Garfinkel maintains, members typically 'talk past' each other in everyday life why, especially when so artful a manipulator as Agnes is involved, should a professional ethnomethodologist be immune from their strategies?
53. Ibid., p. 35.
54. Ibid., p. 33.
55. A. V. Cicourel, 'Basic and Normative Rules in the Negotiation of Status and Roles', in H. P. Dreizel (ed.) (1970), p. 41.
56. R. J. Hill and K. S. Crittenden, (eds) (1968), p. 258.
57. J. Douglas (1967).
58. H. Garfinkel (1967), p. 57.
59. Ibid., pp. 108–12.
60. H. Wagner, 'The Scope of Phenomenological Sociology: Considerations and Suggestions', in G. Psathas, (ed.) (1973).
61. H. Sacks (1963).
62. See Chapter 1 and 7.
63. D. and J. Willer (1973), p. 134.
64. H. Garfinkel (1967), p. 1.
65. P. Winch (1958), pp. 33 and 39.
66. Ibid., p. 44.
67. The quote is from Durkheim's review of A. Labriola's 'Essais sur la conception materialiste de l'histoire', cited in ibid., p. 23.
68. Ibid., p. 23.
69. Ibid., p. 128.
70. See E. Gellner, 'The New Idealism – cause and meaning in the social sciences', in Gellner (1973).
71. J. Goldthorpe (1973).
72. R. G. Lipsey (1970), p. 230.
73. A. W. Gouldner (1971), (1973).
74. J. Rex (1974*b*), p. 10.
75. Ibid., p. 105.
76. J. Rex (1961), pp. 70–3.
77. J. Rex (1974*b*), p. 105.
78. Ibid., pp. 109–11.

79. Ibid., pp. 16–7.
80. Ibid., pp. 15–6.
81. Ibid., pp. 45–6.
82. Ibid., pp. 47–9.
83. Ibid., pp. 49–50.
84. Ibid., pp. 81–2.
85. J. Rex (1961), p. 123.
86. Ibid., p. 123.
87. J. Rex (1973), pp. 3–14.
88. J. Rex (1974b), p. 132.
89. Ibid., pp. 117–8.
90. Ibid., pp. 130–1.
91. Ibid., p. 145.
92. Ibid., pp. 30–1.
93. Ibid., p. 131.
94. Ibid., pp. 230–8.
95. Ibid., p. 250.
96. Ibid., pp. 119–20.
97. Ibid., p. 219.
98. Ibid., p. 250.
99. Ibid., p. 232.

CHAPTER 5

1. J. H. Turner (1973).
2. R. Dahrendorf (1959), pp. 157–65.
3. Ibid., p. 165. For a concise, preliminary version of Dahrendorf's thesis, see R. Dahrendorf (1958).
4. Ibid., p. 158.
5. Ibid., pp. 19–27.
6. Ibid., pp. 10, 12, 21.
7. Ibid., p. 37.
8. Quoted in ibid., p. 13.
9. K. Marx (1972a), p. 157.
10. R. Dahrendorf (1959), p. 33.
11. See M. Nicolaus (1967). This point is discussed in our preceding commentary on Giddens' work.
12. R. Dahrendorf (1959), 34.
13. K. Marx (1972a), pp. 382–3.
14. K. Marx (1959), p. 801.
15. K. Marx (1972a), p. 159.
16. See, for example, C. Hill (1969): 'In most countries official wage rates remained almost unchanged from about 1580–1640, while prices continued to rise.'
17. R. Dahrendorf (1959), pp. 34–5.
18. K. Marx (1972a), p. 448.
19. Sunday Times Weekly Review, 3 March 1974.
20. K. Marx (1972b), p. 13. See also Marx's observations in Capital

concerning the need for a mode of basic economic accounting under at least the first stage of socialism (Marx, (1972a), p. 52.

21. As reference 19.
22. R. Dahrendorf (1959), p. 35.
23. Ibid., p. 76.
24. Ibid., p. 165. See also R. Dahrendorf (1956).
25. R. Dahrendorf (1959), p. 166.
26. Ibid., p. 176.
27. A. Giddens (1973), pp. 53–9.
28. Ibid., p. 72.
29. R. Dahrendorf (1959), p. 195.
30. Ibid., p. 174.
31. Ibid., pp. 197–8.
32. Ibid., p. 168.
33. A. Giddens (1973), p. 73.
34. Ibid., p. 74.
35. R. Dahrendorf (1959), pp. 171–2.
36. This stagnation of workers' incomes is documented in D. Jackson, H. A. Turner and F. Wilkinson (1972).
37. 'Out of Utopia', in Dahrendorf (1968), p. 121.
38. 'Market and Plan', in ibid., p. 169. See also 'Liberty and Equality', in ibid., pp. 202–4.
39. 'On the Origin of Inequality among Men', in ibid., p. 169. See also 'Liberty and Equality', in ibid., pp. 202–4.
40. 'On the 'Origin of Inequality', in ibid., p. 151.
41. 'Market and Plan', in ibid., pp. 225–6.
42. Ibid., p. 225.
43. 'Liberty and Equality', in ibid., p. 205.
44. 'Origin of Inequality', in ibid., p. 171.
45. Ibid., p. 174.
46. R. Dahrendorf (1959), p. 198.
47. Ibid., p. 303.
48. Ibid., p. 306.
49. A. B. Atkinson (1972), p. 21.
50. *Sunday Times*, 24 February 1974.
51. K. Renner (1949), pp. 114–22.
52. K. Marx (1972a), Preface to First Edition, p. 1.
53. 'Homo Sociologicus', in Dahrendorf (1968), pp. 2–39, 68–72.
54. R. Dahrendorf (1959), p. 249.
55. This rejection is quite explicit. See ibid., p. 168.
56. J. S. Mill (1925), p. 121.
57. 'Market and Plan', in Dahrendorf (1968), p. 251.
58. Ibid., p. 217.
59. Sir I. Berlin (1967), p. 141. Maitland, 'Liberty', quoted in E. F. Carritt (1967), p. 133.
60. 'Market and Plan', in Dahrendorf (1968), p. 251.
61. 'Values and Social Science. The Value Dispute in Perspective', in ibid., p. 14.

62. R. Dahrendorf (1959), p. 227.
63. Lecky, 'Democracy and Liberty', quoted in E. F. Carritt (1967), p. 128.
64. E. Burke (1917), p. 145.
65. R. Dahrendorf (1975), p. 49.
66. 'Homo Sociologicus', in Dahrendorf (1968), pp. 75−6.
67. Ibid., p. 79.
68. I. Kant (1959), p. 29.
69. Ibid., p. 53.
70. Ibid., p. 9.
71. Ibid., p. 4.
72. 'Homo Sociologicus', in Dahrendorf (1968), p. 81.
73. Ibid., pp. 85−6.
74. 'Sociology and Human Nature', in ibid., p. 102.
75. 'Origin of Inequality', in ibid., p. 155.
76. J. H. Turner similarly notes that in rejecting Marx's analysis of class interests, Dahrendorf 'forfeits a genuine causal analysis of conflict' (J. H. Turner, (1973), p. 239). Turner's tentative solution is to 'revise' Dahrendorf's schema so as to include 'a series of propositions that indicate the conditions under which legitimatized role relations in imperatively coordinated associations create antagonistic relations of domination and subjection'. Such a reformulation leaves the ideological basis of Dahrendorf's schema untouched, however. Mere internal elaboration of his analysis does nothing to alter the unscientific nature of his conception of class structuration.
77. 'Value and Social Science. The Value Dispute in Perspective', in R. Dahrendorf (1968), p. 17.
78. Ibid., p. 15.
79. This confidential discussion paper is summarised in The Sunday Times, 9 May 1976.
80. R. Dahrendorf (1975), p. 4.
81. R. Dahrendorf (1959), p. 257.
82. R. Hyman (1972), p. 27.
83. R. Dahrendorf (1975), p. 11.
84. Ibid., p. 14.
85. Ibid., p. 46.
86. Ibid., pp. 3−4.
87. Ibid., p. 32.
88. Ibid., p. 24.
89. Ibid., pp. 27−8.
90. Ibid., p. 20.
91. Ibid., p. 81.
92. Ibid., p. 6.
93. Ibid., p. 92.
94. Ibid., p. 96.
95. H. J. Laski (1937), p. 87.
96. R. Dahrendorf (1975), p. 81
97. Politics and Money, 4, No. 1 (Jan−March 1973) 30.
98. R. Dahrendorf (1975), pp. 25−7.

CHAPTER 6

1. L. Horowitz (ed) (1964).
2. See Chapters 3 and 4 respectively.
3. Mills (1967), p. 297.
4. Mills (1970).
5. Another leading oppositional orientation within the academic social studies at this time was the critical theory of the Frankfurt School.
6. Mills (1970), p. 31.
7. Ibid., p. 42.
8. Ibid., pp. 162–71.
9. Ibid., p. 83.
10. 'Two Styles of Social Science Research', in Mills (1967), p. 556.
11. 'The New Left', in ibid., p. 249.
12. Mills (1959), p. 134.
13. Ibid., p. 144.
14. Mills (1970), p. 20.
15. Ibid., p. 168
16. C. S. Peirce (1931–5), 5, para. 2.
17. Ibid., 1, para. 321.
18. Ibid., 5, para. 420.
19. Ibid., 5 para. 402.
20. H. Blumer (1967), p. 139.
21. J. Dewey (1970), p. 218.
22. W. James, 'Pragmatism', in James (1918), p. 199. James' attitude towards religious belief is discussed in A. J. Ayer (1968), pp. 219–23.
23. Ibid., p. 203.
24. J. Dewey (1916), p. 330.
25. James (1918), 'Pragmatism', p. 213.
26. James, 'The Varieties of Religious Experience', in ibid., pp. 254–5.
27. L. Kolakowski (1972), pp. 188–200.
28. Mills (1966), pp. 363–4.
29. J. Dewey (1965), pp. 311–15.
30. Dewey (1970), pp. 219–20.
31. These themes are elaborated and demonstrated in Mills (1966), pp. 375–95.
32. Dewey (1965), p. 307.
33. Ibid., p. 299.
34. Dewey (1960), pp. 286–7.
35. Dewey, 'Freedom and Culture', quoted in Mills (1966), p. 427.
36. Dewey (1929), pp. 255–6.
37. H. Gerth and C. W. Mills (1970), p. 11.
38. Mills, 'Language, Logic and Culture', in Mills (1967), pp. 426–7.
39. Gerth and Mills (1970), p. 274.
40. Mills (1966), p. 467.
41. Mills, 'Language, Logic and Culture', p. 431.
42. 'Situated Actions and Vocabularies of Motives', in Mills (1967), p. 451.

43. 'Language, Logic and Culture', p. 433.
44. Gerth and Mills (1970), p. 277.
45. 'The Cultural Apparatus', in Mills (1967), p. 412.
46. Ibid., p. 405.
47. 'Language, Logic and Culture', p. 425.
48. See K. Marx and F. Engels (1970), especially pp. 50—1.
49. Ibid.,
50. Marx and Engels (1965), G. Plekhanov (1937), p. 72.
51. Mills (1963), pp. 29—30.
52. Gerth and Mills (1970), pp. 288—91.
53. Ibid., p. 294.
54. 'Language, Logic and Culture', pp. 435—6.
55. 'The Sociology of Stratification', in Mills (1967), p. 318.
56. Gerth and Mills (1970), p. 430.
57. 'The Professional Ideology of Social Pathologists', in Mills (1967).
58. 'Culture and Politics', in ibid., p. 238.
59. Mills (1951).
60. 'The Competitive Personality', in Mills (1967), p. 268.
61. Ibid., p. 270.
62. 'The Decline of the Left', in ibid., p. 227.
63. 'The Nazi Behemoth', in ibid., p. 178.
64. 'The New Left', in ibid., p. 251.
65. 'Mass Society and Liberal Education', in ibid., pp. 360—3.
66. 'Man in The Middle: The Designer', in ibid., p. 386.
67. Mills (1956), pp. 360—1.
68. 'Mass Education and Liberal Education', in Mills (1967), pp. 360—3.
69. Ibid., pp. 366—7.
70. 'Liberal Values in the Modern World', in Mills (1967), p. 194.
71. 'The New Left', p. 253.
72. 'Liberal Values in the Modern World', p. 191.
73. 'The Political Gargoyles: Business as Power', in Mills (1967), p. 75.
74. 'On Knowledge and Power', in ibid., p. 613.
75. Mills (1959), p. 144.
76. Ibid., p. 100.
77. See footnote 73.
78. See footnote 63.
79. Mills (1948).
80. 'The Labour Leaders and The Power Elite', in Mills (1967), p. 256.
81. 'The New Left', in ibid., p. 256.
82. Mills (1963), p. 126.
83. 'Two Styles of Social Science Research', pp. 553—4.
84. Ibid., p. 566.
85. Mills (1970), p. 30.
86. Ibid., p. 12.
87. Mills (1970), p. 220.
88. Mills (1963), p. 101.
89. Ibid., p. 105—7.
90. For some central Marxist statements on the question of class, see V. I.

Lenin (1965), p. 421; L. Trotsky (1968), pp. 19–20; and K. Marx (1959), pp. 877–86.

91. Mills (1963), p. 108.
92. Marx (1973a), Chapters 6–9.
93. Mills (1963), p. 108.
94. 'The Problem of Industrial Development', in Mills (1967), p. 150.
95. Ibid., p. 152. The same point is made in Gerth and Mills (1970), pp. 475–9.
96. Mills (1963), p. 119.
97. P. A. Baran (1973), p. 133.
98. Mills (1963), p. 120.
99. H. Marcuse (1964), M. Kidron (1970), P. A. Baran and P. M. Sweezy (1968).
100. Some of these themes are taken up in detail in P. Walton and A. Gamble (1976).
101. Mills (1963), p. 114.
102. K. Marx (1959), p. 244.
103. Mills (1963), pp. 87–8.
104. V. I. Lenin (1972), p. 129. Far from representing an élitist deviation from Marx and Engels' views concerning revolutionary strategy, the Leninist revolutionary party embodies the organisational principles established in *The Communist Manifesto*:

> The Communists are . . . on the one hand, practically, the most advanced and resolute section of the working-class parties of each country, that section which pushes forward all others; on the other hand, theoretically, they have over the great mass of the proletariat the advantage of clearly understanding the line of march, the conditions, and the ultimate general results of the proletarian movement. [Marx and Engels (1967), p. 95]

Lenin's 'What Is To Be Done' develops the implications of the need for theory and decisive organisational forms in the working class in a period when mass social democratic parties had become a significant political force on a world scale. Like Marx and Engels, Lenin insisted that the body of trained revolutionaries can only be of political consequence when it develops deep and organic roots within the masses of the working class. Political substitutionism is not inherent in the Leninist party form.

105. Marx (1972a), p. 45.
106. Mills (1963), p. 88.
107. Marx and Engels (1970), p. 123. (Marx, 'Theses on Feuerbach'.)
108. Mills (1963), pp. 40–1.
109. Marx and Engels (1970), p. 122.
110. Dewey, quoted in Mills (1966), p. 412.
111. See Mills' own critical appraisal of Mead's 'generalized other', in 'Language, Logic and Culture', pp. 426–7.
112. Marx (1973b), p. 107.
113. Ibid., p. 116.
114. Mills (1963), p. 28.

115. Mills (1970), p. 9.
116. 'The Man in The Middle: The Designer', in Mills (1967), p. 386.
117. 'The Decline of the Left', in ibid., p. 235.
118. 'The Social Role of the Intellectual', in ibid., pp. 299–300.
119. 'The Decline of the Left', in ibid., p. 231.
120. Mills (1956), p. 361.
121. See G. R. Morrow (1969), Chapters 4–5.
122. J. S. Mill (1875), p. 575.
123. Marx (1973c), p. 158.
124. Mills (1963), p. 128.
125. Ibid., pp. 128–9, footnote.
126. 'Decline of the Left', p. 235.
127. Mills (1951), p. xvii.
128. Gerth and Mills (1970), p. 13.
129. Mills (1951), p. xvi.
130. Gerth and Mills (1970), p. 480.
131. See the series of appreciative essays in I. L. Horowitz (1964).
132. In this conclusion we disagree with the view that Mills was, in his later writings, approaching a Marxist viewpoint. We hope we have shown, however, that Mills' most basic philosophical and sociological assumptions did not alter in his later studies, even after his conversion to 'Plain Marxism'. For a different interpretation, see I. Deutscher (1971), pp. 68–70.

CHAPTER 7

1. Perhaps the most widely read general critique is that of Gouldner (1971). See also D. Walsh's phenomenological critique (1972).
2. T. Parsons (1968), pp. 719–20.
3. A. Comte (1910), p. 69.
4. R. Fletcher, (ed) (1974), pp. 162–8.
5. Ibid., p. 126.
6. A. Comte (1910), pp. 8–9.
7. Ibid., pp. 402–3.
8. H. Spencer (1915), p. 291.
9. H. Spencer (1894), p. 19.
10. F. W. Hutton (1899), pp. 22–5.
11. C. Darwin (1968), Chapters 1, 2, 3, 4, 10 and 14.
12. Plato (1955), pp. 174–83.
13. N. S. Timasheff (1957), pp. 221–3.
14. E. Durkheim (1962), p. 57.
15. Ibid., p. 88. Spencer similarly denied a complete parallel between societies and biological organisms. The former, in particular, are 'far less specific, far more modifiable, far more dependent on conditions that are never twice alike' (H. Spencer (1894), p. 58). This wide scope for variability of functions in human societies is, ironically, precisely the grounds on which Nagel rejects the classical teleological functionalist

argument as 'in the main very dubious' (E. Nagel (1961), pp. 534–5). Organicist social theory has an uneven and sometimes questionable history, but its principal proponents are in fact innocent of many of the charges directed at them by their popular opponents.

16. E. Durkheim (1964), 226.
17. Ibid., p. 173.
18. Ibid., p. 174.
19. Ibid., p. 227.
20. Appendix A, in T. Parsons and R. F. Bales (1956), pp. 395–9.
21. Ibid., p. 399.
22. See P. Sorokin (1928), Chapter 1.
23. H. Spencer (1894), p. 6.
24. The view expressed by Kingsley Davis (K. Davis (1959), pp. 757–8).
25. See, for example, Pareto's discussion of economic equilibrium, in W. Pareto (1971), pp. 108–10.
26. For a discussion of Parsons's perceived homology between the social system and the planetary system see, for example, T. Parsons and E. A. Shils (1962), pp. 107–8.
27. Ibid., p. 107.
28. T. Parsons (1951), p. 4.
29. Ibid., p. 7.
30. Ibid., p. 19.
31. L. Coser (1965), p. 5.
32. Ibid., pp. 21–2.
33. G. Simmel, 'Soziology', quoted in ibid., p. 10.
34. G. Simmel (1964), pp. 76–8.
35. Ibid., p. 13.
36. A. W. Small (1972), p. 198.
37. R. E. Park (1967), p. 226.
38. L. T. Hobhouse (1966), pp. 207 and 212.
39. Ibid., p. 87.
40. H. Garfinkel (1967), p. 4.
41. D. H. Wrong (1961).
42. T. Parsons (1951), p. 12.
43. Ibid., p. 21.
44. T. Parsons (1968), pp. 635–9.
45. M. Weber (1968), p. 4.
46. T. Parsons (1968), p. 636.
47. T. Parsons (1951), pp. 493–4.
48. Ibid., p. 251.
49. Ibid., p. 297.
50. T. Parsons (1967), p. 394.
51. Ibid., pp. 400–1.
52. T. Parsons and E. A. Shils (1962), pp. 171–2.
53. T. Parsons and R. F. Bales (1956).
54. T. Parsons (1968), p. 291.
55. T. Parsons (1951), p. 321.
56. 'An Analytical Approach to the Theory of Social Stratification', in T.

Parsons (1964), pp. 72–3.

57. 'A Revised Analytical Approach to the Theory of Social Stratification', in Ibid., p. 388.

58. K. Davis and W. E. Moore (1945), pp. 242–3.

59. B. Barber (1957), p. 9.

60. M. Tumin (1953), p. 393.

61. E. Durkheim (1964), pp. 380–1. The meritocratic theme in Durkheim's work is examined in P. Walton, I. Taylor and J. Young (1973).

62. R. D. Schwarz (1955).

63. Thus, Schwarz's comparative study of two Israeli kibbutzim, while concluding that both communities have developed egalitarian ways to fill socially important positions, assesses their success in terms of system integration, measured by the technical effectiveness with which positions are filled (R. D. Schwarz (1955), p. 430).

64. 'On the Concept of Political Power', in Parsons (1967), p. 324.

65. T. Parsons (1960), p. 113.

66. Ibid., p. 113.

67. J. K. Galbraith (1969), p. 128.

68. H. I. Ansoff (1968), p. 44.

69. K. Marx (1959), p. 370.

70. Monopoly trends became increasingly pronounced during the last quarter of the nineteenth century. A. Hunter's detailed empirical analysis identifies a decisive merger boom in the United States during 1879–1903 and in Britain between 1898–1904. Hunter concludes that the mergers of this period 'crystallized the industrial structures of the United States and Britain into a concentration pattern that persists to the present day' (A. Hunter (1969), p. 100).

71. J. Burnham (1945).

72. S. Aaronovitch and P. Sawyer (1974), p. 15.

73. B. Rowthorn (1971), p. 42, from Table 12.

74. A. Peaker (1974), pp. 7–11.

75. M. Burrage (1973).

76. *National Institute Economic Review*, 71 (Feb. 1975), 14, from Table 4.

77. For Britain, A. Glyn and B. Sutcliffe document a fall in the post-tax rate of profit in the industrial and commercial sectors from 6·7 per cent to 4·1 per cent over 1950–60 (Glyn and Sutcliffe (1972), p. 66). Comparable declines are reported by J. L. Walker (1974), p. xli; M. Panic and R. E. Close (1973), p. 25; and G. W. Burges and A. J. Webb (1974). Some of the theoretical and methodological issues raised by the relatively minor variations between these studies are discussed in my unpublished M.Litt. thesis, *Sociology and the State. Some Recent Theories, with special reference to post-war Britain*, University of Glasgow, 1976. Despite often heated controversies, however, an informed consensus on the steadily downward drift of profits in British industry has emerged since the late 1960s. For a systematic analysis of the similar trend in the United States, see W. D. Nordhaus (1974).

78. 'Evolutionary Universals in Society', in T. Parsons (1964), p. 503.

79. Ibid., p. 508.

80. K. Marx (1973*b*), pp. 165–6.
81. T. Parsons (1951), p. 62.
82. I. Kant (1959*b*), p. 56.
83. K. Marx (1973*b*), p. 166.
84. E. Preiser (1971), p. 130.
85. F. Parkin (1972), pp. 81–2.
86. See our discussion of ideology and revolutionary consciousness in Chapter 6.
87. The library shelves are stacked with studies of working-class communities, old and new. Perhaps the most valuable from the point of view of the relation between social conditions and consciousness is N. Dennis, F. Henriques and C. Slaughter's study (1969) of a Yorkshire coalmining community.
88. T. Parsons (1951), p. 120.
89. Ibid., p. 120.
90. Ibid., p. 121.
91. Ibid., p. 123.
92. Ibid., p. 126.
93. 'On the Concept of Political Power', in Parsons (1967), p. 301
94. Ibid., p. 303.
95. 'The Distribution of Power in American Society', in Parsons (1969)', 199.
96. 'On the Concept of Political Power', p. 306.
97. G. Simmel (1964).
98. 'Some Reflections on the Place of Force in Social Process', in Parsons (1967), p. 295.
99. T. Parsons (1951), p. 126.
100. 'Certain Primary Sources and Patterns of Aggression in the Social Structure in the Western World', in Parsons (1967), pp. 311–14.
101. 'Some Comments on the Sociology of Karl Marx', in Ibid., p. 303.
102. 'An Analytical Approach to the Theory of Social Stratification', in Parsons (1964), pp. 76–83. See also 'Social Classes and Class Conflict in the Light of Recent Sociological Theory', in ibid., pp. 326–7.
103. Parsons thus writes:

> (The)... dominant pattern of the occupational sphere requires at least a relatively high degree of 'equality of opportunity', which in turn means that status cannot be determined primarily by birth or membership in kinship units. ['An Analytical Approach', pp. 78–9']

104. Ibid., p. 83.
105. C. W. Mills (1956), J. K. Galbraith (1969).
106. G. W. Domhoff (1967), p. 44.
107. Alexis de Tocqueville (1956), p. 52.
108. Quoted in S. Bruchey (1965), p. 65.
109. De Tocqueville (1956), pp. 226–8.
110. S. Bruchey (1965), pp. 194–201.
111. The recorded income share of the richest 10 per cent of North Americans varied little between 1910 and 1959 (34 per cent and 29 per cent of total

respectively), while that of the poorest fifth substantially declined over the fifty years prior to 1963 (G. Kolko (1962), p. 14). See also G. W. Domhoff (1967).

112. C. B. Macpherson (1962), pp. 46–68.
113. M. Weber (1968), p. 941.
114. Ibid., 139.
115. Ibid., pp. 13–18.
116. T. Parsons (1968), p. 652.
117. M. Weber (1968), pp. 24–6.
118. 'A Critique of Eduard Meyer's Methodological Views', in M. Weber (1949), p. 124.
119. M. Weber (1968), p. 53.
120. T. Parsons, 'Evolutionary Universals in Society', in Parsons (1964).
121. Weber's methodological and philosophical assumptions are discussed in greater detail in Chapter 1.
122. H. Gerth and C. W. Mills (1970), p. 55, footnote.
123. M. Weber (1968), p. 938.
124. 'Speech for the General Information of Austrian Officers in Vienna', in J. E. T. Eldrige (ed.) 1971b), p. 219.
125. Weber's political writings and speeches are examined in some detail in D. Beetham (1974). See also W. J. Mommsen (1974), J. P. Mayer (1956) and K. Jaspers (1965).
126. 'The Meaning of Ethical Neutrality', in Weber (1949), pp. 26–7.
127. Quoted in J. P. Mayer (1956), p. 41.
128. 'Gesammelte Politische Schriften', quoted in W. J. Mommsen (1974), p. 32.
129. W. J. Mommsen (1974), pp. 112–13.
130. Gesammelte Politische Schriften', quoted in D. Beetham (1974), p. 106.
131. R. Aron (1964), p. 88.
132. J. P. Mayer (1956), p. 91.
133. 'Politics as a Vocation', H. H. Gerth and C. W. Mills (1970), pp. 77–8.
134. M. Weber (1968), p. 922.
135. Ibid., p. 925.
136. Ibid., p. 926.
137. Ibid., pp. 905–9.
138. Ibid., pp. 921–2.
139. Ibid., p. 98.
140. D. Beetham (1974), p. 173.
141. M. Weber (1968), p. 994.
142. Ibid., 1460.
143. 'Speech for... Austrian Officers', p. 215.

CHAPTER 8

1. V. G. Childe (1965), pp. 206–10.
2. A. R. and M. B. Hall (1964), p. 19.
3. Ibid., p. 22.

4. Plato (1955), p. 103.
5. Ibid., p. 167.
6. Ibid., pp. 336–7.
7. Ibid., pp. 236–7.
8. Plato (1965), p. 70.
9. Ibid., p. 65.
10. Ibid., p. 81.
11. Plato (1955), p. 183.
12. Ibid. pp. 160–1.
13. Frankfurt Institute for Social Research (1973), p. 18.
14. Plato (1955), p. 103.
15. Ibid., pp. 102–6.
16. Aristotle (1912), p. 7.
17. See J. D. Bernal (1969), pp. 223–34.
18. Aristotle (1912), p. 29.
19. Ibid., p. 19.
20. Ibid., pp. 8–9.
21. Ibid., p. 18.
22. Ibid., pp. 78–9.
23. Ibid., p. 127.
24. 'Ethics', Book 6, in Aristotle (1963), p. 347.
25. See, for example, Aristotle's reified account of social relations within the city (Aristotle (1912), p. 4).
26. G. Leff (1958) gives a useful account of both the continuity and the controversy of this period.
27. 'Novum Organum', in F. Bacon (1892), pp. 256–7.
28. Ibid., p. 290.
29. 'Of Atheism', in ibid., pp. 25–6.
30. Descartes, *Discourse on Method*, not dated, p. 11.
31. Ibid., p. 141.
32. Ibid., pp. 73–4.
33. Ibid., p. 22.
34. Ibid., p. 23.
35. 'Letter to the Grand Duchess Christiana', in Galileo (1957), p. 183.
36. See C. Singer (1959), pp. 170–1.
37. *Discourse on Method*, not dated, p. 69.
38. T. Hobbes (1914), p. 28.
39. 'De Corpore Politico', in M. Hollis (ed.) (1973), pp. 183–4.
40. Hobbes (1914), p. 63.
41. Ibid., p. 49.
42. Ibid., pp. 87–90.
43. In *Behemoth*, Hobbes suggests that the chief instigators of the civil war were 'ambitious ministers and ambitious gentlemen' who challenged the authority of church and state respectively (Hobbes (1969), p. 23).
44. Hobbes (1914), p. 64.
45. De Corpore Politico', in Hobbes (1962), p. 282.
46. Lord Herbert of Charbury, 'De Verita', in M. Hollis (ed.) (1973), p. 42.
47. Ibid., p. 44.

48. 'Of Civil Government', Book 2, in J. Locke (1963), 5, p. 394.
49. Ibid., pp. 353–4.
50. Ibid., pp. 366–7.
51. Ibid., p. 388. The magistrate, Locke contended, is obliged by 'the laws of public justice and equity' to guarantee the 'just possession' of the money, land and property of his subjects ('A Letter Concerning Toleration', in Locke (1963), 6, p. 10).
52. Locke, *Essay Concerning Human Understanding*, not dated, p. 281.
53. Ibid., pp. 59–61, 141–4, 443–6.
54. 'Some Thoughts Concerning Education', in Locke (1963), 9, p. 7.
55. D'Alembert (1963), pp. 83–6.
56. Ibid., p. 122.
57. 'Of Civil Government', Book 2, in Locke (1963), vol. 5.
58. C. L. Becker (1932), p. 39.
59. Voltaire (1961), p. 40.
60. Montesquieu (1902), I, p. 348.
61. C. L. Becker (1932), Chapter 3. See also H. Vyverberg (1958), Chapter 10 for a helpful discussion of the views held by Turgot and Condorcet on historical progress.
62. E. Gibbon (1892), 2, pp. 1025–38.
63. 'The Social Contract', in Rousseau (1913), p. 73.
64. E. Gibbon (1892), 2, p. 1033.
65. Ibid., p. 1038.
66. See the relevant readings in D. D. Raphael (1969), 1.
67. Locke, *Essay Concerning Human Understanding*, not dated, p. 160.
68. Richard Cumberland, 'De Legibus Naturae', in D. D. Raphael (1969), 1, p. 91.
69. An Inquiry Concerning the Principles of Morals', in D. Hume *Essays*, not dated, p. 486.
70. Ibid., p. 423.
71. Ibid., p. 419.
72. Mandeville (1970), p. 64.
73. O. Gierke (1934), pp. 35–9. On the history of natural law doctrines, see also A. P. D'Entrèves (1970).
74. Morelly 'Code de la Nature', quoted from C. H. Driver (1930).
75. M. De Mirabaud (Baron D'Holbach) (1834), 2, p. 309.
76. Ibid., p. 312.
77. See E. G. Barber (1967), pp. 99–140.
78. Voltaire (1966), p. 356.
79. Rousseau advocated a compulsory civil religion, comprising of a few simple principles and presented 'without explanation or commentary', in order to ensure that each citizen will 'love his country' ('The Social Contract', in Rousseau, 1913, pp. 113–14). Such a resort, however minimal, to a socially binding and obligatory theological creed was hardly consistent with the more radical enlightenment claims for the power of reason in social life. With the already mentioned notable exception of Morelly, the philosophes saw reason as the preserve of an elect élite, and the lower classes were to share its social benefits rather

than effect its realisation.

80. D'Alembert (1963), p. 62.
81. Voltaire (1966), p. 353.
82. Ibid., p. 356.
83. Quoted in P. Gay (1970), p. 512.
84. G. Plekhanov (1956), Chapter 1.
85. M. De Mirabaud (D'Holbach) (1834), 1, p. 9.
86. Ibid., p. 13.
87. 'Discourse on the Arts and Sciences', in Rousseau (1913), p. 131.
88. Ibid., p. 129.
89. 'The Origin of Inequality', in ibid., p. 192.
90. 'The Social Contract', in ibid., pp. 22–3.
91. 'A Discourse on Political Economy', in ibid., p. 236.
92. 'The Social Contract', in ibid., p. 12.
93. Montesquieu (1902), 2, p. 253.
94. F. Engels (1934), p. 23.
95. Montesquieu (1902), 1 and 2.
96. See E. Durkheim (1967), p. 165.
97. A. Comte, 'A Plan of the Scientific Operations Necessary for Reorganiz-ing Society', in R. Fletcher (ed.) (1974), p. II.
98. A. Comte (1877), 2, p. 125.
99. A Comte (1910), p. 49.
100. Ibid., p. 411.
101. Ibid., pp. 411–12.
102. Ibid., p. 145.
103. Ibid., pp. 143–4.
104. A. Gouldner, 'Introduction' to E. Durkheim (1967), pp. 23–6.
105. A. Comte (1910), p. 143.
106. H. Spencer (1894), p. 53.
107. Ibid., p. 35.
108. 'Individual and Collective Representations', in E. Durkheim (1953), p. 29.
109. E. Durkheim (1952), p. 38.
110. A. Giddens (1971), p. 89.
111. 'Individual and Collective Representations', in E. Durkheim (1953), p. 34.
112. E. Durkheim (1962), p. 145.
113. E. Durkheim (1964), p. 227.
114. Ibid., p. 174.
115. Ibid., p. 179.
116. Ibid., p. 182.
117. Ibid., p. 173.
118. Ibid., p. 174.
119. Ibid., p. 40.
120. Ibid., p. 360.
121. 'The Principles of 1789 and Sociology', in Durkheim (1973), pp. 35–41.
122. Durkheim (1964), pp. 380–1.
123. The meritocratic theme in Durkheim's work is examined in more detail

in P. Walton, I. Taylor and J. Young (1973).

124. 'Individualism and the Intellectuals', in Durkheim (1973), p. 45.
125. Ibid., p. 49.
126. Durkheim (1964), pp. 387–8.
127. R. N. Bellah, 'Introduction' to Durkheim (1973), p. xiv.
128. 'If political economy as a subject has progressed further than sociology, this is to a large extent due to the fact that its concern is with logical actions' ('Treatise on General Sociology', in W. Pareto (1966), p. 196.
129. Durkheim (1964), p. 386.
130. Ibid., p. 382.
131. Ibid., p. 384.
132. Ibid., p. 370.
133. Ibid., p. 377.
134. Ibid., p. 374–81.
135. Ibid., p. 25, footnote.
136. Ibid., p. 179.
137. Although Durkheim far from implied a literal identity between the two types of organism. He contrasted, for example, the relative constancy of biological species to the potential for the rapid development of new types of organisation within the social realm (Durkheim (1962), p. 88).
138. Durkheim (1964), p. 386.
139. Ibid., p. 387. Durkheim elsewhere makes the same point in even stronger terms: ' . . . society is nature arrived at a higher point in its development, concentrating all its energies to surpass, as it were, itself' ('Value Judgements and Judgements of Reality', in Durkheim (1953), p. 97).
140. M. Weber, 'On Law in Economy and Society', in J. E. T. Eldridge (ed.) (1971b), pp. 174–84.
141. By the mid-nineteenth century the concept of a social Law of nature was under attack from a number of directions. Sir Henry Maine, for example, questioned the historical basis of such a law, characterising it as 'a superstition of the lawyers' (Ancient Law, pp. 51–3). While Maine noted the important part played by the law of nature in the development of international law, his thesis of the increasingly dominant influence of contract in history directed attention away from immutable natural laws towards the historically specific forms of contractual relations. The achievement of Weber and Durkheim was to systematically define the terms of sociology in the absence of this once revolutionary, but now transparently ideological, body of ideas.
142. G. Myrdal (1953), p. 155.
143. H. Stuart Hughes (1967), p. 74.
144. Ibid., pp. 96–7.
145. 'Les Systèmes Socialistes', in W. Pareto (1966), p. 140.
146. Thierry (1859), pp. 42–3.
147. A. Mignet (1868), pp. 1–20.
148. Ibid., p. 2.
149. 'Letter to Weydemeyer, 5 March, 1852', in K. Marx and F. Engels (1965), p. 57.

Bibliography

Aaronovitch, S. and Sawyer, P. (1974), '*The Concentration of British Manufacturing*', *Lloyd's Bank Review*, no. 114.

Abendroth, W. (1972), *A Short History of the European Working Class* (London, New Left Books).

Andrewes, A. (1971), *Greek Society* (Harmondsworth, Penguin).

Ansoff, H. I. (1968), *Corporate Strategy* (Harmondsworth, Penguin).

Aristotle, (1912), *A Treatise on Government* (London, Dent and Sons).

—— (1963), *The Philosophy of Aristotle*, ed. R. Bambrough (London, New English Library).

Aron, R. (1964), *German Sociology* (New York, The Free Press of Glencoe).

Atkinson, A. B. (1972), *Unequal Shares* (London, Allen Lane).

Ayer, A. J. (1968), *Studies in Pragmatism* (London, Macmillan).

Bacon, Francis (1892), *Essays, Advancement of Learning, Novum Organum* (Ward Lock and Bowden and Co.).

Baldamus, W. (1961), *Efficiency and Effort. An Analysis of Industrial Administration* (London, Tavistock).

Baran, P. A. and Sweezy, P. M. (1968), *Monopoly Capital* (Harmondsworth, Penguin).

Baran, P. A. (1973), *The Political Economy of Growth* (Harmondsworth, Penguin).

Barber, B. (1957), *Social Stratification*, (New York, Harcourt, Brace and Wold).

Barber, E. G. (1967), *The Bourgeoisie in France* (Princeton University Press).

Bauman, Z. (1976), *Towards a Critical Sociology* (London, Routledge and Kegan Paul).

Becker, C. L. (1932), *The Heavenly City of the Eighteenth Century Philosophers* (New York, Yale University Press).

Beetham, D. (1974), *Max Weber and the Theory of Modern Politics* (London, Allen and Unwin).

Bendix, R. and Roth, G. (1971), *Scholarship and Partisanship: Essays on Max Weber* (Berkeley, University of California Press).

Berg, M. (1975), 'Vulgar Economy and Marx's Critics', in *Bulletin of the Conference of Socialist Economists*, 4, no. 2.

Berlin, I. (1967), *Two Concepts of Liberty*, reprinted in A. Quinton (ed), *Political Philosophy* (1967) (London, Oxford University Press).

Bernal, J. D. (1969), *Science in History, Vol. 1. The Emergence of Science* (Harmondsworth, Penguin).

Bhaduri, A. (1969), 'On the Significance of Recent Controversies on Capital Theory: A Marxian View' *Economic Journal*, 79.

Blumer, H. (1967), 'Society as Symbolic Interaction', in J. G. Manis and B. N. Meltzer (eds), *Symbolic Interaction. A Reader in Social Psychology* (Boston, Allyn and Bacon).

Bottomore, T. B. (1966), *Elites and Society* (Harmondsworth, Penguin).

Bruchey, S. (1965), *The Roots of American Economic Growth 1607–1861. An Essay in Social Causation* (London, University Library).

Bukharin, N. (1972), *Economic Theory of the Leisure Class*, (New York, Monthly Review Press).

Burgess, G. W. and Webb, A. J. (1974), 'The Profits of British Industry', *Lloyd's Bank Review*, 112 (April).

Burke, E. (1917), *Reflections on the Revolution in France*, (London, University Tutorial Press).

Burnham, J. (1945), *The Managerial Revolution* (Harmondsworth, Penguin).

Burns, T. ed. (1969), *Industrial Man* (Harmondsworth, Penguin).

Burrage, M. (1973), 'Nationalization and the Professional Ideal, *Sociology*, 7.

Carritt E. F. (1967), *Liberty and Equality*, in A. Quinton, op. cit.

Cassels, J. M. (1950), 'On the Law of Variable Proportions, in *American Economic Association Readings in the Theory of Distribution* (London, Allen and Unwin).

Chamberlin, E. H. (1950), 'Monopolistic Competition and the Productivity Theory of Distribution', *American Economic Association*.

Champernowne, D. G. (1973), *The Distribution of Income between Persons* (Cambridge University Press).

Childe, V. Gordon (1965), *What happened in History* (Harmondsworth, Penguin).

Clark, J. M. (1950), 'Distribution', in *American Economic Association*.

Comte, A. (1970), *Republic of the West. Order and Progress. A general view of Positivism* (London, Routledge).

—— (1877), *System of Positive Polity*, Franklin Philosophy Monograph Series, 4 vols, reprint of 1877 editions.

Coser, L. (1965), *George Simmel* (New Jersey, Prentice Hall Inc.).

Coulter, J. (1971), 'Decontextualised Meanings: Current Approaches to Verstehende Sociology, *Sociological Review*, 19.

Dahrendorf, R. (1956), 'Social Structure, Class Interests and Social Conflict, *Transactions of the Third World Congress of Sociology*, 3.

—— (1958), 'Toward a Theory of Social Conflict, *Journal of Conflict Resolution*, 2.

—— (1959), *Class and Class Conflict in an Industrial Society* (London, Routledge and Kegan Paul).

—— (1967), *Conflict After Class; New Perspectives in the Theory of Social and Political Conflict* (London, Longmans).

—— (1968), *Essays in the Theory of Society* (London, Routledge and Kegan Paul).

—— (1969), 'The Service Class', in T. Burns (ed), op. cit.

—— (1975), *The New Liberty. Survival and Justice in a Changing World* (London, Routledge and Kegan Paul).

D'Alembert (1963), *Preliminary Discourse to the Encyclopedia of Diderot* (New York, Bobbs-Merrill).

Darwin, C. (1968), *The Origin of Species* (Harmondsworth, Penguin).

Davis, K. (1959), 'The Myth of Functional Analysis as a Special Method in Sociology and Anthropology, *American Sociological Review*, 24.

Davis, K. and Moore, W. E. (1945), 'Some Principles of Stratification, *American Sociological Review*, 10.

Dennis, N. Henriques, F. and Slaughter, C. (1969), *Coal is Our Life. An Analysis of a Yorkshire Mining Community* (London, Tavistock Publications).

Descartes, R. (not dated), *The Discourse on Method and Metaphysical Meditations* (London, Scott).

Deutscher, I. (1971), *Marxism in our Time* (Berkeley, Ramparts Press).

Dewey, J. (1916), *Essays in Experimental Logic* (University of Chicago).

—— (1929), *Quest for Certainty* (New York, Putnam).

—— (1960), *On Experience, Nature and Freedom*, ed. R. J. Bernstein (New York, Bobbs-Merrill).

—— (1965), *Philosophy, Psychology and Social Practice*, ed. J. Ratner (New York, Capricorn Books).

—— (1970), 'Logic, The Theory of Enquiry', extract in D. P. Verne, *Man and Culture, A Philosophical Anthropology* (New York, Laurel).

Dilthey, W. (1961), *Meaning in History. W. Dilthey's Thoughts on History and Society*, ed. H. P. Rickmann (London, Allen and Unwin).

Dobb, M. (1937), *Political Economy and Capitalism* (London, Routledge).

Domhoff, G. W. (1967), *Who Rules America?* (New Jersey, Prentice-Hall).

Douglas, J. (1967), *The Social Meanings of Suicide* (Princeton University Press).

Dreizel, H. P. (ed) (1970), *Recent Sociology No. 2. Patterns of Communicative Behaviour* (London, Collier-Macmillan Ltd).

Driver, C. H. (1930), 'Morelly and Mably', in F. J. C. Hearnshaw, ed,

The Social and Political Ideas of Some Great French Thinkers of the Age of Reason (London, George Harrap and Co. Ltd).

Durkheim, E. (1952), *Suicide. A Study in Sociology* (London, Routledge and Kegan Paul).

—— (1953), *Sociology and Philosophy* (London, Cohen and West).

—— (1956), *Education and Sociology* (New York, Free Press).

—— (1960),*Montesquieu and Rousseau. Forerunners of Sociology* (University of Michigan Press).

—— (1962), *The Rules of Sociological Method* (New York, Free Press of Glencoe).

—— (1964), *The Division of Labour in Society* (New York, Free Press of Glencoe).

—— (1967), *Socialism*, ed. A. W. Gouldner (London, Collier-Macmillan).

—— (1973), *On Morality and Society*, ed. R. N. Bellah (University of Chicago Press).

Ehrenberg, V. (1968), *From Solon to Socrates* (London, Methuen).

Eldridge, J. E. T. (1971a), *Sociology and Industrial Life* (London, Nelson).

—— (1971b), *Max Weber. The Interpretation of Social Reality*, (London, Michael Joseph).

Engels, F. (1934), *Anti Dühring*, (London, Martin Lawrence).

d'Entrèves, A. P. (1970), *Natural Law* (London, Hutchinson University Library).

Ferguson, A. (1966), *An Essay on the History of Civil Society* (Edinburgh, The University Press).

Filmer, P. *et al.* (1972), *New Directions in Sociological Theory* (London, Collier-Macmillan).

Fletcher, R. (ed.) (1974), *The Crisis of Industrial Civilization. The Early Essays of Auguste Comte* (London, Heinemann Educational Books).

Foster, J. (1974), *Class Struggle and the Industrial Revolution* (London, Weidenfeld and Nicolson).

The Frankfurt Institute for Social Research (1973), *Aspects of Sociology* (London, Heinemann Educational Books).

Freud, S. (1962), *Two Short Accounts of Psychoanalysis* (Harmondsworth, Penguin).

—— (1966), *The Psychopathology of Everyday Life* (London, Ernest Benn).

Freund, J. (1972), *The Sociology of Max Weber* (Harmondsworth, Penguin).

Friedrich, C. J. (ed.) (1954), *The Philosophy of Hegel* (New York, Random House).

Galbraith, J. K. (1969), *The New Industrial State* (Harmondsworth, Penguin).

Galileo (1957), *Discoveries and Opinions of Galileo*, ed. S. Drake (New York, Doubleday).

Garfinkel, H. (1967), *Studies in Ethnomethodology* (Englewood Cliffs, Prentice-Hall).

Gay, P. (1970), *The Enlightenment: An Interpretation. Vol. 2. The Science of Freedom* (London, Weidenfeld and Nicolson).

Gellner, E. (1973), *Cause and Meaning in the Social Sciences* (London, Routledge and Kegan Paul).

George, K. D. (1971), *Industrial Organization. Competition, growth and structural change in Britain* (London, Allen and Unwin).

Gerth, H. and Mills, C. W. (1970), *Character and Social Structure. The Psychology of Social Institutions* (London, Routledge and Kegan Paul).

Gibbon, E. (1892), *The History of the Decline and Fall of the Roman Empire, Vol. 2* (London, Routledge).

Giddens, A. (1971), *Capitalism and Modern Social Theory* (Cambridge).

—— (1973), *The Class Structure of the Advanced Societies* (London, Hutchinson and Co.).

—— (1974), 'Elites in the British Class Structure', in P. Stanworth and A. Giddens, *Elites and Power in British Society* (Cambridge).

Gierke, O. (1934), *Natural Law and the Theory of Society* (The University Press, Cambridge)

Gillman, J. M. (1965), *Prosperity in Crisis* (Marzani and Munsell).

Glass, D. V. (ed.) (1954). *Social Mobility in Britain* (London, Routledge and Kegan Paul).

Glyn, A. and Sutcliffe, B. (1972), *British Capitalism, Workers and the Profits Squeeze* (Harmondsworth, Penguin).

Goldthorpe, J. H. (1973), 'A Revolution in Sociology?', *Sociology*, 7, no. 3.

Gouldner, A. W. (1971), *The Coming Crisis of Western Sociology* (London, Heinemann).

—— (1973), *For Sociology. Renewal and Critique in Sociology Today* (London, Allen Lane).

Gross, B. M. (1966), *The State of the Nation. Social Systems Accounting* (London, Tavistock Publications).

Hall, A. R. and B. M. (1964), *A Brief History of Science* (New York, Signet).

Hamilton, P. (1974), *Knowledge and Social Structure* (London, Routledge and Kegan Paul).

Heathfield, D. H. (1971), *Production Functions* (London, Macmillan).

Hill, C. (1969), *Reformation to Industrial Revolution* (Harmondsworth, Penguin).

Hill, R. J. and Crittenden, K. S. (1968). *Proceedings of the Purdue Symposium on Ethnomethodology* (Purdue University).

242 BIBLIOGRAPHY

Hobbes, T. (1914), *Leviathan* (London, Dent and Sons).
—— (1962), *Body, Man and Citizen*, ed. R. S. Peters (New York, Collier Books).
—— (1969), *Behemoth Or the Long Parliament*, ed. F. Toënnies (London, Frank Cass).
Hobhouse, L. T. (1966), *Social Development, its Nature and Conditions* (London, Allen and Unwin).
Hobsbawm, E. J. (1972), *Industry and Empire* (Harmondsworth, Penguin).
Hollis, M. (ed.) (1973), *The Light of Reason. Rationalist Philosophers of the Seventeenth Century* (London, Fontana-Collins).
Honigsheim, P. (1968), *On Max Weber* (New York, Free Press).
Horowitz, I. L. (1964), *The New Sociology. Essays in Social Science and Social Theory in Honor of C. Wright Mills* (New York, Oxford University Press).
Hughes, H. S. (1967), *Consciousness and Society. The Reorientation of European Social Thought, 1890-1930* (London, MacGibbon and Kee).
Hume, D., *Essays. Literary, Moral and Political* (London, not dated, George Routledge and Sons).
Hunt, E. K. and Schwartz, J. G. (eds) (1972), *A Critique of Economic Theory* (Harmondsworth, Penguin).
Hunter, A. (1969), 'The Measurement of Monopoly Power', in A. Hunter (ed.), *Monopoly and Competition* (Harmondsworth, Penguin).
Hutton, F. W. (1899), *Darwinism and Lamarckism* (London, Duckworth and Co.).
Hyman, R. (1972), *Strikes* (London, Fontana-Collins).
Jackson, D., Turner, H. A. and Wilkinson, F. (1972), *Do Trade Unions Cause Inflation?* (University of Cambridge Department of Applied Economics. Occasional Paper 36, Cambridge University Press).
James, W. (1918), *Papers on Philosophy* (London, Dent and Sons).
Jaspers, K. (1965), 'Max Weber as Politician, Scientist and Philosopher', in *Leonardo, Descartes, Max Weber* (London, Routledge and Kegan Paul).
Jevons, S. (1970), *The Theory of Political Economy* (Harmondsworth, Penguin).
Kant, I. (1959a), *Critique of Pure Reason* (London, Dent and Sons).
—— (1959b), *Foundations of the Metaphysics of Morals* (Indianapolis, Bobbs-Merrill).
Kidron, M. (1970), *Western Capitalism Since The War* (Harmondsworth, Penguin).
Kolakowski, L. 1972), *Positivist Philosophy. From Hume to the Vienna Circle* (Harmondsworth, Penguin).
Kolko, G. (1962), *Wealth and Power in America* (New York, Praeger).

Lange, O. (1950), 'A Note on Innovations', in *American Economic Association*.

Laski, H. J. (1937), *Liberty in the Modern State* (Harmondsworth, Penguin).

Lassman, P. (1974), 'Phenomenological Perspectives in Sociology', in J. Rex (ed.) (1974*a*).

Leff, G. (1958), *Medieval Thought. St. Augustine to Ockham* (Harmondsworth, Penguin).

Lenin, V. I. (1965), 'A Great Beginning', in *Collected Works*, 29 (London, Lawrence and Wishart).

—— (1971), *A Characterisation of Economic Romanticism* (Moscow, Progress Publishers).

—— (1972*a*), *What is to be Done?* (Peking, Foreign Languages Press).

—— (1972*b*), A Note on the Question of the Market Theory, in *Collected Works*, 4 (London, Lawrence and Wishart).

Lipset, S. M. and Bendix, R. (1959), *Social Mobility in an Industrial Society* (University of California Press).

Lipsey, R. G. (1970), *An Introduction to Positive Economics* (London, Weidenfeld and Nicolson).

Locke, John (1963), *The Works of John Locke, vols. 1–10*, reprinted by Scientia Verlag Aalen, Germany.

—— *An Essay Concerning Human Understanding* (London, not dated, George Routledge and Sons).

Lundberg, G. A. (1964), *Foundations of Sociology* (New York, David McKay).

Machlup, F. (1950), 'On the Meaning of the Marginal Product', *American Economic Association*.

Macpherson, C. B. (1962), *The Political Theory of Possessive Individualism. Hobbes to Locke* (Oxford University Press).

Maine, Sir Henry, *Ancient Law* (London, not dated, Dent and Sons, Everyman edition).

Mandeville (1970), *The Fable of the Bees* (Harmondsworth, Penguin).

Marcuse, H. (1955), *Reason and Revolution* (London, Routledge and Kegan Paul).

—— (1964), *One Dimensional Man* (London, Sphere Books).

—— (1968), *Negations* (Harmondsworth, Penguin).

Marshall, A. (1946), *Economics of Industry* (London, Macmillan).

Marshall, T. H. (1950), *Citizenship and Social Class* (Cambridge).

Marx, K. (1959), *Capital Vol. 3*, (Moscow, Progress Publishers).

—— (1967), *Capital Vol. 2*, (Moscow, Progress Publishers).

—— (1954), *The Eighteenth Brumaire of Louis Bonaparte* (Moscow, Progress Publishers)

Marx, K. (1969), *Theories of Surplus Value, Part 1* (Moscow, Progress Publishers).

—— (1972*a*), *Capital Vol. 1*, (London, Dent and Sons).

—— (1972*b*), *Critique of the Gotha Programme* (Peking, Foreign Languages Press).

—— (1972*c*), *Theories of Surplus Value, Part 3* (Moscow, Progress Publishers).

—— (1973*a*), *Wages, Price and Profit* (Peking, Foreign Languages Press).

—— (1973*b*), *The Economic and Philosophic Manuscripts of 1844* London, Lawrence and Wishart).

—— (1973*c*), *Grundrisse* (Harmondsworth, Penguin).

Marx, K. and Engels, F. (1965), *Selected Correspondence* (Moscow, Progress Publishers).

—— (1970), *The German Ideology* (London, Lawrence and Wishart).

—— (1967), *The Communist Manifesto* (Harmondsworth, Penguin).

Mayer, J. P. (1956), *Max Weber and German Politics* (London, Faber and Faber).

Meek, R. L. (1956), *Studies in the Labour Theory of Value* (London, Lawrence and Wishart).

Menger, C. (1950), *Principles of Economics* (Glencoe, The Free Press).

Merton, R. K., Gray, A. P., Hockey, B. and Selvin, H. C. (1964), *Reader in Bureaucracy* (Free Press of Glencoe).

Mignet, F. A. (1868), *History of the French Revolution from 1789 to 1814* (London, Bell and Daldy).

Mill, J. S. (1875), *Principles of Political Economy* (London, Longmans Peoples Edition).

—— (1925), *Utilitarianism, Liberty and Representative Government* (London, Dent).

Mills, C. W. (1948), *The New Men of Power: America's Labour Leaders* (New York, Harcourt, Brace and Company).

—— (1951), *White Collar: the American Middle Classes* (New York, Oxford University Press).

—— (1956), *The Power Elite* (New York, Oxford University Press).

—— (1959), *The Causes of World War Three* (London, Secker and Warburg).

—— (1966), *Sociology and Pragmatism: The Higher Learning in America* (Oxford University Press).

—— (1967), *Power, Politics and People* (London, Oxford University Press).

—— (1963), *The Marxists* (Harmondsworth, Penguin).

—— (1970), *The Sociological Imagination* (Harmondsworth, Penguin).

De Mirabaud (Baron D'Holbach) (1834), *Nature and Her Laws, as applicable to the Happiness of Man, Living in Society, contrasted with superstition and imaginary systems* (London, James Watson).

Mommsen, W. J. (1974), *The Age of Bureaucracy: perspectives on the political sociology of Max Weber* (Oxford, Blackwell).

Montesquieu (1902), *The Spirit of the Laws* (London, George Bell and Sons).

Morrow, G. R. (1969), *The Ethical and Economic Theories of Adam Smith* (New York, Kelley).

Myrdal, G. (1953), *The Political Element in the Development of Economic Theory* (London, Routledge and Kegan Paul).

Nagel, E. (1961), *The Structure of Science. Problems in the Logic of Scientific Explanation* (London, Routledge and Kegan Paul).

Nicolaus, M. (1967), 'Proletariat and Middle Class in Marx', *Studies on the Left* (Jan-Feb.)

Nordhaus, W. D. (1974), 'The Falling Share of Profits', in A. M. Okun et al, *Brookings Papers on Economic Activity*, no. I (Washington).

Palloix, C. (1976), 'The Labour Process: from Fordism to neo-Fordism', in *Conference of Socialist Economists Pamphlet No. 1*, Stage 1 (London).

Panic, M. and Close, R. E. (1973), 'Profitability and British Manufacturing Industry' *Lloyd's Bank Review*, no. 109.

Pareto, W. (1966), *Sociological Writings*, ed. S. E. Finer (London, Pall Mall Press).

―― (1971), *Manual of Political Economy* (London, The Macmillan Press).

Park, R. E. (1967), *On Social Control and Collective Behaviour*, ed. R. H. Turner (University of Chicago Press).

Parkin, F. (1972), *Class Inequality and Political Order* (London, Paladin).

Parsons, T. (1951), *The Social System* (New York, Free Press).

―― (1960), *Social Structure and Process in Modern Societies* (New York, Free Press).

―― (1964), *Essays in Sociological Theory* (Toronto, Free Press of Glencoe).

―― (1967), *Sociological Theory and Modern Society* (New York, Free Press).

―― (1968), *The Structure of Social Action* (London, Collier-Macmillan).

―― (1969), *Politics and Social Structure* (New York, Free Press).

Parsons, T. and Bales, R. F. (1956), *Family: socialization and interaction process* (London, Routledge and Kegan Paul).

Parsons, T. and Shils, E. A. (1962), *Towards a General Theory of Social Action* (New York, Harper and Row).

Peaker, A. (1974), *Economic Growth in Modern Britain* (London, Macmillan).

Peirce, C. S. (1931–5), *The Collected Papers of Charles Sanders Peirce*, 6 vols (Harvard University Press).

Pilling, G. (1972), 'The Law of Value in Ricardo and Marx, *Economy and Society*, no. 3.

Plato (1955), *The Republic* (Harmondsworth, Penguin).

—— (1965), *Timaeus* (Harmondsworth, Penguin).

Plekhanov, G. (1937), *Fundamental Problems of Marxism* (London, Lawrence and Wishart).

—— (1956), *The Development of the Monist View of History* (Moscow, Progress Publishers).

Preiser, E. (1971), 'Property, Power and the Distribution of Income', in K. W. Rothschild (ed.), *Power in Economics* (Harmondsworth, Penguin).

Psathas, G. (ed.) (1973), *Phenomenological Sociology* (London, Wiley).

Raphael, D. D. (1969), *British Moralists 1650–1800*, 2 vols (Oxford University Press).

Rees, A. (1961), *Real Wages in Manufacturing. 1890–1914* (Princeton, Princeton University Press).

Renner, K. (1949), *The Institutions of Private Law and their Social Functions* (London, Routledge and Kegan Paul).

Rex, J. (1961), *Key Problems of Sociological Theory* (London, Routledge and Kegan Paul).

—— (1973), *Race, Colonialism and the City* (London, Routledge and Kegan Paul).

—— (ed.) (1974*a*), *Approaches to Sociology: An Introduction to Major Trends in British Sociology* (London, Routledge and Kegan Paul).

—— (1974*b*), *Sociology and the Demystification of the Modern World*, (London, Routledge and Kegan Paul).

Ricardo, David (1911), *The Principles of Political Economy and. Taxation* (London, Dent and Sons).

—— (1951), 'Absolute Value and Exchangeable Value', in *Works*, ed. P. Sraffa, 4 (Cambridge University Press).

Robinson, J. and Eatwell, J. (1973), *An Introduction to Modern Economics* (London, McGraw-Hill).

Roll, E. (1938), *A History of Economic Thought* (London, Faber and Faber).

Rousseau, J. J. (1913), *The Social Contract and Discourses* (London, Dent and Sons).

Roth, G. (1976), 'History and Sociology in the Work of Max Weber', *British Journal of Sociology*, 27, no. 3.

Routh, G. (1965), *Occupation and Pay in Great Britain* (Cambridge University Press).

—— (1975), *The Origin of Economic Ideas* (London, Macmillan).

Rowthorn, B. (1971), *International Big Business, 1957–67. A Study of Comparative Growth*, University of Cambridge Department of Applied Economics Occasional Paper 24.

—— (1974), Neo-Classicism, Neo-Ricardianism and Marxism', *New Left Review*, no. 86.

Runciman, W. G. (1972), *A Critique of Max Weber's Philosophy of Social Science*, (Cambridge University Press).

Sacks, H. (1963), 'Sociological Description', *Berkeley Journal of Sociology*, 8.

Sampson, N. (1968), *The Enlightenment* (Harmondsworth, Penguin).

Schumpeter, J. A. (1959), *History of Economic Analysis* (London, Allen and Unwin).

Schutz, A. (1962), *Collected Papers. Vol. 1. The Problem of Social Reality* (The Hague, Martinus Nijhoff).

Schutz, A. and Luckmann, T. (1973), *The Structures of the Life-World. Vol. 1* (London, Heinemann).

Schwartz, R. D. (1955), 'Functional Alternatives to Inequality', *American Sociological Review*, 20.

Seligman, B. B. (1963), *Main Currents in Modern Economics* (New York, Free Press of Glencoe).

Sewall, H. R. (1968), *The Theory of Value Before Adam Smith* (New York, Kelley).

Simmel, G. (1964), *Conflict* (London, Free Press of Glencoe).

Singer, C. (1959), *A Short History of Scientific Ideas to 1900* (Oxford University Press).

Small, A. W. (1972), *Adam Smith and Modern Sociology* (New Jersey, Augustus).

Smith, A. (1970), *The Wealth of Nations* (Harmondsworth, Penguin).

Sorokin, P. (1928), *Contemporary Sociological Theories* (New York, Harper and Row).

Spencer, H. (1894), *The Study of Sociology* (London, Williams and Norgate).

—— (1915), *A System of Synthetic Philosophy. Vol. 1. First Principles* (London, Williams and Norgate).

Tawney, R. H. (1938), *Religion and the Rise of Capitalism* (Harmondsworth, Penguin).

Therborn, G. (1974), 'The Economic Theorists of Capitalism', *New Left Review*, 87–8.

Thierry (1859), *The Formation and Progress of the Tiers Etat* (London, Henry G. Bohn).

Ticktin, H. H. (1973), 'Political Economy of the Soviet Intellectual', *Critique*, no. 2.

Timasheff, N. S. (1957), *Sociological Theory: Its Nature and Growth* (New York, Random House).

Tocqueville, Alexis de (1956), *Democracy in America* (New York, Mentor).

Trotsky, L. (1968), *The Class Nature of the Soviet State* (London, New Park Publications).

Tumin, M. (1953), 'Some Principles of Stratification: a Critical Analysis', *American Sociological Review*, 18.

—— (1955), 'Rewards and Task-Orientations', *American Sociological Review*, 20.

Turner, J. H. (1973), 'From Utopia to Where? A Strategy for Reformulating the Dahrendorf Conflict Model', *Social Forces*, 52.

Turner, R. (ed.) (1974), *Ethnomethodology. Selected Readings* (Harmondsworth, Penguin).

Urban, W. M. (1949), *Beyond Realism and Idealism* (London, Allen and Unwin).

Ure, J. (1973), 'Towards a Structural Theory of the Middle Class', *Acta Sociologica*, 16, no. 3.

Veblen, T. (1954), *The Engineers and the Price System* (New York, Viking Press).

Voltaire (1961), *Philosophical Letters* (New York, Bobbs-Merrill).

—— (1966), *The Age of Louis XIV* (London, Dent and Sons).

Vyverberg, H. (1958), *Historical Pessimism in the French Enlightenment* (Cambridge, Massachusetts, Harvard University Press).

Walker, J. L. (1974), 'Estimating Companies Rate of Return on Capital Employed', *Economic Trends*, no. 253 (H.M.S.O.)

Walras, L. (1954), *Elements of Pure Economics* (London, Allen and Unwin).

Walsh, D. (1972), 'Functionalism and Systems Theory', in P. Filmer *et al* (1972).

Walton, P., Taylor, I. and Young, J. (1973), *The New Criminology* (London, Routledge and Kegan Paul).

Walton, P. and Gamble, A. (1976), *Capitalism in Crisis* (London, Macmillan).

Warner, W. Lloyd (1960), *Social Class in America. The Evaluation of Status* (New York, Harper and Row).

Weber, M. (1949), *Methodology of the Social Sciences* (New York, Free Press).

—— (1957), *The Theory of Social and Economic Organization* (Glencoe).

—— (1968), *Economy and Society*, 3 vols (New York, Bedminster Press).

—— (1970), *The Protestant Ethic and the Spirit of Capitalism* (Unwin University Books).

—— *General Economic History* (London, not dated, Allen and Unwin).

Westergaard, J. H. (1972), 'Sociology: the Myth of Classlessness', in R. Blackburn (ed.), *Ideology in Social Science* (London, Fontana).

Whittaker, E. (1960), *Schools and Streams of Economic Thought*, (Chicago, McNally).

Whyte, W. H. (1957), *The Organization Man* (New York).

Winch, P. (1958), *The Idea of a Social Science and its Relation to Philosophy*, (London, Routledge and Kegan Paul).

Willer, D. and J. (1973), *Systematic Empiricism: Critique of a Pseudoscience* (New Jersey, Prentice-Hall).

Windelband, W. (1958), *A History of Philosophy. Vol. 2* (New York, Harper and Row).

Wrong, D. H. (1961), 'The Oversocialized Conception of Man in Modern Sociology', *American Sociological Review*, 26, no. 2.

Yaffe, D. (1973), 'The Crisis of Profitability: a Critique of the Glyn-Sutcliffe Thesis', *New Left Review*, no. 80.

Index